OBERLIN COLONY
The Story of a Century

BY

WILBUR H. PHILLIPS

OBERLIN, OHIO
JUNE, 1933

This volume was printed at the Press of the Oberlin Printing Company, Oberlin, Ohio. The type is Caslon. The paper is Linweave Text.

Four hundred and fifty numbered copies have been made of this edition.

This is number

A Facsimile Reprint
Published 2000 by

HERITAGE BOOKS, INC.
1540E Pointer Ridge Place
Bowie, Maryland 20716
1-800-398-7709
http://www.heritagebooks.com

ISBN: 0-7884-1491-7

To the Memory of
JOHN W. STEELE
CITIZEN   SOLDIER   JURIST

PREFACE

The author presents his story of the first century of the history of Oberlin Village with thorough appreciation of its probable inadequacy as a permanent record. The work has been done under pressure of conflicting duties and has been made possible very largely by the loyal cooperation of his associates in business, who have carried forward most of the work pertaining to his vocation, while he has been occupied by an avocation which has been marked by both pleasure and disappointment. The pleasure growing out of the task has been found in a study and transcription of the records of the town of his adoption. The disappointment came from a growing appreciation of the fact that a proper writing of such a record should be a matter of years, rather than of months. It has seemed to the author that a publication attempting to cover the first one hundred years of Oberlin's history should appear at the Centennial Anniversary. The apparent need to meet this publication date has not made it possible, in all instances, to check records not original in character.

For the early history of the colony the author has drawn liberally upon President Fairchild's excellent work, *Oberlin: The Colony and the College,* and occasionally upon Dr. Leonard's history. Original sources consulted for the period prior to the Civil War have included the *Oberlin Evangelist,* the minutes of the Oberlin Society, the original records of the Board of Trustees of Oberlin College, and of the Prudential Committee of Oberlin College, and such early records of an official character as are to be found in the village archives. Foundation material of unquestioned authenticity was secured from Professor G. Frederick Wright's *History of Lorain County* and *The History of Early Oberlin* by Mr. Henry Matson, former librarian of Oberlin College. The year-by-year story of village development since the Civil War has its basis very largely in the records of the Lorain County News, the Oberlin News, and the Oberlin Tribune.

In the course of the task the author has had valuable and much appreciated assistance from Mr. Julian S. Fowler, librarian of Oberlin College, Mr. George M. Jones, secretary of Oberlin

College, Professor William H. Chapin, an authority on Oberlin history, Mr. William B. Gerrish, Mrs. Louise Margaret Dittrick of Cleveland, Mr. Peter L. Pease of New York, and from others whose courteous cooperation is acknowledged with thanks.

A difficulty apparent at the outset was that of attempting to write a record of Oberlin dealing primarily with the village. The history of Oberlin Village and Oberlin College is more or less an inseparable story. The author has been obliged to exercise his own judgment in references to college growth and in references to the relations between community and college. He has had no purpose to serve in this writing other than that of such exactness as was possible under the pressure of limited time. He believes that the inseparable nature of college and town and the primary differences between Town and Gown are fairly set forth in the sketches of Colonel John W. Steele and Honorable James Monroe. Mr. Monroe was selected as a man of letters who rendered conspicuous service to his community and his country. Judge Steele was chosen as unquestionably the outstanding citizen in the history of the village. Other men of the community have been unselfish in their contributions to public life. Other members of the faculty of Oberlin College have given generously of their time and thought to the promotion of community affairs. Residents of Oberlin in the new century will remember with increasing gratitude the citizenship of Henry Churchill King, Edward Increase Bosworth, John M. Ellis, and many others who have served both college and community.

WILBUR H. PHILLIPS.

Oberlin, Ohio, May 10, 1933.

CONTENTS

BEFORE THE CIVIL WAR

JOHN W. STEELE

IN THE BEGINNING

CHAPTER I

OBERLIN had its beginning when Peter Pindar Pease, on April 19, 1833, brought his wife and children from their pioneer home in Brownhelm to take up their residence in his log cabin on the campus, near the site of the Historic Elm. This modest home, the construction of which began three days before, was the first building put up in Oberlin. Deacon Pease, the first citizen to make his home in the forests here, was the advance guard and breaker of ways for that stout band of hardy builders who came in response to the call of the founders of Oberlin College for men of pious and self-denying nature to build and support the College and the Colony.

But for the firm belief of John J. Shipherd,[1] that something must be done at once to "save the perishing world," a belief shared by Philo P. Stewart,[1] his friend and associate in missionary work, there would have been no Oberlin College nor Oberlin Community in the wilderness. Three strong men stand out as the builders and sustainers of college and colony in the first two or three decades after their founding. Shipherd and Stewart made the beginning of the school and community. Charles Grandison Finney was mainly responsible for keeping alive both the community and the college. Mr. Shipherd, a man whose life was marked by unselfish devotion to the things he thought were right, had caught the spirit of the great evangelistic movement which was sweeping America in the early thirties. The outstanding leader in this march of evangelism and missionary fervor was Mr. Finney, later president of Oberlin College and for years the dominant personality in the molding not only of the thought but of the course of conduct of the people of college and community. It was the personal pleas of Mr. Shipherd with prospective colonists which permitted the building at one and the same time of school and village.

---

1 See Appendix A.

Oberlin Colony

Peter Pindar Pease, first citizen of Oberlin, came in response to an appeal from Mr. Shipherd. This is true of other pioneers who gathered here from Brownhelm, from other Ohio communities, and from the New England states, where Mr. Shipherd traveled in an effort to find not alone pupils for the school which he and Mr. Stewart had planned, but as well citizens and builders for the village. In those beginning years the interests and activities of the college and community were so nearly identical that it would have been difficult then to have discerned a dividing line. Both were making a stern struggle for survival and growth, and college and colony shared alike in the sacrifices and privations which were a part of pioneering.

Whether consciously or not, Mr. Shipherd was influenced in his plan to "plant a colony and school . . . whose chief aim shall be to glorify God and do good to men," by the preaching of Mr. Finney. He was supported unselfishly by Mr. Stewart and was aided in no small degree by the "pious" character and fine courage of the colonists who had been called to the scene by strong belief in Mr. Shipherd and his purpose. The promise of permanent growth of both college and community was still in some doubt when, after two years of existence, it received the accession from Lane Seminary and, more important still, the addition to the faculty of Mr. Finney. The commercial and financial crash which marked the late thirties and the early forties could not have been met had it not been for aid secured from friends of the school in Great Britain. Again, that aid would not have been forthcoming had the school failed in 1835 to go on record through its trustees as willing to admit colored students and as consequently another champion of the cause of anti-slavery. While this action of the board was taken at the direct insistence of Mr. Shipherd, it was due in the main to the demands of Arthur Tappan, New York capitalist, who had agreed to finance the coming here of Mr. Finney and other outstanding teachers and who at the same time insisted upon this declaration in behalf of the Negro by the Board of Trustees. Mr. Tappan was one of the early leaders in the anti-slavery cause. English gifts in time of dire need and distress were due not only to Oberlin's apparent anti-slavery attitude but in great degree to the knowledge of the givers across the sea that Oberlin had on its teaching staff in Mr. Finney an evangelist who had won their respect and affection by his preaching in the British Isles.

In the preliminary conferences between Mr. Shipherd and Mr. Stewart, Mr. Shipherd was inclined to stress the missionary activity of the proposed school and to take joy in the belief that it would be called into being to give new life to the church and "cheer our benighted world." It was Mr. Stewart's thought that the school should place emphasis on the furnishing of manual labor to students, as was the rule at Pawlet Academy. The two seemed to have agreed as to the principle of co-education. Within a few years it was found impracticable to furnish labor to all students. The school suffered the usual criticism for pioneering in the field of education with its offer of equal opportunities to women. It is significant that nothing in the published correspondence of either of the two founders and nothing in the Oberlin Covenant makes reference to the evil of slavery. Despite this fact Oberlin's course was fixed and her growth finally assured both as a community and a college by the ambiguous decision of the Board of Trustees, construed to record a stand for Abolition, and by the steady course of evangelical effort under the direction of Mr. Finney. Neither college nor colony had gone on record prior to the formal declaration of the board on the anti-slavery question. The reluctance of the trustees to take action reflected the indifference and mild antagonism of the community toward the course proposed. It followed, of course, that the colony endorsed the new stand when once made and that from that time forward Oberlin was active in the anti-slavery cause.

It was in the summer of 1832 that Mr. Shipherd and Mr. Stewart, who had been students together at Pawlet, Vermont, reached an agreement for the founding of a Christian school in the Connecticut Western Reserve.[2] Mr. Shipherd was then

---

2 See Appendix B.

pastor of a church in Elyria and Mr. Stewart, formerly a missionary to the Choctaw Indians in the State of Mississippi, was his guest. It was only after long discussion and much fervent prayer that the two arrived at their conclusion.[3] It was almost a year before land had been procured and a plan in detail approved by the two. The first tangible fruits of these discussions came when colony and college alike had their beginnings in the log cabin built by Peter Pindar Pease.

It was no chance determination made by Stewart and Shipherd which resulted in the founding of the college and community. Mrs. Stewart's health had failed in their missionary service, and Mr. Stewart, after correspondence with Mr. Shipherd, came to Elyria from the East to consider a possible new field of missionary work. This was in the spring of 1832. Soon after his becoming an inmate of the Shipherd home he and Mr. Shipherd began their discussions about the founding of a Christian school. These two pioneers in education and religion had much in common, but were unlike in temperament. They were close friends, and each had great respect for the opinion of the other. In their preliminary discussion both dwelt upon the need of caring for the wants of the "Mississippi Valley." Mr. Shipherd laid emphasis on the establishment of a community of Christian families from which to a great extent worldly influences should be excluded and where gospel principles should prevail in place of worldly views and fashions. He seemed to incline even to a community of property, but it was no part of his plan to concentrate the interest of the community upon itself.[4] Mr. Stewart, leaning rather toward the material development of their proposed enterprise, emphasized the need of a school providing manual labor for students and urged the necessity for co-education. Both these proposals were part of the program in the Pawlet Academy where Shipherd and Stewart had been students, and the two founders were agreed as to their merit. The name Oberlin for

---

[3] The house in which Mr. Shipherd then lived and in which the two held their conferences was still standing in Elyria in 1933.
    [4] President Fairchild, *Oberlin: The Colony and the College.*

both college and community was selected by the two who had recently been reading a life of the Alsatian pastor, John Frederic Oberlin.

In a letter to his parents dated August 6, 1832, Shipherd said: "I propose through God's assistance to plant a colony somewhere in this region whose chief aim shall be to glorify God and do good to men, to the utmost extent of their ability. They are to simplify food, dress, etc., to be industrious and economical and to give all over their current or annual expenses for the spread of the Gospel." This same letter makes reference to the establishment of work-shops and firms in connection with the school and to four hours daily labor on the part of students. He further says: "These schools will also educate school teachers for our desolate valley and many ministers for our dying world. To do this we want some twenty-five or more *good* families, and $2,000 outfit for the school." In pursuit of these principles Mr. Shipherd resigned the pastorate of the Elyria church October 29, 1832, and he and Stewart set to work to give the breath of life to their vision.

It was known to the two that Street and Hughes of New Haven, Connecticut, were owners of a large tract of land in Russia Township and that they had offered upon certain conditions 500 acres for educational purposes. Offers of a site for the school and college were made by Judge Ely of Elyria and by residents of Brownhelm. These were refused, apparently because the tracts suggested seemed too small for the purpose and because of the opportunity to secure lands at the site selected at less expense. The isolated location of the future Oberlin, offering a barrier to those not moved by the missionary spirit, doubtless had weight in the decision.

The day following their agreement as to the name of the school Shipherd and Stewart rode from Elyria about nine miles west to the site of what is now Oberlin. Several years previous surveyors had made a rough road by some clearing north out of Oberlin. Tradition says that the two men knelt under a tree, now identified as the Historic Elm, on the southeast corner of the campus, to pray to God for guidance. After their prayer a hunter reported to them that he had seen a bear and two cubs climb down from a tree, approach their horses, look them over, and turn away. For some reason this was interpreted by the two as an indication from on high that they should here establish their school and colony.[5]

Mr. Shipherd was sustained by his firm belief that God was guiding him in his enterprise. He was gifted with persuasive eloquence and so undertook the task of going to New Haven to see Street and Hughes about the land. He started the journey in November, 1832. In two weeks he was in New Haven and after several days of conference with the landowners they yielded to his request. He received from them a gift of 500 acres for his school and secured a tentative sale by the owners of 5,000 acres at $1.50 per acre which was to be sold again to colonists at an increase of $1.00 an acre, thus providing funds for the operation of the school. This transfer was to become effective after the school had been in operation a given period of time and had under its care at least 100 students. For this reason the deed bears date of 1836. The original is now in the office of the treasurer of Oberlin College.

No better statement of the purpose of the founders in establishing their school and community can be found than that set forth in the Oberlin Covenant, which was signed by original colonists as they came on the ground. While after two or three years the Covenant was not appealed to as a definite and enforceable mandate, many of its principles were honored alike by the college and community over a long period.

---

[5] At the celebration in 1883 of the Fiftieth Anniversary of the founding of the college and colony Mrs. Amanda Pease Williams, daughter of Peter Pindar Pease, in commenting on the accepted story of the bears said: "I think there was not a bear in the woods at that time, neither did one come down the tree while Shipherd and Stewart were kneeling." In response to this, President Fairchild stated at the time that he had in his possession a letter from Mrs. John J. Shipherd confirming the accuracy of the bear story and its effect on Shipherd and Stewart. Mr. Fairchild said: "There is no such improbability in the story as to warrant its rejection." Mr. Fairchild further said that he knew of the presence of bears in the woods in those days. Mrs. Williams in the course of the statement quoted said that her father slept under the Historic Elm when he came to Oberlin to build his cabin. Her father and Addison Tracy, she said, piloted Shipherd and Stewart through the woods on the occasion of their first visit to the site. The four knelt by a log in prayer to consecrate the land to its purpose. Tracy gave the first $5.00 into the treasury of the new school.

The Story of a Century

Covenant of the Oberlin Colony

Lamenting the degeneracy of the church and the deplorable condition of our perishing world, and ardently desirous of bringing both under the entire influence of the blessed gospel of peace; and viewing with peculiar interest the influence which the valley of the Mississippi must assert over our nation and the nations of the earth; and having, as we trust, in answer to devout supplications, been guided by the counsel of the Lord: The undersigned covenant together under the name of the Oberlin Colony, subject to the following regulations, which may be amended by a concurrence of two-thirds of the colonists:

First, Providence permitting, we engage as soon as practicable to remove to the Oberlin Colony, in Russia, Lorain County, Ohio, and there to fix our residence, for the express purpose of glorifying God in doing good to men to the extent of our ability.

Second. We will hold and manage our estates personally, but pledge as perfect a community of interest as though we held a community of property.

Third. We will hold in possession no more property than we believe we can profitably manage for God as his faithful stewards.

Fourth. We will, by industry, economy, and Christian self-denial, obtain as much as we can, above our necessary personal or family expenses, and faithfully appropriate the same for the spread of the Gospel.

Fifth. That we may have time and health for the Lord's service, we will eat only plain and wholesome food, renouncing all bad habits, and especially the smoking, chewing, and snuffing of tobacco, unless it be necessary as a medicine, and deny ourselves all strong and unnecessary drinks, even tea and coffee, as far as practicable, and everything expensive, that is simply calculated to gratify the palate.

Sixth. That we may add to our time and health, money for the service of the Lord, we will renounce all the world's expensive and unwholesome fashions of dress, particularly tight dressing and ornamental attire.

Seventh. And yet more to increase our means of serving Him who bought us with his blood, we will observe plainness and durability in the construction of our houses, furniture, carriages and all that appertains to us.

Eighth. We will strive continually to show that we, as the body of Christ, are members one of another; and, will while living, provide for the widows, orphans, and families of the sick and needy as for ourselves.

Ninth. We will take special pains to educate all our children thoroughly, and train them up in body, intellect and heart, for the service of the Lord.

Tenth. We will feel that the interests of the Oberlin Institute are identified with ours, and do what we can to extend its influence to our fallen race.

Eleventh. We will make special efforts to sustain the institutions of the Gospel at home and among our neighbors.

Twelfth. We will strive to maintain deep-toned and elevated personal piety, 'to provoke each other to love and good works', to live together in all things as brethren, and to glorify God in our bodies and spirits, which are His.

In testimony of our fixed purpose thus to do, in reliance on divine grace, we hereunto affix our names.

The original of the Covenant bearing the signatures of early pioneers is carefully kept in the safe in the Library of Oberlin College. While the final signature bears the date April 18, 1839, the majority of the signatures were appended in the years 1833, 1834, 1835. There are a few recorded as having been attached in 1836. Prior to this later date, however, the Covenant had more or less ceased to have effect as a document binding the colonists. A letter from Mrs. Philo P. Stewart, dated April 27, 1872, says of the Covenant: "I do not know when it was 'laid aside.' As long as Mr. Stewart and myself stayed it was adhered to except among the students who furnished their parlors and dressed themselves to some extent more expensively than the Covenant allowed. I think no formal action was ever taken, but it being unpopular with the officers and colonists it was carelessly dropped out of sight and mind."

The name of John J. Shipherd very properly heads the list of signers. Next following the signature of Father Shipherd are names of members of his family and then the names of Peter

The Story of a Century

Pindar Pease, his wife and children. Those who are listed as having signed the Covenant in 1833 are: John J. Shipherd, Esther R. Shipherd and their children, Peter Pindar Pease and Ruth H. Pease and their children, Philip James and Matilda O. James and one child, Harvey Gibbs, Pringle Hamilton and Almira K. Hamilton, Asahel Munger and Sarah E. Munger and children, Philo P. Stewart and Eliza C. Stewart, Bela Hall, Elizur M. Leonard, Otis Janes, Sophronia Janes, T. S. Ingersoll, Lydia B. Ingersoll and children, Daniel Morgan, Isaac and Anna Cummings and family, Sarah Munger, William H. Hoisington, William Lewis, I. F. Samson.

Signers who arrived in Oberlin after 1833—most of them in the years 1834 and 1835—were: Brewster Pelton, Thirsa Pelton, Sarah N. Warren, Ruel Alden, Nelson Scovell, Thomas P. Turner, Lydia Turner and family, Anna G. Moore, Nehemiah Brown and Lydia Brown, James S. Brown, Betsy Stephens, Jacob J. Safford, Jane R. Safford, William Hosford, Linda Hosford, Elihu Hosford, Josiah B. Hall, Roseana Hall, James Dascomb, Marianne Dascomb, James B. Campbell, Lucena S. Campbell, Diana Samson, Johnathan S. Campbell, O. S. Campbell, Fay Hopkins, Elizabeth Hopkins, Sarah F. Hopkins, R. E. Gillett, Mary A. B. Gillett, Steven Hull, Fanny Hull, Daniel Stillman, Eunice Stillman, Martin Leonard, Elizabeth Leonard, Asa Mahan, Mary H. Mahan, Daniel B. Kinney, Betsey Kinney, Oliver Eastman, Laura Eastman, Sally Miller Ward, Nathan P. Fletcher, Lucretia A. Fletcher, Chloe Cummings, Hiram A. Pease, Lydia R. Pease, Horace Crosby, Celina M. Crosby, Joseph H. Marsh, Lua M. Marsh, Edwin Dowd, Lyman Farrar, Jose Woodman, Debora Woodman, Henry Cowles, Alice W. Cowles, Elvira L. Miller, Sarah S. Case, Sylphyna Tracy, Anson Penfield, Minerva D. Penfield, Paul Shipherd, Alonso Jones, Henry Chapin, Mary Chapin, Harriet Chapin, Baxter Chapin, David Holtslander, Sally S. Holtslander, James M. Holtslander, Herman Chapin, Rhoda Chapin, Nehemiah A. Hunt, Luther Turner, Norman Bedortha, Eliza Sill, Ebenezer T. Penfield, Maria H. Penfield, Eliza Branch, E. P. Ingersoll, Louisa F. Ingersoll, H.

Oberlin Colony

W. Fairfield, M. B. Fairfield, R. H. Penfield, Homer Penfield, Emily A. Penfield, Maria Penfield, Elihu Spencer, Harriet A. Spencer, Nancy L. Hall, John Morgan, S. C. Hinsdall, D. Jeffers, L. D. Butts, William H. Green, John T. Pierce, Rowlins Brown, Abel Stockwell, Ebenezer Rolfe, Smith Sturgis, Moses W. Henderson, William Weir, William Hills, Mayo G. Smith, Charles Gerrish, I. I. Gardner, E. N. Bartlett, C. A. Kellogg, Elihu Babcock, Benjamin Cole, I. S. Holmes, Robert Ridell, Silas G. Tyler, Elmira C. Tyler, Anna Butler.

Signers to the Covenant, excluding those not heads of families—mainly children of mature signers—number one hundred and forty from the date of the signature of Mr. Shipherd to the time of the signature of Anna Butler.

In his history of Oberlin, President Fairchild says: "This is not a church covenant but a colonial covenant, and secured its end in presenting the purpose of the colony, and in turning away some that might have been drawn into the enterprise by consideration of wordly advantages. In so far as it goes beyond a general expression of christian consecration, it subsequently afforded occasion of earnest discussion, and sometimes, perhaps, of uncharitable judgment. It was at length found necessary to leave the determination of personal duty in practical affairs to the individual conscience; and thus, after a year or two, the covenant was no longer appealed to in the settlement of differences of opinion upon these subjects. It doubtless had its part in giving form to the social and religious life of the place."

While absent in the East Mr. Shipherd, in addition to reaching an agreement with Street and Hughes, gave time to an effort to secure funds, colonists, and students for the school which he planned to open in the fall of 1833. In September of that year he returned to Oberlin. Meantime, while Mr. Shipherd was in the East, Peter Pindar Pease, first resident here, had kept his agreement with Shipherd and Stewart and had begun with Mrs. Pease housekeeping in his new log cabin on the campus which he occupied April 19, 1833. While Pease and other early colonists

MAP OF COLONY 1835

were clearing the forests for the school and community the school itself had made a start by the selection of a "Board of Trust," the members of which were John J. Shipherd and Peter Pindar Pease of Oberlin, Henry Brown of Brownhelm, Captain E. Redington of Amherst, Reverend Joel Talcott of Wellington, Addison Tracy and Philo P. Stewart of Elyria, J. Burrell of Sheffield, and Reverend John Keys of Dover. This board held its first meeting in a cleared space near the southwest corner of the present college campus, used many years prior by Indians as an encampment. Deacon Pease meanwhile took care of his part of the task, handicapped by the failure on the part of Mr. Shipherd to have a steam sawmill, owned by the college, in operation in the early summer.

A letter from Mr. Stewart to Mr. Shipherd early in 1833 says: "I would suggest for your consideration the question whether it would not do to dispose of some of the Colonist lands to persons of a certain character who are not pious. This might be better than to have the colony very small and surrounded by a corrupt and irreligious population." Stewart, later in the year, after the failure of the sawmill to arrive, says in a letter to Fayette Shipherd, brother of John J. Shipherd: "Brethren Ayers, Hall, Gibbs, Morgan, and Safford have arrived. They are considerably disappointed in regard to the sawmill. You will recollect that to lay a plan is not the same thing as to carry it into execution. Brother Pease has been on the ground about four weeks, has four hands at work, has chopped over five acres." A little later in the same letter Mr. Stewart says: "It seems to me we ought studiously to avoid raising expectations which cannot be realized."

Notwithstanding these discouraging features, so frankly pointed out by Mr. Stewart, the project went forward.[6] Colonists came in and went eagerly to work. The records show but one man who came from the East, got homesick in Elyria, and, feeling no better when he arrived in Oberlin, turned back to his

---

[6] See Appendix C.

former home. So steady had been the accessions that on June 11, 1833, a letter to Mr. Shipherd from "the few sheep that are collected at Oberlin" was signed by Peter Pindar Pease, Brewster Pelton, Samuel Daniels, Philip James, Pringle Hamilton, William Hosford, Asahel Munger, Harvey Gibbs, Jacob J. Safford, and Daniel Morgan. In addition there were three or four women in the colony. Several other families came before fall. The steam engine finally arrived in October and was soon put to work.

When the school opened December 3, 1833, there were eleven families in the colony. Forty-four students were in attendance for the winter term,—twenty-nine young men and fifteen young women. The school was chartered by the State in February, 1834, as the Oberlin Collegiate Institute.

The first circular issued by the college, framed by Reverend John J. Shipherd, announced that the hopes of the Institute were: "To give the most useful education at the least expense of health, time, and money; to extend the benefit of such education to both sexes" and thus contribute to "the elevation of female character, by bringing within the reach of the misjudged and neglected sex all the instructive privileges which have hitherto unreasonably distinguished the leading sex from theirs."

The college attendance of 44 in the initial winter term of 1833-34 had increased to 101 for the summer term of 1834. In 1835 the total attendance was 276, of whom 73 were women. The following year the total was 310. In 1837, in the midst of a panic, the college had not funds with which to publish a catalogue, so there is no record. Attendance of 391 in 1838 had grown to 534 in 1850. At that latter date there were 217 women students. Added financial ability and increased interest in education resulted in 1852 in a total attendance of 1020. The following year the attendance was 1305. This notable increase in attendance over the previous year was due to the establishment of endowment funds in 1852 through gifts and scholarships. The high mark for the years before the Civil War was reached in 1860 when attendance was 1311.

PETER PINDAR PEASE

THE FIRST COLONIST

CHAPTER II

PETER PINDAR PEASE, who as first settler in Oberlin Colony may well be considered the father of the Oberlin community, was a direct descendant of Robert Pease, who lived in Great Baddow, Essex County, England, in the early seventeenth century. The genealogy of the Pease family shows that Margaret, widow of Robert Pease, came to America with the family of a son and joined the church at Salem, Massachusetts, in 1639. Robert, the son, received a land-grant at Salem, Massachusetts, in 1637. Later in the seventeenth century the American descendants of Robert Pease settled at Enfield, Connecticut. The grandfather of Peter Pindar Pease, Nathaniel Pease, left Enfield about 1760 and settled at Norfolk, where he died in 1818 at the age of ninety.

Phineas Pease, father of Peter Pindar Pease, was the oldest son of Nathaniel. Phineas Pease was a tanner and shoemaker and served as a musician in Washington's army in the War of the Revolution. He was born at Enfield in 1756, four years before the departure of his father for Norfolk. Phineas married Betsy Lawrence of Canaan, Connecticut, in 1779. He died in 1836 at Stockbridge, Massachusetts, at the age of 82. His wife died in 1837.

Peter Pindar Pease was one of a family of twelve children born to Phineas and Betsy Pease. He was born at Stockbridge, Massachusetts, April 12, 1795. Other members of the family were Flavius, Sarah, Pelia, Martha, Elizabeth, Electa, Phineas, Hiram Abif, Alonzo, Aurelia, and Amanda. Hiram Pease was born April 19, 1797, and came to Oberlin as a pioneer in May, 1834, a little over a year after the arrival of his brother Peter Pindar, the first settler. Family tradition has it that Peter Pindar Pease was named by his parents in honor of an English minor poet and satirist, who used the pen name of Peter Pindar. Correspondence of the Pease family dating back to the early part of the nineteenth century, some of which is in the possession of Mrs.

Oberlin Colony

Robert E. Brown of Oberlin, a grand-niece of Peter Pindar Pease, indicates that members of the family habitually called Deacon Pease by his middle, rather than his first, name.

Oberlin's first citizen had through life an unquestioned reputation for both piety and integrity. These same characteristics seem to have marked the Pease family of older days. The story is told of Phineas Pease, father of Peter Pindar, that he had bought certain lands of an Indian in the East and had made only part payment. The balance, a considerable amount, was put in a note which was given to the former owner. Mr. Pease was startled one day when the Indian called upon him and explained that he was going to a distant hunting ground and, expecting to be gone a long time, asked Mr. Pease to hold the promissory note until the owner should return. When the Indian said, "Take him and keep him," Mr. Pease advised his creditor against such a course as being a violation of good business. "No," said the Indian, "Mr. Pease be a good man—he be honest—he no cheat poor Indian." In face of such a tribute Mr. Pease took the note and, needless to say, on the return of the Indian gave the note to him and eventually paid it with interest.

In 1816 Peter Pindar Pease attained his majority. In the fall of that year he left his paternal home, Stockbridge, Massachusetts, and came with Judge Henry Brown to aid in the development of a settlement in the forest at a point now known as Brownhelm. At that time, of course, the spot had neither name nor habitation. Mr. Pease remained on the site during the winter of 1816 with two other young men and these three built the first house in Brownhelm, the home of Judge Henry Brown. Judge Brown, with other early colonists, returned to the East and came back to Brownhelm in the spring of 1817 to complete the work of establishing the village. Meantime Pease and his associates were busy clearing the forests and providing timber for the building of homes for the settlers. It was in work of this kind, building houses for others and constructing roads for the use of the pioneers, that Mr. Pease spent the greater portion of the next four or five years. He married Miss Ruth H. Crocker, of Amherst, in 1821, and settled on one of the unbroken wilderness farms, which he must clear with his own hands and payment for which was made by himself and his wife with their own labor. It is interesting to note that he paid the government at the rate of $6.00 an acre. Only a few years after that time land was sold to colonists in Oberlin at $2.50 an acre. The Brownhelm land, however, was better fitted for agriculture. Elyria, the nearest town, was but a hamlet in those days. There was little or no market for surplus crops and the problem of Mr. and Mrs. Pease was mainly one of growing from their wilderness farm sufficient for a living for themselves.

Tradition has it that when Deacon Pease was a resident of Brownhelm, before coming to his work in Oberlin, he and his wife and other members of the colony were suffering for lack of food. It was in the midst of a hard winter and game was scarce. One Sunday morning a large buck appeared near the Pease cabin and stood quietly for some time. To a man of Deacon Pease's intense religious temperament shooting a gun on what was then habitually known as the Sabbath was a serious offense. Mr. Pease and the buck both meditated for a time and the good deacon soon reached the conclusion that the buck was sent by the hand of God to furnish food for his own and other families. Mr. Pease was as accurate in his shooting as he was religious in his thought and it required but one effort to bring the buck to the ground.

It was doubtless while Peter Pindar Pease was a resident of Brownhelm that he first made the acquaintance of Reverend John J. Shipherd, one of the two founders of Oberlin College. The record shows that Mr. Shipherd in seeking colonists for Oberlin "thought first of Mr. Pease." This grew out of the fact that Deacon Pease possessed the piety, religious character, and practical industry desired by Mr. Shipherd and Mr. Stewart in those who should make up the Oberlin colony. Pease and Shipherd doubtless met in the church at Brownhelm, of which Mr. Pease was a member at the time of its organization June 10, 1819. Just prior to 1830, when Mr. Shipherd had in contemplation his educational plan, there was a great religious movement in the land in connection with which protracted meetings were first extensively introduced, commonly known, says President James H. Fairchild, in his *History of Brownhelm* as "four-day meetings." The Brownhelm church participated in these and Mr. Pease was one of the leaders of the church. Mr. Shipherd, then a pastor in Elyria, was one of the ministers in charge of the work. At these four-day meetings the people gathered in the morning, taking a luncheon for themselves and for visitors from abroad, and the entire day was devoted to preaching, prayer, and inquiry meetings. Evening meetings followed. Such a protracted meeting was held in Brownhelm in the summer of 1831 under a bower in the forest, since the meeting house was not large enough to accommodate all comers. Mr. Shipherd, it may be assumed, was present at such an outstanding gathering and no doubt talked with Peter Pindar Pease on this occasion. Mr. Pease had a reputation as a pioneer builder. He helped in the construction of the first log church at Brownhelm and was a leader in the organization not alone of the church, but of the Sunday School which followed.

Supplementing these indications of good citizenship, industry, and church interest, Mr. Pease had a part in the opening in Brownhelm in the summer of 1830 by Reverend Harvey Lyon of the first academy in Lorain County, in a small house built for the purpose near the home of Mr. Pease. It is of record that Mr. Pease was interested in this initial movement for higher education in the county, since he furnished board at his own home for students of the new school and gave those attending opportunity to pay for such board by labor on his farm. This little school was the first classical school in the county and preceded by two years the high school at Elyria and by more than three years the opening of Oberlin College. So it was an appreciation on Mr. Shipherd's part of the interest of Mr. Pease in religion and in education that brought about the latter's enlistment in aid of the plans of Mr. Shipherd and Mr. Stewart for establishing a school at 'Oberlin.

The Story of a Century

When Mr. and Mrs. Pease arrived by oxcart in Oberlin on April 19, 1833, it was to enter their new home built on the southeast corner of the campus near the site of the Historic Elm. Tradition has it that Peter Pindar Pease first came to Oberlin to look over the ground on March 15, 1833, when he cut down the first trees felled on the site. On April 3 Mr. Pease came from Brownhelm with two other men and these three cut an ox-wagon road through the forest. The third visit was on April 10 of the same year when he came with a nephew, Alonzo Pease, son of Hiram A. Pease, to make arrangements for the building of the log cabin which was to be his home. Logs were drawn and prepared for the new structure and aid was secured from other pioneers living in small settlements near Oberlin.[1] The actual work of construction began April 16, 1833, and the home was ready for occupancy when Mr. and Mrs. Pease arrived three days later, accompanied by their five children. Signatures on the Oberlin Covenant of Peter Pindar Pease and his wife Ruth H. Pease are supplemented by the names of these children with their ages as follows: Amanda 10, Flavius 8, Eliza 6, Samantha 3, and Margaret, an infant. Other children later born to Mr. and Mrs. Pease were: Walter, Frederic, Franklin, Herbert, Lucius, and Phineas.

In the oxcart of Deacon Pease, when he came with his nephew to begin clearing for the building of his home here, were boards and tools and camping utensils. The first work was to stand the boards against a tree near the Historic Elm to make a temporary shelter. This was the home of the two for four days. The pious character of Deacon Pease is attested in a letter written ten years after the founding of Oberlin by Flavius E. Pease, his oldest son, who said: "I remember my eighth birthday, April 17, 1833. On the 19th our father moved our family to the log cabin on the site of the future Oberlin. The first Sabbath we spent in Oberlin our father called his own family together and

---

[1] Mr. Pease was told while his work was going on that he could not get men to help unless he furnished them liquor. "If I can't," said he, "let the work stop. There can be no ardent spirit on that ground." But there was no lack of laborers. Among those who helped was Peter Bender, great-grandfather of Miss Pearl Eppley, O. C., '12.

said in substance, 'We are away from our own home but we can worship God together.' So he read something; we sang and prayed; he then went over our Sunday School lesson with us children, as he would at our own church. This I remember distinctly because of the novelty of the situation, and the solemn impression which I received which remains with me to this day."

After the cabin ceased to be used as a place of worship, and Mr. Pease no longer occupied it, it became the first abode of many new families in succession, and was the first home in Oberlin of President Mahan.[2]

That John J. Shipherd and Philo P. Stewart, founders of Oberlin College, placed great confidence in Deacon Pease is shown by the fact that, by arrangement with Mr. Shipherd, Mr. Pease was first on the ground and to him was committed the duty of preparing for the reception of colonists later to arrive. He had general oversight of building operations for the college for the first two or three years of the history of the school. In the language of President Fairchild, "Mr. Pease at once entered upon the work necessary to prepare the way for the colony and the school, without reference to his personal interests as a colonist. He was to make such provision as was possible for the reception of the colonists as they should arrive, and superintend and hasten forward the work upon the building which was to receive the school." That his associates in this great work had confidence in his judgment as well as in his industry is shown by the fact that Mr. Pease had been made a member of the "Board of Trust," already constituted, of the Oberlin Collegiate Institute,

---

[2] A letter from Mrs. Marianne P. Dascomb to her mother, dated Oberlin, April 7, 1835, gives this sprightly description of the cabin of Peter Pindar Pease: "As I wrote this I stopped my pen and raised my eyes to laugh, and as my eyes rested on an object seen from my window, my risibility increased, as I thought I would describe it to Hannah. It was the palace of President Mahan. It was not originally erected for him, being the first house erected in Oberlin. It was made of the bodies of the monarchs of our forest in their native state, no hammer or saw being allowed to mar their pristine beauty. The mansion is on Centre Street, being at the north end of a block of buildings in the same style of architecture. In front of this dwelling is one door, and a few inches from it one window. This whole pile having become somewhat dilapidated by the encroachment of time, or the depredation of village school boys who have been trained there for a few months past, has been repaired, and a shanty of rough boards added to make more numerous apartments. I have not been in recently to observe modern improvements, but the president says they shall have a fine suite of apartments, a parlor, kitchen, bedroom, etc."

although the school had not yet been incorporated. When the Charter was granted by the state a few months later Mr. Pease was made a charter member of what finally came to be called the "Board of Trustees" and he served faithfully on this board until his death in 1861.

Peter L. Pease, a grandson of Peter Pindar Pease, now living at 551 Fifth Avenue, New York City, has in his possession a scrap book made by Amanda Pease, eldest daughter of Deacon Pease. Among the items contained in the book is the only known existing letter or document, aside from deeds, in the handwriting of Deacon Pease. This document bears no date, but the concluding sentence indicates that it was written by Mr. Pease late in life, after his companions in the building of Brownhelm had all died. It reads as follows:

In 1816 Colonel Henry Brown, of Stockbridge, Massachusetts, visited Ohio for the purpose of selecting a location for a colony as a settlement for about one dozen families who were engaged in the enterprise. On the fourth of July he set his foot on Township No. 6, Nineteenth Range in the Connecticut Western Reserve (now Brownhelm) and concluded to make a purchase of the same. Himself and two young men, D. S. Baldwin and William Lincoln, spent a week or more reconnoitering the township, then an unbroken wilderness, and commenced opening a pathway for wagons from the lake back to the center and south part of the town and succeeded in getting about four miles—then returned to Stockbridge and on October 23 left with three young men for the new settlement and arrived the tenth of November. The names of the young men: Elihu Millard, Mr. Risley and Peter Pindar Pease. They commenced building the first house in town—logs of course. December 2 Brown left for the East, leaving us three to winter in this dense forest, to chop down and clear the heavy timber and commence cultivating the soil. Novelty kept up our spirits for a month or two till our small library had been well perused and several jew's harps worn out, then we felt lonesome and began to sigh for society—so we continued till about the first of March when William Lincoln arrived with an ox team loaded with pork and tools, furniture, bedding, etc. Then we took a new start and went on cheerfully . . . June 3, 1817, came the first family or families. Brown's family did not arrive until May, 1818. By this time about one dozen families had settled in town. All the first winter we sat on stools without backs and found we were getting very crooked. With elbows on our knees on rainy days, wanting something to do, several of us set to work to make backs to our chair stools. In the course of the day three chairs appeared of different construction. Our tools consisted of an ax, auger and jackknife. Ten of these were too frail to endure the hardship of the wear. They and the individuals who made them have long since passed away. *This one only remains, and, by the blessing of God, its author is with you today. P. P. Pease.

Without question Mr. Pease was the acknowledged leader of the colonists in these early days. His name appears first in a letter to Mr. Shipherd written June 11, 1833, giving a bird's-eye view of the condition of the colony, both physical and spiritual. For some weeks the Pease home was the only building on the college site and Mr. and Mrs. Pease were glad to keep open house and temporarily care for those who came as colonists or as prospective students.

There could be no question but that Deacon Pease was in entire sympathy with the high purpose of the founders of the school. Over the door of the humble cabin, which he largely built with his own hands, he put the words "Present your bodies a living sacrifice." Mrs. Marianne P. Dascomb, wife of Dr. James Dascomb, member of the faculty of the college, writing to her parents in the East in April, 1835, says: "We removed from the boarding house last winter to Deacon Pease's, and find our situation far preferable to what it was last summer. Mrs. Pease is a pleasant woman, and manages her children well. She thinks much of making her boarders happy. Deacon Pease is more like Deacon Willson than anyone I know of. He looks like Uncle Tenney, who is ardently pious." This opinion of Mrs. Dascomb is reënforced by a statement made at the Oberlin Jubilee in 1883 by Reverend John M. Williams of Chicago, who came to Oberlin in September, 1833. Mr. Williams said: "I was first introduced into the family of Deacon Pease—a good man whose countenance seemed a benediction."

It was the good fortune of Mr. Pease to sustain this fine reputation throughout his life. At the time of his death, in October, 1861, the Lorain County News said of him: "His counsel and prayers and labors were valuable contributions to the prosperity

---

* Reference is made to one of the chairs made by Deacon Pease and still in the possession of a descendant of Judge Brown a number of years after the death of Peter Pindar Pease.

of the school and to the place in those early days; and to the day of his death his interest did not fail. He was able to rejoice in the prosperity of others, although his own share in that prosperity was not such as to man's judgment might seem appropriate. His estimate of himself and his labors was very modest. His opinion was always given quietly, but definitely and forcibly. Though naturally quick in his impulses, his temper was kept under such control that those most intimately associated with him never heard a word that they could wish recanted, an utterance that was not marked by candor and gentleness."

Deacon Pease was known throughout his life as a builder. Speaking of the relations of the colony and the college at the Jubilee celebration Reverend William H. Ryder said: "The college was Oberlin, and Oberlin was the college. Deacon Pease and Deacon Turner with handsaw and jackplane were as important to the college as Dr. Dascomb with his retort and blow pipe." Mr. Pease worked on many of the early college buildings and aided in the building of the First Church. He was more or less active in this manner to the time of his death. One of the final entries in the records of the Prudential Committee respecting Mr. Pease is dated August 13, 1861, and notes that a "bill of Peter Pindar Pease for work about the foundation of the Ladies Boarding Hall was submitted to Professor J. H. Fairchild to inquire and report." This work was done in the spring of 1861. The records do not show final action on the bill prior to the death of Mr. Pease the following October.

Since none of the early colonists came to 'Oberlin with the idea of attaining wealth, it is not surprising that, despite his early efforts and his work at his trade of builder, Deacon Pease did not gain a worldly fortune. The trustees of Oberlin College, early in 1834, passed a resolution that Mr. Pease should have credits to his account of scholarships for his children for compensation for the service of himself and his wife during the past year on behalf of the Institution. In November, 1837, the Prudential Committee of the College voted to take a deed for ten acres of land on Mill Street from Brother Peter Pindar Pease at $300 on his debt to the Institution. Later Deacon Pease was allowed $15 for his interest in the wheat on this lot. In August, 1842, the trustees recommended to the Prudential Committee the granting of a lease to Pease for a period of ten years of ten acres of woodlot adjoining his land. In February of the next year two children of Deacon Pease were allowed to attend the Institution free "until Commencement." In August, 1852, the Trustee Records contain a note as follows: "Peter Pindar Pease having presented a request for a permanent lease of thirty acres of land in consideration of early services in the founding of this Institution, for which services he received no compensation and did not then expect any; Resolved, that while we highly appreciate the arduous and self-denying labors of Brother Pease and those of his wife at the period referred to, yet that we cannot accede to his request for the reasons that we have no right to make such a disposal of our present means and that we think it unwise because it might establish a precedent for numerous other claims of like character."

In August, 1854, a contract was made with Deacon Pease and Lyman Hill for putting up the frame timbers, shingling, etc., for the new Chapel for $600. Mr. Pease was also appointed as a committee to make an estimate of Chapel costs. Four years later he was made a member of a committee to report on the cost of repairs to the cupola of Tappan Hall. This date in 1858 is the final date indicating work of this character for Oberlin College. He had, however, retained his membership on the Board of Trustees and in addition served on the Prudential Committee 1834-39 and 1850-51.

It is of record that Deacon Pease was a man of extreme modesty. His active life following the first few years of laying the physical foundations of the village and the college was devoted largely to his trade of carpenter and builder and to his routine duties to his family, the church, and the community. He apparently did not have an acquisitive disposition and the records would indicate that he approached the end of his days with the need to accept the fact that his conspicuous services in the pioneer

The Story of a Century

days could not be counted upon to relieve him from the anxiety incident to the lack of a sound competence in old age. That he felt the need to reënforce his small fortunes is shown in the dignified request he made in 1852 to the trustees of the college for a permanent lease on thirty acres of land. Mr. Pease passed from life in October, 1861. The only paper then published in Oberlin gave a three-line notice of his death at the time and promised a longer appreciation the following week. Civil War was the living issue then and it was two weeks before a sketch appeared of Deacon Pease.[3]

In almost thirty years a new generation had come upon the scene, made up largely of men to whom the early founders were an uncertain memory. Mr. Pease had become a nice old gentleman who did odd jobs of carpentry work about the village. The editor of the paper, immersed in thoughts of war, paid belated tribute to the passing of a good man and noted that in his death an epoch in the history of the village had closed.[4]

---

[3] The author is indebted to Mr. P. L. Pease of New York City, a grandson of Peter Pindar Pease, for the following list of direct descendants of Peter Pindar Pease who were still living in 1933: H. A. Pease, Gladstone, Mich.; Mrs. W. T. Ream, West DePere, Wis.; P. L. Pease, New York City; Mrs. Chas. S. Norton, Gladstone, Mich.; Mrs. Harry Blair, Milwaukee, Wis.; Mrs. C. M. Ray, Columbus, O.; Mrs. Alva Dittrick, Jr., Cleveland, O.; Miss Ruth Pease, New York City; Mrs. L. S. McConaghy, Mobile, Ala.; Lillian Locke, Winchester, Ontario; L. D. Pease, Drummond, Wis.; Edward Pease, Spooner, Wis.; Gertrude Hull, Minneapolis, Minn.; Mary A. Pease, Arthur Pease, Fred Pease, Aldridge Pease, Tacoma, Wash.; Mrs. Jessie Pease, New York City; Marshall Pease, Detroit, Mich.; Delia L. Freestone, Usk, Wash.; Elsie Pease Hasse, Anacortis, Wash.; Clifford Hoag, Spokane, Wash.; Fred Hull, Brainerd, Minn.; Mrs. M. Claire Turner, Portland, Ore.; Maud Hoag Campbell, Port Gamble, Wash.; F. C. Deery, Los Angeles, Cal.; Ruth Deery Foote, Rice Lake, Wis.; Mrs. Arthur D. Hull, Spokane, Wash. This list is supplemented by the following list of descendants of Frederic H. Pease, supplied by his son Marshall Pease, 1509 Broadway, Detroit, Mich: Max L. Pease, and Philip and Josephine Pease, Sumter, N. C.; Marjorie Pease King and John, Josephine, Maxine, and Charles King, 932 Gladstone Ave., Detroit, Mich.; A. B. Pease, Virginia, and Nancy Pease, Boston, Mass.; Marshall Pease, Jr., Cincinnati, O.; Patrica Pease, 1260 Bishop Rd., Detroit, Mich.; Frederic I. Pease, 3941 Pinegrove Ave., Chicago, Ill.; Elinore Pease, Kalamazoo, Mich.; Mrs. Ruth Johnston, and Frederic, Robert, Jessica, and Ruthann Johnston, 12 MacKenzie Rd., Toronto, Canada.

[4] Mr. Peter L. Pease of New York City has in his possession a powder horn used in the War of the Revolution. The horn bears two inscriptions as follows: "Phineas Pease of Stockbridge, Massachusetts, 70 years old, 9th of January, 1826, presents this to Peter P. Pease of Ohio."

"P. Pindar Pease, born 12th of April, 1795, died October 22, 1861, to Walter C. Pease, born Oberlin, Ohio, June 17, 1837, died Cumberland, Wisconsin, December 6, 1900."

Mr. Walter C. Pease was the father of Mr. Peter L. Pease.

THE WORK OF THE BUILDERS

CHAPTER III

THAT Mr. Shipherd and Mr. Stewart were able to see the realization of their hopes in the opening of Oberlin Collegiate Institute in its own building on December 3, 1833, was due to persistent effort on the part of Deacon Pease and the ten or more pioneers who appeared upon the scene soon after the completion of the first log cabin here in April of that year. All through the summer was heard in the forest the sound of the ax wielded by pioneers who were clearing the way for the building of college and colony. Two or three modest homes were erected soon after the completion of Mr. Pease's cabin. First consideration was properly given to the needs of the college, since preparation must be made for the coming of students. The community was for the first year so small that there was little in the way of activity beyond the construction of small homes and the putting up of the needed college structures. The first of these was Oberlin Hall.[1] This building, started in the summer of 1833, was ready for use at the opening of the school. It was a wooden structure, 35x40, two stories in height, and it included a boarding hall, chapel, meeting house, school room, college office, professors' quarters, and private rooms for forty students. It was located on the south side of College Street, west by south of the Historic Elm. While a few prospective students were on the ground in late summer and gave aid in the work, the greater part of the construction was done by the colonists.

The second college building, the carpenter shop,[2] was built in the fall of 1835 and stood west of Oberlin Hall. It was used for a time for lecture rooms and for sleeping quarters for students.

Colonists and students had part also in the building of the

---

[1] Oberlin Hall, partaking of the primitive character in construction and fittings of the buildings in Oberlin of that day, was sold in 1860, the college having abandoned its use. The building was used for business purposes until 1886, when it was destroyed by fire.

[2] The shop was used for business purposes for half a century. It was destroyed by fire in 1886.

The Story of a Century

First Ladies Hall,[3] which was begun in the summer of 1834 and completed in the autumn of 1835. It stood on the northeast corner of the lot on West College Street now occupied by Wright Laboratory, formerly the Second Congregational Church.

Cincinnati Hall, also known as Slab Hall, was built in 1835 to accommodate students coming from Lane Seminary. It was built of rough green lumber and had passed from existence about 1840. It stood near the site of Sturges Hall.

Another college building project of the year 1835 was the erection of a two-story brick home for Professor Charles G. Finney. This stood on the site of Finney Chapel. This same year saw the building of a home for President Mahan. It was a two-story brick house and stood on the present site of Warner Hall on North Professor Street.[4]

A modest building project in the year of 1835 was the construction of Walton Hall, a two-story frame building of twelve rooms, located on South Main Street opposite the old high school building. Funds for its building were given by the Presbyterian Church of Walton, New York.

The year 1836 marked the completion of Colonial Hall, begun in the autumn of 1835. It was located west of Ladies Hall, near the southwest corner of West College and Professor Streets. This building was named Colonial Hall because the residents of the community, then known as colonists, subscribed about half of the five thousand dollars which the building cost. It was agreed by the college that the lower floor of the building should be used for community Sunday services. This building was divided into dwelling houses about 1866 and removed to other locations.[5]

Tappan Hall, also begun in 1835, was completed in 1836. Arthur Tappan, of New York City, generous friend of the col-

---

[3] In 1865, on completion of the new Ladies Hall, this building was divided into five sections and used as dwelling houses in various parts of town. One section was bought by Lyman Hill, grandfather of J. V. Hill, Oberlin merchant, and placed on North Pleasant Street.

[4] The Mahan home was bought in 1850 by Professor Morgan and used by him until 1881, when it was bought by the Conservatory of Music. Two years later it was torn down that Warner Hall might occupy its site.

[5] A section of the building, almost a century old, still stands (1933) as a dwelling at the southeast corner of Woodland Avenue and West Lorain Street.

lege in those pioneer days, gave $10,000 for its construction. It stood at the center of the college campus and for a number of years the campus was called "Tappan Square." This structure was of brick and was described at the time as "The ultimate idea of comfort and convenience in a college dormitory." Despite this strong approval it was torn down in 1885, "because of grave imperfections of constitution."

The only structure built in 1838 was the old Chemical Laboratory, a one-story brick building 30x50 feet. It stood south of Colonial Hall.[6]

In the building of their modest homes the pioneers made use of Main Street, which was the first thoroughfare cleared by the settlers. These first homes were on the east side of the street, between College and Lorain Streets. Building within a few months began on South Main Street where dwellings were put up. The sawmill, which was put up in the late fall of 1833, was located at South Main and Mill (now Vine) Streets. The home of Pringle Hamilton, still standing in 1933 at South Main and Hamilton Streets, was at the time of its building in the midst of the forest.

In 1834 the community building development spread to East College and East Lorain Streets. The following year saw the building on North Professor Street, west of Tappan Square, of homes for President Mahan and Professor Finney. The early plan to confine homes of professors to this street, which at that time extended only from College to Lorain, was soon abandoned. Pleasant Street from College to Lorain and West Lorain Street were opened early, but no homes were built on them in the first year or two of the development of the colony.

Early in the year 1834, while minor building operations in the way of homes were in progress on the part of the community, a colonial meeting was held at which the Oberlin Covenant principles were drawn upon for the determination of the question of

---

[6] The building program of the college prior to the Civil War was completed by the construction of the College Chapel, begun in 1854 and dedicated in 1855. It was of brick, two stories high, and stood on the campus south of Tappan Hall.

color for houses. The majority opinion was reached that red was the most durable and least expensive color and that consequently the houses of the village should be painted red. This color was placed on three dwelling houses and the college carpenter shop. Aside from these indications of obedience to the community meeting, each builder exercised his own judgment in the application of paint. "So early," says President Fairchild, "under the Oberlin Covenant, did taste begin to prevail over stern utility."

Oberlin had, however, at this time at least one colonist who took such matters very seriously. In a letter to the trustees of the college on March 9, 1836, T. S. Ingersoll asked: "Will you suffer a word from one who loves the cause in which you are engaged?" After pointing out that the trustees are agents for God, Mr. Ingersoll quotes from the text, "Ye cannot serve God and mammon." He drives this statement home with the following specifications: "In the house which is built for Brother Mahan, I have found some forty or more dollars worth of work in the two north rooms which I cannot find for my life any good reason for, except it be to please the taste of a vitiated world. An impenitent master-builder remarked to me the other day that he thought President Mahan's house might have been built $300 cheaper, taking size and style, and have it answer the object for which it ought to be built. There is a plain, neat, simple style of building which commends itself to every enlightened good sense, and still will not be highly esteemed by the world, neither is it an abomination in the sight of God." Mr. Ingersoll, who had never had opportunity to see the new Theological Quadrangle of Oberlin College nor the Allen Art Building, closes with the advice to the trustees that they draw their models from the word of God and not "from some human architect."

Writing many years after the building of Oberlin, C. S. Hopkins, long a resident here and the son of a pioneer settler, says: "When the colonists first began to put up dwelling houses here in Oberlin they were built with heavy timbers. The sills were usually 8x10 or 12 inches and the beams were a little smaller. It was very difficult to get stones for the foundations then, so many of the houses were put upon wooden blocks; oak was generally used, for that was more durable than other kinds of timber. The blocks were put in the ground two or three feet and then the sills were laid on the blocks and the frame put up. To make the dwellings more comfortable in the winter, boards were nailed around on the blocks and then banked up with earth or sawdust.

"When Daniel B. Kinney built his house on West Lorain Street—the farm was later owned by D. P. Reamer—he procured the stone for the cellar wall and foundation on his farm on the northwest corner near the road. He removed the earth for a piece about fifty feet square and quarried out the stone. The stone seemed to lay in thick layers about four or five inches thick. It required a great deal of hard work to get stone for building purposes. It was all brought in in wagons, mostly from Amherst. I remember one place where we got the stone, it cropped out in great ledges some fifteen or twenty feet high. The writer has brought a great many loads of stone to town with an ox team. It was considered a good day's work to get a load. . . ."

Mr. Hopkins in writing of the building of the College Chapel which preceded Finney Chapel said: "Peter Pindar Pease, the first pioneer of Oberlin, put on the roof and built the attic. A. L. Morris and Deacon Herschel Reed had the job of finishing the interior. The lumber for the seats and in fact all the finishing stuff was done by hand. We took it just as it came from the mill after it was kiln dried. . . . With the exception of about two days' work, the writer laid all the floors in the building. The flooring was gotten out by S. B. Ellis, father of the late Professor John M. Ellis. They did not understand getting out flooring then as well as nowadays. I remember in laying it I had to use an awful sight of power to get it together; and some of the boards were badly sprung and after a great deal of sweat (not swearing) I laid the floor in good shape, all for $1.25 a day."

One of the first buildings of a community character was a hotel conducted in 1833 by Brewster Pelton on the site of the present 'Oberlin Inn, at East College and Main Streets. The year after the building of the log hotel Mr. Pelton moved the smaller house to the rear of the lot and built on the site a large frame hotel, which gave good service until it was destroyed by fire in January, 1866. In 1834 Theodore S. Ingersoll opened on North Main street the first store in Oberlin, conducting it for about two years. He himself put up the building.

The business center of the town in these early days ran north and south on Main Street from the present public square. There were, of course, no business blocks on the west side of Main Street between College and Lorain, as this was college property. Several small frame business buildings were built on Main street, just south of the present block of the Oberlin Savings Bank Company. At the same time there was a business development north on Main Street from the hotel corner which finally became the Merchants Exchange. Two stores were built in this section by Brewster Pelton, both of them before the year 1840. Business men of the late 30's and early 40's included Jonas Jones, T. De-witt Eells, J. W. Mason, Lewis Holtslander, George Kinney, Sidney Bedortha, O. R. Ryder, Brewster Pelton, and others.

Fire in 1848 destroyed a business block belonging to O. R. Ryder, as well as the book store and printing office of J. M. Fitch, who printed the Oberlin Evangelist. These buildings were located on South Main Street. Brewster Pelton, who seems to have been most active in construction business in the early days, formed a partnership in 1843 with Philo Weed of New York. In 1850 Weed withdrew from the firm and formed a partnership with Woolston Beckwith. The two partners bought out the tin shop of B. Pelton & Company and went into business on East College Street, operating one of the first stores in that section. Mr. Pelton finally sold all his interests of a business character to Johnson & Kellogg.

In April, 1852, George Kinney and Frank Carpenter opened a dry goods store, Mr. Kinney retiring in 1856. Two years later he formed a partnership with D. P. Reamer. In 1849 George W. Ells opened a tailoring shop which he conducted for more than a quarter of a century. Five years later Hiram A. Bunce opened a drug store near the Ells shop on South Main Street.

The small manufacturing interests of the early days seemed to center on Plum Creek near what is now Vine Street. The first steam mill was built by Oberlin College in October, 1833, on South Main near Plum Creek. This was both a flour and grist mill. It was later sold to Isaac Chamberlain and by him to Henry Wilcox. It was owned by Beebe & Horton when it burned in 1846. A saw mill was built in 1841 on the east side of Water Street by Ellis, Wilder & Reed. It was soon abandoned, and in 1856 L. M. Hall used the old boiler to furnish steam for a flour mill built near the spot. In 1846 Lewis Holtslander built a grist mill on the west side of Water Street, south of Hall's mill.

The earliest cabinet maker in the village was David S. Ingham, one of the Lane Seminary students. He made the bedsteads for Tappan Hall and the college furniture generally. A large chair shop was located in the early years south of the creek, about midway between Main and Professor Streets. It was burned in 1849. Walton Hall, built for college use in 1835, was used as a chair factory for a number of years.

In 1838 three students put up a building on South Main Street to be used as a factory where students depending on manual labor for support might be employed. President James H. Fairchild, then a student in college, made the window frames for the building, twenty in number, for a contract price of fifty cents each. The student proprietors began the manufacture of sashes and doors and put in a mortising machine. In 1840 a shoepeg factory was installed and a few years later a small factory, owned by Jennings, Wilder & Ellis, was established. For a while this was the only cabinet shop in Oberlin. In 1848 a curtain and dress making machine was installed and did an extensive business.

Anson Penfield opened the first blacksmith shop and wagon factory near the college mill in December, 1834. In 1838 he was caught by a power belt and killed. His brother, Isaac Penfield, continued the shop after his death. At the same time Hiram A. Pease, brother of Peter Pindar Pease, had a wagon shop which he later sold to Penfield & Avery. Mr. Pease carried on wagon making at his home for many years after the sale. Prior to his appointment as postmaster in 1843 E. F. Munson worked at blacksmithing here. He had conducted a shop in Elyria before coming to Oberlin. In 1843 Allen Jones owned a blacksmith shop on North Main Street. He made some of the iron work used in the construction of the First Church. About the year 1834 Bela Hall had a blacksmith shop on South Main Street. He was the first smith in Oberlin.[7]

In 1836, when college and community were both feeling the pinch of "hard times" due to the panic and the great fire in New York, Mr. Shipherd got into communication with the Reverend E. B. Coleman, who persuaded the Oberlin man that the manufacture of silk would solve the financial difficulties of both college and community. At this time, with much of the needed clearing of the land done, the college was finding it difficult to furnish manual labor to all students applying. It was doubtless with the thought of curing this trouble, as well as of increasing the growth of the school, that Mr. Shipherd persuaded the trustees to invest more than $2,000 in 60,000 mulberry trees. These were meant to feed about 1,000,000 silk worms, with the assurance from Mr. Coleman that at the end of a year the expense would be met and there would be continuing profits thereafter. Colonists and stu-

---

[7] Writing more than a generation after the founding of Oberlin, E. M. Leonard, himself one of the pioneers, tells of the experience of Bela Hall. Mr. Leonard relates that Hall, who arrived on the scene before he brought his wife to Oberlin, built one of the most "aristocratic" log houses in the community. It had a shingle roof, two rooms—one used as a living room and the other as a kitchen—a chimney made of brick, with two fireplaces, and a finished stairway leading to an attic. This was located on South Main Street. When this home in the wilderness was completed Mr. Hall sent word to his wife, who was a semi-invalid of nervous disposition. She came to Oberlin with apparent misgivings as to her ability to remain in the new country. Mr. Hall thought he had conquered this obstacle in the little home which he had built for her. As it developed Mrs. Hall could not become reconciled to physical conditions here and returned to her home in Vermont. Mr. Hall, who remained and aided in the building of the community, is described by Mr. Leonard as "A man in constant communion with Heaven." The home which Hall built was later sold and used for some years as a cooper's shop. A part of the lot was for a number of years in possession of the Leonard family.

Oberlin Colony

dents united in the planting of the trees and in support of the venture. Recitations were suspended for a week while mulberry trees were set out. A cocoonery was built for the purpose of manufacturing, but a dry summer, combined with Oberlin clay soil, spelled disaster for the mulberry trees and consequently for the silk making. No leaves were ever picked and no silk was ever manufactured. The failure of this plan was one incident in the effort on the part of the trustees to furnish manual labor to all students. Appeal was finally made to the colonists for help in the problem. In 1849 there was discussion as to the possibility of renting the college farm. Three years later it was decided to lease the land perpetually, with a clause requiring the lessees to furnish a certain amount of labor if it should be called for. Much of the most desirable residence property in Oberlin is held in this fashion and is transmitted on sale to new owners without question, although instead of the usual warranty deed the passing of ownership is by way of a ninety-nine year lease renewable forever.[8]

---

[8] It was ascertained that a single family, as a rule, afforded as much employment to students as several acres of farm land, managed as the college had been able to do it, and this without any expense or supervision on the part of the college. After mature consideration, it was decided to lease permanently the inalienable lands of the college, with the provision that the leaseholders should furnish a certain amount of labor to students. Thus the college farm was opened to occupation for residence, and is now covered by that part of the village lying between Lorain and Morgan Streets and west of Main Street.—President Fairchild, *Oberlin: The Colony and the College.*

REBELS SAVE THE COLONY

CHAPTER IV

EARLY in the year 1835 occurred the accession to the college of the "Rebels" from Lane Seminary, an event which, with its various ramifications, had more to do with shaping the character and destiny of Oberlin College, and consequently of Oberlin Village, than any other occurrence in the first half century of the school's existence. The coming of these students was accompanied by enlarged finances for the school, the addition of Charles Grandison Finney to the faculty, and the strengthening generally of the teaching force by the acquisition of educators of high standing. But more than all these, it brought about a declaration by the Board of Trustees of the Institute construed to be an endorsement of the anti-slavery movement. This last act fixed the character of the college and, combined with the international reputation of Mr. Finney as a leader in theology and evangelism, made certain the future of both college and colony.[1]

Lane Seminary was located at Cincinnati. Many of its students were drawn from Oneida Institute in New York. Some of these were convinced by the arguments of William Lloyd Garrison against slavery and some had sat under the evangelistic preaching of Finney. These students had arranged for a series of debates at Lane on the slavery question and these went forward for eighteen successive evenings. Anti-slavery views grew in strength among the student body and the debates were a matter of common knowledge in Cincinnati. The growing interest disturbed the Board of Trustees, who met and made a ruling prohibiting the discussion of slavery among the students, both in public and private. This stand was taken without consultation with the faculty. At this same meeting a message was sent to Professor John Morgan, a member of the faculty, then in New York City, that his services were no longer desired. Students immediately went "on strike" and four-fifths left as a body.

---

1 The fortunes of college and colony were at low ebb early in 1835 and there was grave doubt of the final success of the venture.

Oberlin Colony

This was the condition late in 1834 at the close of the first year of operation of Oberlin College. "Father" Shipherd at this season set forth to secure funds for the further work of the school and to look for a president and a professor of mathematics. Tradition has it that after a season of fasting and prayer, his habit when considering matters of grave importance, he received a call from "on high" to go to Cincinnati. This inspired message is said to have reached Mr. Shipherd at Columbus, at which point he had intended to go directly eastward. For a time he resisted, but finally, after prayer, changed his course to Cincinnati.[2]

After a day of rest at Cincinnati Mr. Shipherd called on Reverend Asa Mahan, pastor of the Sixth Street Presbyterian Church, who gave him in detail the story of the Lane Rebellion.

At the time of the visit of Mr. Shipherd to Cincinnati the "Lane Rebels" had been for about five months continuing their studies in a temporary building not far from the city. Arthur Tappan, of New York, who was to become in time one of the chief contributors to Oberlin College in its early days, had offered $5,000 for a building for these striking students on condition that they establish a school under anti-slavery principles. It is significant that Mr. Mahan had been a trustee of Lane Seminary and that he resigned because of his failure to agree with other members of the Board in their effort to prevent free speech among the students.

In December, 1834, Mr. Shipherd wrote the Board of Trustees saying: "I desire you, at the first meeting of the trustees, to secure the passage of the following resolution to-wit: '*Resolved,* That students shall be received into this institution *irrespective of color.*' This should be passed because it is a right prin-

---

[2] In his *Story of My Life* Professor G. Frederick Wright has this more credible version of Shipherd's trip. "The national road was then built and furnished the easiest way to reach the Atlantic Coast from the central west. Mr. Shipherd went from Oberlin to Columbus to take advantage of this new lane of communication. At Columbus he chanced to meet Theodore Keep, a son of one of the earliest friends of Oberlin, who was coming from Cincinnati where he had been one of the seceding students from Lane Seminary. Keep told Mr. Shipherd of the situation at Lane and urged him to go down to Cincinnati and see if some arrangement might not be made for the advantage of all parties concerned. Though suffering from a temporary illness Shipherd changed his original plan and rode to Cincinnati. Mr. Mahan at once fell in with Mr. Shipherd's proposition that the Lane students should come up to Oberlin."

ciple, and God will bless us in doing right. Also because thus doing right we gain the confidence of beneficial and able men, who probably will furnish us some thousands. Moreover, Brothers Mahan and Morgan will not accept this invitation unless this principle rules. Indeed, if our Board would violate right so as to reject youth of talent and piety because they are *black,* I should have *no heart* to labor for the upbuilding of our Seminary, believing that the curse of God would come upon us, as it has upon Lane Seminary, for it is unchristian abuse of the poor slave."

Those of the present generation, having in mind the long and honorable record of Oberlin College and Community in underground railroad history, in the Wellington Rescue, in advocacy of the Republican party, when in its infancy it was battling against the slave evil, might assume that this request of Mr. Shipherd met with hearty endorsement. Such was not the fact. There was nothing in the Oberlin Covenant touching on slavery. In the summer before the submission of Mr. Shipherd's request to the trustees there had been discussion of slavery by the students and colonists in the Oberlin Lyceum. These debates showed that with the exception of Mr. Shipherd and a few students both Town and Gown were Colonizationists. Mr. Shipherd had suggested a thing entirely new in education in the West and the founders of Oberlin, other than "Father" Shipherd, both within and without the school, were men and women of conservative belief and training. There was opposition both in the colony and the college. The fear that the college would be overrun by colored students caused much discussion and considerable excitement. The idea did not appeal. Young women students, in Oberlin for the long vacation then held in the winter, declared that if colored students were admitted to the institution they would return to their homes in the East if they had to wade Lake Erie. Because of the bitter opposition and the excitement prevailing here in Oberlin, the trustees decided to hold their meeting in Elyria, where it had been said the atmosphere would be more congenial to deliberation. A petition submitted to the trustees

Oberlin Colony

at this meeting, signed by the chief colonists and by certain students who were then in Oberlin, was worded in a fashion that indicated a desire of the signers to place the responsibility for a decision upon providence and the trustees. The petition read:

> Whereas, there has been, and is now, among the colonists and students of the Oberlin Collegiate Institute a great excitement in their minds in consequence of a resolution of Brother J. J. Shipherd, to be laid before the Board, respecting the admission of people of color into the institution, and also of the Board's meeting at Elyria: now, your petitioners feel a deep interest in the Oberlin Collegiate Institute, and feel that every measure possible should be taken to quell the alarm that there should not be a root of bitterness springing up to cause a division of interest and feeling (for a house divided against itself cannot stand): Therefore, your petitioners request that your honorable body will meet at Oberlin, that your deliberations may be heard and known on the great and important questions in contemplation. We feel for our black brethren—we feel to want your counsels and instructions; we want to know what is duty, and, God assisting us, we will lay aside every prejudice, and do as we shall be led to believe that God would have us to do.

Possibly feeling that no additional light had been shed on the subject by this petition, the trustees failed to take a definite action at the Elyria meeting with respect to the admission of colored students. They had appointed President Mahan and Professor Morgan in compliance with a request of Mr. Shipherd, but supplemented this action by the following record:

> Whereas, information has been received from Reverend J. J. Shipherd, expressing a wish that students may be received into this institution irrespective of color; therefore, resolved, that this Board does not feel prepared till they have more definite information on the subject, to give a pledge respecting the course they will pursue in regard to the education of the people of color, wishing that this Institute should be on the same ground, in respect to the admission of students, with other similar institutions of our land.

It is a fact that one or two eastern schools were at this time admitting Negro students. The stand of Oberlin for co-education, taken at the time of the founding of the school, was more out of line with practices in eastern educational circles than was the final determination to admit colored students. Meantime, it is well to record the fact that, following his conference with Mr. Mahan at Cincinnati, Mr. Shipherd, in company with Mr.

The Story of a Century

Mahan, went to New York to consult with Arthur Tappan as to the financial affairs of the college and the probability that he would do for Oberlin under similar conditions at least what he had promised to do for the rebellious Lane Seminary students. Mr. Shipherd was advised of the failure of the Board to take action and also of the petition filed by Oberlin colonists. He made responses to this latter in a pastoral letter to the people of Oberlin in which he said: "My fears are excited by your recent expressions of unwillingness to have youth of *color* educated in our institution. Those expressions were a grief to me, such as I have rarely suffered. Although I knew that with some of you the doctrine of expediency was against the immediate obliteration of slavery, because the slaves are not qualified for freedom, I supposed you thought it expedient and duty to elevate and educate them as fast as possible; that, therefore, you would concur in receiving those of promising talent and piety into our institution. So confident was I that this would be the *prevailing sentiment* of 'Oberlin in the colony and institution that about a year ago I informed eastern inquirers that we received students according to character irrespective of color." Mr. Shipherd points out that inter-marriage is not asked and need not be feared, and that there need be no intimate social relations between colored and white students. After the statement that, "If we refuse to deliver our brother, now drawn unto death, I cannot hope that God will smile upon us," Mr. Shipherd gives reasons of a more material character to support his attitude. He says: "The men and money which would make our institution most useful cannot be obtained if we reject our colored brother. Eight professorships and $10,000 are subscribed upon condition that Reverend C. G. Finney become Professor of Theology in our institution; and he will not unless the youth of color are received, nor will President Mahan nor Professor Morgan serve unless this condition is complied with; and they all are men we need irrespective of their anti-slavery sentiments."

Near the close of his letter Mr. Shipherd makes the statement that unless his wishes are respected in this matter he will have to abandon the Oberlin effort. His language is: "Such is my conviction of duty in this case that I can not labor for the enlargement of the 'Oberlin Collegiate Institute if our brethren in Jesus Christ must be refused because they differ from us in color. You know, dear brethren and sisters, that it would be hard for me to leave that institution, which I planted in much fasting and prayer and tribulation, watering it with my sweat and my tears; but I have pondered the suggestion well with prayer and believe that if the injured brother of color, and consequently Brothers Finney, Mahan, and Morgan with eight professorships and $10,000, must be rejected, I *must* join them; because by doing so I can labor more effectively for a lost world and the glories of God; and believe me, dear brethren and sisters, *for this reason only*."

Faced with the fairly open threat of Mr. Shipherd to abandon the enterprise, then still in its infancy, both trustees and colonists came to accept his views. That Mr. Shipherd moved faster in the way of change than did most of his associates is demonstrated by the fact that Philo P. Stewart, then a member of the Board of Trustees, voted against the proposal for the admission of colored students. In time, of course, he became an earnest abolitionist.

It was at a meeting held February 9, 1834, at the home of Mr. Shipherd in Oberlin, built the summer before on West Lorain Street opposite the north side of the college square, that the Board finally took the action requested. Tradition says that it was at the suggestion of "Father" Keep, who, as president, cast the deciding vote for Mr. Shipherd's resolution, that the women of the community under the leadership of Mrs. Shipherd had a season of prayer during the deliberations of the Board, asking that God determine their judgment. The resolution finally passed by the Board is termed by President Fairchild as seeming to be "The expression of timid men who were afraid to say precisely what they meant." This is its language:

> Whereas, there does exist in our country an excitement in respect to our colored population and fears are entertained that on the one hand they will be left unprovided for as to the means

of a proper education, and on the other that they will in unsuitable numbers be introduced into our schools, and thus in effect forced into the society of the whites, and the state of public sentiment is such as to require from the Board some definite explanation on the subject; therefore, resolved, that the education of people of color is a matter of great interest, and should be encouraged and sustained in this institution.

The language of the resolution is anything but clear, but the effect was that sought by Mr. Shipherd and Mr. Tappan in that from that hour Oberlin was on record as favoring the anti-slavery movement. No other action or formal statement was demanded or required. Mr. Finney came on as Professor of Theology. Mr. Mahan was made president and Mr. Morgan took up his duties on the faculty. Mr. Tappan immediately pledged $10,000 for a new building for the Department of Theology and agreed to secure a loan of a similar amount for other improvements. Coincident with these happenings the "Lane Rebels" came to Oberlin and were housed in Cincinnati Hall, built for their accommodation. These additions to the faculty and the definite establishment of a fund for building and operation really changed the character of the college from an educational standpoint. The Institute with its various departments then became a college, although the name was not changed to Oberlin College until 1850.

When action had been taken by the trustees for the admission of colored students, the colonists, who had been at first startled by the suggestion, fell quickly into line and "the house was not divided against itself." Whole-hearted approval was given of the course taken, and Oberlin people, both of colony and college, were pioneers in the anti-slavery movement in the Western Reserve.[3] It was thus a gradual and progressive advance through the preaching of President Finney to the Wellington Rescue, to

---

[3] The attitude of college and community toward slavery after the writing of the record at the demand of Mr. Shipherd may be read in a note in the Oberlin Evangelist of September 18, 1841, telling of the death here of Charlotte Temple, an escaped slave: "She was ignorant of her own age, but her hoary head and furrowed cheeks showed that her years had not been few. The numerous scars upon her body told of the extent of inhuman barbarity inflicted upon her. The slavery from which she fled still retains in its grasp all her relatives. Children and grandchildren survive her, but they are not present to smooth her dying brow, nor follow her to the grave. The mother died alone, and was buried by strangers without one from among her numerous offspring to follow her to the grave, for they are all shut up in the prison house of slavery."

more or less sympathy with the futile attempt of John Brown to free the slaves with a corporal's guard, and to the final contribution of Oberlin College and Colony to the suppression of rebellion and to liberation of the Negro race.

President Finney in setting forth in his memoirs the story of his coming to Oberlin tells how the change grew out of the Lane Rebellion. The first suggestion for Mr. Finney's taking charge of the Lane students came from Arthur Tappan. This was apparently prior to the visit of Messrs. Shipherd and Mahan to New York, since Mr. Finney says that Tappan suggested that if he would go to "some point in Ohio" where he could instruct these young men he (Mr. Tappan) would bear the entire expense. Mr. Finney further tells of the visit of Mr. Shipherd and Mr. Mahan and of their effort to persuade him to go to Oberlin as Professor of Theology. He says: "These Lane students had themselves proposed to go to Oberlin, in case I would accept the call. This proposal met the views of Arthur and Lewis Tappan, and many of the friends of the slave. The brethren in New York offered, if I would go and spend half of each year in Oberlin, to endow the institution, so far as the professorships were concerned." Mr. Finney relates that he made it a condition precedent of his accepting that there should never be interference on the part of the trustees with the internal regulations of the school and that the school should receive colored people on the same conditions as it did white people and that "there should be no discrimination made on account of color." He further tells of the promise of Arthur Tappan that he would give almost all his income of $100,000 a year to Oberlin to make sure that the work would be carried forward, if Mr. Finney would accept. The great evangelist then made the decision to come to Oberlin and carry forward the work here.

Soon after the coming of Mr. Finney occurred the panic which swept the country in 1836, the force of which was felt for several years. Mr. Tappan was caught in the crash and was unable to give the help he had counted upon. Oberlin College and Colony felt at this time not only the inconvenience of small and uncertain wages but as well the suffering incident to poverty. Temporary relief for the school was secured largely through the reputation of Mr. Finney in contributions obtained in England by Reverend John Keep and William Dawes, who were sent as agents for the college.[1] The decision for abolition and the selection of Mr. Finney as a faculty member had much to do with the small contributions given at this time from people in the northern states who, says Mr. Finney, were "abolitionists and friends of revivals." The extent of the industrial calamity, as it affected Oberlin, is shown in this statement made by Mr. Finney in the story of his life: "At one time I saw no means of providing for my family through the winter. Thanksgiving Day came and found us so poor that I had been obliged to sell my traveling trunk, which I had used in my evangelistic labor, to supply the place of a cow which I had lost. I rose on the morning of Thanksgiving and spread my necessity before the Lord. I finally concluded by saying that, if help did not come, I should assume that it was best that it should not; and would be entirely satisfied with any course that the Lord would see it wise to take. I went and preached, and enjoyed my own preaching, as well, I think, as I ever did." Mr. Finney's lifelong belief in the efficacy of prayer was justified in this instance by his finding, when he returned home from church, a letter containing a check for $200 from Josiah Chapin of Providence, Rhode Island. Mr. Finney says: "Mr. Chapin had been here the previous summer, with his wife. I had said nothing about my wants, as I never was in the habit of mentioning them to anybody, but in the letter containing the check he said he had learned that the endowment fund had failed and that I was in want of help. He intimated that I might expect more, from time to time. He continued to send me $600 a year, for several years; and on this I managed to live."

---

1 The debt of the college in 1839 was $40,000, a large sum for those days. The visit of the college agents to England resulted in gifts amounting to $30,000.

AS THE COLONY GREW

CHAPTER V

ALMOST coincident with the foundation of the college and community, attention was given to two or three essentials above and beyond building expansion. For the first two or three years Dr. James Dascomb of the college faculty served as physician for the college and town. His academic duties finally prevented this private service and, in 1836, Dr. Alexander Steele came from New York to Oberlin to practice medicine and continued in this work until his death in 1872. He was followed by Dr. Isaac Jennings in 1839, and in succeeding years by Dr. Homer Johnson, Dr. William Bunce, Dr. Dudley Allen, and others. That the health of the new community was generally good is shown by the fact that the total of deaths to 1840 was 28. In 1839, with a total population of 1000 students and citizens, there were only nine deaths.

One of the first needs of the new colony was a burying ground. In December, 1835, the 'Oberlin Society began a movement looking to the establishment of a cemetery, and, with the coöperation of the colony and the college, a piece of ground lying between Professor and Main Streets along the north side of Morgan Street, which included the present site of the Episcopal Church and of the General Shurtleff home, was set aside for this purpose. The following year the Society supplemented its good work by naming a committee of four, "to act as managers in assembly on funeral occasions." A resolution was later passed as follows: "Persons hereafter buried in 'Oberlin shall be laid in a line; running from south to north beginning at the southwest corner of the ground appropriated for this purpose; thence running north, the heads of the graves being on a line parallel with the east line of lot, six feet from line of lot running north and south." This plot of ground was used for burial purposes for more than thirty years, but after a few years the graves were removed from the lots on Main Street and only the land in the rear was used. This old ground was leased to the Oberlin Society by the college for cemetery purposes and was returned to the college when Westwood Cemetery was established after the opening of the Civil War. Bodies in the old cemetery were, over a period of years, removed to Westwood.

The problem of education of the children of the community was not easily solved. The college undertook primary work in the first year of its existence, with Miss Eliza Branch as teacher, but at the end of the year decided that teaching of this character belonged properly to the community. Accordingly June 7, 1834, the citizens of the colony met to organize a school district. This meeting elected Brewster Pelton, chairman, J. B. Campbell, clerk, Bradstreet Stevens, treasurer, and D. Marsh, Isaac Cummings, and William Hosford, directors. Empowered to provide school facilities, the directors procured George Fletcher's "shop Chamber" as a temporary school building. In August the directors elected William Hosford moderator and voted to build a school house. In April, 1836, the voters of the district approved the raising of $200 to build a school house "20 by 24 feet, one story high, 9 foot posts, underpinned with stone, well lighted entry." This house was built this year on the "parsonage lot," near the site of James Brand House. The new school was built by Bradstreet Stevens. Its use began in 1837.[1]

The new school could not care for all pupils, since an enumeration in the fall of 1837 showed 236 children of school age in the village. The overflow was cared for in rented rooms, the early records showing schools conducted in Mrs. Penfield's front room, President Mahan's school room, Mr. Fletcher's shop, and other places. The first community common school was taught in a part of the house belonging to Deacon T. P. Turner by Miss Anna Moore. Later this school was moved into a shop near the

---

1 When early in 1851 the colony approved the request of the school board for a new school house this old building was acquired by Elizur Leonard, who then lived on the site of the present municipal building on South Main Street. Mr. Leonard placed the building on the south side of the lot, where it still stands, just south of the Town Hall. It was occupied for years by a daughter of Mr. Leonard and is now a part of the home of Mr. and Mrs. A. E. Cassells. It is the middle section of the Cassells home.

corner of Main and East College Streets. Prior to 1837, when the first school house was built and in less degree for several years thereafter, the common schools of the village were moved from place to place as necessity demanded.

The good fathers of the community in that day were not a unit in the support of the program of building a school house for the children. Some considered it a worthy step forward and upward in the cause of education, while others frankly called it an unwarranted piece of extravagance. At the outset rough boards were furnished for seats. Later rough tables were placed around the wall and chairs built in front of the tables with backs to the fireplace and the teacher. This one-room building was the only school house in operation in the village until 1851, although the number of pupils doubled and tripled during these twelve years. Meantime every room and shop that was not in use for any other purpose served as a house for the schools. Private schools were numerous.

A report of the directors of the common schools of the village in 1840 indicates that four schools had been in operation in the district for periods ranging from five to fourteen weeks within that year. Teachers were Jeremiah Butler, Catherine G. Stevens, Laurett L. Turner, and Mary Hall.[2] The directors were Bradstreet Stevens and John Grannis. In 1842 the school enumeration showed a total of 224. This included all persons in the district between the ages of four and twenty-one years. In 1844 eight schools were in operation. There was no great increase in school attendance until about 1850, when the enumeration suddenly doubled, with a total of 428, thirty-four of whom were colored. This increase was due in part to the enlargement of the school district. During all these years the numerous schools

---

[2] Records of the original school show Butler to have been employed for three and one half months at $18 a month "finding him board and washing." Equal suffrage was still years away and Catharine Stevens was employed at $2.50 a week, "she boarding herself." The record further shows that John L. Hunter taught on trial, his wages having been determined at the end of the quarter. That the trial was satisfactory is shown by the fact that he was employed in 1841 at $90 a quarter to have supervision over all the schools of the district.

were struggling for an existence with but little life. The rooms were small and inconvenient, with no furniture in most cases.[3]

Among the early directors were Deacon Peter Pindar Pease, D. B. Kinney, Deacon Thomas P. Turner, Henry Cowles, and Henry Peck. Among the teachers was Margaret Pease, daughter of Peter Pindar Pease, of whom the superintendent said, "She seems industrious and well earned her money."

Oberlin public schools received new impetus when in 1851-52 a new brick school building was built on Professor Street west of Tappan Hall. This was two stories high and contained three school rooms and one recitation room. The rooms were well-furnished for the period. For the first time an attempt was made to grade the schools. It is interesting to note that the building of a second new school house met with much opposition, although there were more than 400 pupils with but one school house for accommodation. In 1854 the schools were re-organized and Joseph H. Barnum was elected superintendent. During his term of office two wings were added to the building, two stories high, providing seven school rooms. The schools were continued in the fall of 1857 without a superintendent. At the opening of the winter term Deacon W. W. Wright was selected by the school board to have general supervision over the schools and to teach some of the classes. He served for the rest of the school year. No superintendent was employed for 1858 and 1859 and the schools suffered by that fact. A change came when in 1860 the Union School District was first organized under the law of 1849. Samuel Sedgwick was made superintendent.

While the work of education was going forward in town and college and buildings needed for community life and for the conduct of the schools were being erected, citizens began early to

---

3 C. S. Hopkins, who was a pupil in the public schools here in the forties, tells of the attendance in a school in the West Lorain Street district in 1846 of an Indian boy known as Charlie Pawnee. The boy was brought to Oberlin by George Gaston in 1845 from a mission established among the Pawnee Indians. Charlie, a boy of fifteen, seemed to like his school work, and joined in the games of the day. After about a year of attendance here the Indian lad slipped away one Sunday and was never seen again in Oberlin. He took his school books with him and set out for his home in the far west, where he finally arrived. Upon his return to his tribe he took off the clothes of civilization and donned the Indian blanket. A year or two later he was killed in Indian warfare.

turn their attention to the problem of good roads. When the community was founded there were, of course, no roads in the real sense of the word leading in and out of Oberlin. In the fall of 1833, when Mr. and Mrs. John J. Shipherd drove from Elyria to Oberlin, "The last two miles of the road before reaching Oberlin was only a track of cleared underbrush, winding among the trees, the roots of which extending across the track, made it so rough that Mrs. Shipherd could not keep her seat and she walked that portion of the way with her babe in her arms." [4]

Speaking of this same time President Fairchild in his history of Oberlin says: "The trees had been cut from the college square, but the stumps were still strong in the ground. The roads near the center had been open to the sunlight but not thrown up or ditched, and teams were sometimes mired in front of the college building. At a greater distance the roads were only tracks through the forests, and it was not an uncommon thing for even young women, coming to the school, to walk the last two or three miles of the way."

In the establishing of the village and college the first streets in the settlement were those surrounding the campus, Main and Professor running north and south and College and Lorain Streets east and west. Despite the fact that the center of the Oberlin tract is at the northeast corner of the campus, the first building in the village was placed in the southeast corner and this determined the center of the growing community. The tendency to grow to the south was increased by the location on Plum Creek of small mills and factories at an early day. As a result of this Pleasant, Morgan, and Mill Streets, the latter now Vine Street, were among the earlier streets.

The most important road in the early days was that leading to Elyria, and citizens and the teachers and students of the col-

---

[4] That Mr. Shipherd had appreciation of the temporal side of college and colony is shown by this paragraph from a pastoral letter to Oberlin people written at New York, January 27, 1835: "And as property is convertible into moral power, look well to the state of your farms, shops, and all your temporal interests; 'be diligent in business,' remembering pastor Oberlin's plea that good roads be made for Christ's sake."

lege joined in giving time and money to repairs and construction. The road building of those early days was crude in character, and the nature of the soil made frequent rebuilding and repairing necessary. This same clay soil made the construction of streets and sidewalks in the village a grave problem before the time of brick and concrete. The first sidewalks were of whitewood plank, three inches thick, laid end to end. When these were renewed the planks were made thinner and laid crosswise. With the coming of the railroad, construction of sidewalks of stone secured from Berea began. A plank road from the intersection of Main and College Streets to the depot was followed by one of broken sandstone. This was soon ground into the clay, and sandstone blocks followed this second venture in road building. At a much later date came the present modern brick paved street. The solution of the road question for the purpose of community and college, prior to the Civil War, came with the construction of the Cleveland, Norwalk and Toledo Railroad in 1852. For the building of this road the township subscribed $20,000 to the stock and residents of Oberlin a like amount.

COLONIAL GOVERNMENT

CHAPTER VI

FOR the first thirteen years of the existence of the community there was no civil authority other than that of the township. The Oberlin Society was incorporated in February, 1834. Its early records indicate that the members recognized it as both religious and secular in character. This grew out of the fact that Ohio laws at that time did not permit the ownership of realty by churches. Early in its existence it is found recommending the employment of Reverend Fayette Shipherd, brother of John J. Shipherd, as pastor of the community church, defeating a proposal that all colonists are at liberty to act with the charter members of the association, defeating a motion to abandon the Charter, considering a resolution for the incorporation of the village, passing a resolution that J. B. Hall be a committee to oversee making and repairing all roads in the place, appointing a committee on January 29, 1835, to consider the building of a school house and the laying out of roads, and, on this same date, passing a resolution that "The conduct of Mr. Townly in disposing of land in Oberlin Colony with the probable intention of speculating, is unjust and contrary to the spirit and intention of the colonists who have settled Oberlin—that we mark such conduct with disapprobation."

In March of the same year a motion that no business, except ecclesiastical, be transacted in this society was lost. On March 3, 1835, a committee was appointed to consider "the extent to which the Charter of this society may be with propriety and can be with safety used under which to transact business." That the society was a forward-looking organization is shown by the appointment early in 1835 of a committee "to explore the route from this place to the mouth of Black River and estimate if possible whether it will be practicable to petition for a railroad from here to that place." Three months later the society jumps from the consideration of national growth through railroads to matters nearer home and resolves that "We disapprove of permitting swine to run at large." In August of that year a resolution passed that "It is inexpedient to sell lands to students." On December 11, 1835, N. P. Fletcher, Deacon Peter Pindar Pease, and P. Hamilton were named a committee to act with the agents of the college in laying out a burying place. In December of this same year a committee was named to investigate fire conditions. On March 1, 1836, the society passed a resolution against swine running at large. This seems to be the first piece of definite village legislation which the society attempted. Again on this date a committee was named to prepare a Charter and forward it to the legislature for the incorporation of Oberlin. A motion on this date that the pastor be exonerated from paying a land tax was lost. At a meeting on May 20, 1836, assessors were named to lay a tax on Oberlin property for the support of the pastor and other necessary expenses of the society. In July of 1836 the society took steps looking to raising $200 to be expended toward the construction of a road to Pittsfield. In August of the same year Asahel Munger was directed to prepare four ladders, two hooks, and two axes and deposit them in a public place for fire protection.

In April of 1837 a new constitution and by-laws were adopted and William Hosford was elected first chairman of the board. The new constitution provided that the society should be composed of such male persons of legal age as are recommended by the board of directors.

The list of incorporators of the Oberlin Society is interesting as furnishing an accurate record of the leading citizens of the community of Oberlin who were on the ground prior to February 26, 1834. The incorporators were: Peter Pindar Pease, Bela Hall, Pringle Hamilton, Philip James, Harvey Gibbs, Bradstreet Stevens, Theodore S. Ingersoll, Daniel Morgan, Daniel Marsh, Isaac Cummings, Origen Cummings, George Fletcher, Asahel Munger, Jonathan L. Simpson, Otis James, Nelson Scovell, Philo P. Stewart, John J. Shipherd, Samuel Daniels,

Oberlin Colony

William Hosford, Jacob J. Safford, Jotham G. Dearborn, Washington George, Brewster Pelton, Paul Sheperd, James Platt, James B. Campbell, E. M. Leonard, and Martin Leonard.

The first list of signers other than incorporators contains the names of several of the early pioneers of Oberlin. These signers were Nathan P. Fletcher, Josiah B. Hall, Fay Hopkins, Daniel B. Kinney, J. P. Turner, N. Brown, O. Eastman, E. T. Penfield, H. A. Pease, Charles Farrow, Anson Penfield, George W. Fletcher, A. H. Boland, James Dascomb, Jonathan S. Campbell, Nathaniel Gerrish, Daniel Stillman, R. Campbell, Edwin Dowd, Lyman Farrar, and Henry Chapin.

Manuscripts for years in the possession of Elizur M. Leonard, pioneer colonist and father of Dr. D. L. Leonard, who made copies of them in 1894, tell of seven meetings held by colonists in the Chapel in 1837. Resolutions introduced at a meeting July 7 included one to the effect that examination should be made of the justice of prices paid for teaming and other work done in Oberlin. A committee appointed under this resolution reported July 21 "that in their opinion the prices of all kinds of labor are too high; also all kinds of trade and the salaries of agents and faculty and officers of the institution." This resolution doubtless reflects the depression which was prevalent in that year following the great fire in New York, and the general panic. A recommendation from a committee as to a policy touching those who had purchased lots from the parsonage plot and conveying the willingness of the purchasers to return the lots on reasonable terms was left with a recommendation to the directors of the Oberlin Society for immediate action. An apparently direct attack on modern banking business was contained in a resolution adopted this same date that "It is a gross violation of the Oberlin Covenant as well as of the sacred scriptures to receive any increase of our poor brothers for moneys lent them." The question of new colonists was taken up at a meeting August 18 and a resolution was passed that "It is inconsistent with our Covenant obligation to encourage any settlers among us who are immoral or unfriendly to our institution, or to dispose of our lands to those we have no reason to believe seek the furtherance of our object." At the same time measures were taken to promote the interest of common schools in the colony. At a meeting August 26 the colonists finally considered and "very unanimously" adopted the following resolution introduced at the suggestion of "Father" Shipherd: "Resolved that the use of tobacco is inconsistent with the principles of this institution and the gospel and the pledge of the Oberlin Covenant, and that we deem it our duty not to patronize any innkeeper or merchant who will vend those articles." A similar resolution was later passed with reference to the sale of tea and coffee.

The Oberlin Society had dual purposes. It was the church organization, and, until the incorporation of the village, was as well the body through which virtually all civic action functioned. We find this society taking charge of taxation and collection and looking after sanitary conditions, as well as calling ministers to have charge of the spiritual welfare of the community and college.

It is doubtful if there was any particular change in the community character which brought about the incorporation of the village in February, 1846. This action was taken by the Ohio Legislature after a record of one or two attempts through the Oberlin Society to bring about this end. The change came largely because the society was itself doubtful of its authority in civic matters, and felt that there would be more satisfaction in the conduct of municipal affairs through the ordinary provisions of the Ohio laws.

At the first election held under the Village Charter, Lewis Holtslander was chosen as mayor. He served two years. James H. Fairchild, later president of Oberlin College, was a member of the first council. Other mayors in the early days were Isaac Jennings, O. R. Ryder, J. W. Merrill, Uriah Thompson, James Dascomb, O. R. Rogers, David Brokaw, A. W. Beecher, and Samuel Hendry. In those days there were no party tickets and nominations were made by a town caucus. This was true for more than seventy years.

The Charter of the village was amended in 1848 to include in the municipality lots 75, 76, 85, 86 of the original survey of

Oberlin Colony

Russia Township. The character of the community is reflected in the fact that the second ordinance passed by council provided a penalty for selling liquor in the village. The first created the necessary offices for the transaction of business. An early enactment provided a minimum fine of 50 cents for playing marbles in the streets.

In 1856 a printed book of ordinances contained only 14 enactments. In 1861 there were 32. In 1932 there were about 150. A measure passed in 1853 created two fire engine companies of not more than forty men and a hook and ladder company of fifteen. A notice on the cover of the ordinance book of 1856 says: "On the occurrence of a fire let every man take with him a pail and also water, if practicable."

When a post office was first opened in Oberlin it was established by the post office department under the name of Russia— the township name. This was on January 10, 1834. David D. Crocker was the first postmaster, serving from the time of the opening of the office until October 20, 1834, when he was succeeded by Harvey Gibbs who walked from Elyria to bring mail to Oberlin. The college and colony were almost two years old when the name of the office was changed to Oberlin on March 16, 1835. When the name was changed a new commission was issued to Gibbs who served until December 11, 1839.[1]

1 The first post office was a two-story frame building on North Main Street, built for the purpose by Harvey Gibbs. This occupied ground later built upon for a residence by Dr. Alexander Steele, and stood just north of the old town hall site, opposite the center of the east side of the campus. On the expiration of the second term of service of Gibbs, Grosvenor D. Reed was named as his successor. Mr. Reed served from December 11, 1839 to June 11, 1841, when he was succeeded by Timothy Dwight Eells. When Mr. Eells was appointed postmaster, in 1841, he moved the office to his store on North Main Street, but a little later he again moved it to a small building a little east of Main Street on the south side of East College Street. From 1843 to 1848 E. F. Munson conducted the office on the site of the present Oberlin Bank Company at Main and East College. When this block was burned in 1848 the office was temporarily placed in the college treasurer's office in Oberlin Hall and was afterwards moved to a house on North Main Street, north of the original 1834 site. In 1850 David McBride became postmaster and moved the office to the W. H. Plumb book store at East College and Main Street. Mr. Munson was again appointed in 1853 and he took the office to his own building on the west side of South Main Street, moving it again in 1855 to a building on the east side of South Main Street. In 1861 George Stevens became postmaster and moved the office to the J. M. Fitch building on East College Street where the business was conducted until 1865, when J. F. Harmon was named postmaster, and he moved it to 11 North Main Street. In 1869 the office was moved to the Carpenter Block on West College. From that place it was removed to 4 North Main Street in 1886. The office was maintained at this North Main Street location (the site of the BeVier-Webber store) until 1869, when it was removed to the Beckwith Block on South Main Street, its location in 1933.

MAKING A CHURCH HOME

CHAPTER VII

IN a community such as 'Oberlin it was natural that among the first organizations aside from the college was a church. The initial steps were taken August 19, 1834, and the organization of the Oberlin church was completed September 13, 1834, with a membership of sixty-one.[1] Nathan P. Fletcher was clerk and Isaac Cummings and Samuel Daniels were temporary deacons. This was the beginning of the present First Church in Oberlin. The pioneer church was named "The Congregational Church of Christ at Oberlin." Reverend John J. Shipherd and Deacon Peter Pindar Pease were delegates to apply to the Presbytery of Cleveland for membership on the part of the church. Mr. Shipherd accepted a call to the pastorate and served until the fall of 1836. He then tendered his resignation and Reverend Charles Grandison Finney, then a member of the faculty of the college, was called to have temporary charge. The relation was finally made permanent and Mr. Finney served as pastor until 1872. In 1836, on the organization of the Congregational Association for the Western Reserve, the Oberlin church withdrew from the Presbytery and became a member of the former organization.

Oberlin Hall, original college building, furnished the first place of meeting. In 1835 colonists and the college united in the building of Colonial Hall, with the understanding that the first floor should be made an audience room for church purposes. This was completed in 1836 and furnished seats for eight hundred people. When in February, 1841, it was found that Colonial Hall could no longer accommodate all attending church services the way was paved for what proved to be the largest building program, viewed from a community standpoint, of the early years of the Colony.

The suggestion to build a church first came from Mr. Finney. At the opening of the spring term in 1841 the hall was crowded

---

[1] At the end of one year the membership had increased to 232 and in less than five years the total membership was 656.

and it was characteristic of Mr. Finney that he proposed, apparently without previous conference with any one, that the congregation meet the next day and talk over the matter of the building of a new church. At this meeting it was determined to go forward, and George Whipple, James Dascomb, Horace Taylor, and Lewis Holtslander were named a committee on building. Mr. Finney made suggestions as to the size and the type of the new structure. Size was emphasized in the plans of the church. The growing congregation made this necessary. It was specified that the new building should be plain and substantial. It was a part of the original plans that rooms for the Institution, as the college was then known, should be included in the building, but this feature was abandoned, largely due to lack of funds.

The year 1841 was spent in an effort to collect money and materials for the new church. Original records of the Oberlin Society and letters of early pioneers disclose that many direct contributions of building material were made, and that in addition many people gave clothing and other articles upon which money for the building operation might be realized. Money in those days was scarce. The college was slowly emerging from one of the worst panics in the country's history and the community of course had shared in these reverses. The end of "hard times" had not come when the building project was first launched. The salaries of the professors in the college were $600 and these sums were not always paid in full. The panic of the late 30's had not spent its force. It had swept away the foundations secured from Tappan and others. Subscriptions for a total of $100,000 finally realized only $6,000. Professor Henry Matson writing of these days says: "Salaries of $600 were no longer possible and for their necessary support the professors could trust only to God." Definite sacrifice was made by members of the congregation and the total cash cost of $13,000 was largely raised through small sums. It is said that the largest individual cash contribution was $100. However, most of the professors pledged $200 each, which of course was not paid in a lump sum. In many instances such givers found it necessary to double their pledges. Many of the

FIRST CHURCH

citizens felt too poor at this time to give in cash and instead donated labor on the building. Some gifts were received from outside Oberlin and were in goods or chattels, later to be converted into cash. Among these gifts were two cows, a wagon, a coat, two pieces of cloth, and a keg of nails. Included in the timber for the church, much of which came from the Whipple farm on what is now Lorain Street, was an oak tree eight feet in diameter. There were a number of whitewood trees seventy feet to the first limb and the beams that support the ceiling of the church were cut from these. The brick used in the building were made on the farm of Pringle Hamilton. Shingles for the church were bought in Canada. The early church records indicate that stone was secured from L. J. Burrell of Elyria. While the record does not show it, tradition says that some of the stones were secured from the quarry on the farm of John Rose near Kipton. Large quantities of lumber were bought from E. Redington of South Amherst. Much of the lumber was donated by the residents of the community. A deacon of the church and an honored resident of the community had accumulated materials for the building of a new house. These he gave to the new church building and spent the rest of his years in his old home. Thus at great sacrifice was the building completed. It is probable that in such times a task so great could not have been performed but for the inspiring leadership of Finney.

The cornerstone of the church was laid June 17, 1842. This was, however, only the beginning of the great task of building, for money and material were increasingly scarce and since much of the work was donated, it was done at odd times rather than continuously. It was after long effort that the end was neared in the putting on of the roof. Advice was sought from a Boston architect, and it was finally finished. Among the carpenters and builders engaged in the project were Lyman Hill, Peter Pindar Pease, and Deacon T. P. Turner. Mr. Hill had much to do with the putting on of the roof, which stands today as an almost perfect piece of workmanship and material.

The Story of a Century

The slow progress of the work is shown by the fact that while commencement exercises were held in the church in August, 1843, five years later a committee was named to consider the painting of the window frames and sashes. The tower was put on in 1845. No carpets were laid until 1851. There was never a formal dedication of the house of worship.

Both town and college were vitally interested in this major piece of construction. The church was for many years the chief assembly room for both college and village. At the time of its completion it was considered "As desirable an audience room as any in the West." It still stands as a handsome and dignified memorial of the excellent taste of our fathers and is still one of the most fitting and imposing church buildings in America. There was unified interest in the building project, as this church and congregation constituted the only church body in 'Oberlin until 1855, when the Episcopal Church was organized. The church of this latter congregation, located on South Main Street, was begun soon after the organization of the congregation, but was not dedicated until May, 1859.

For the first three decades of the life of Oberlin, and possibly for a much longer period, the First Congregational Church was, without question, the most influential organization of a community character within the village. Until close to the time of the Civil War it was the only church in the village, at a period when church membership was almost a prerequisite to comfortable living on the part of community residents. The early colonists signed a Covenant stating in effect that they came to Oberlin to fix their residence, "For the express purpose of glorifying God," and religion, as manifested in outward form, was one of the chief considerations of the community and the college in those days. The First Church, from its forming until the death of President Charles Grandison Finney, very largely reflected the spiritual enthusiasm of this great evangelist. Mr. Finney was ably seconded by President Mahan, Professor Morgan, and other leaders of the time.

Oberlin Colony

Pioneer conditions were in part responsible for the early interest and participation in all the activities of the church. It was a serious age and a sober community had been formed in a section which made little appeal to frivolity. The clearing of the giant forests and the attempt to till a clay soil more or less covered with swamp land was not a matter for jest. The colonists in the early days, as is largely the case now, were poor in the world's goods. They were particularly poor in the first thirty years of the college, since they were dependent in the main on college conditions, and the college itself was then poor. Salaries of professors were small and at times uncertain of payment. Money was scarce. There were neither shows, athletic games, card parties, dances, nor any of the other modern appeals to the lighter side of life. Men doubtless went to church because they desired to do so. But it is probably true that they desired to go to church in some instances because there was no place else to go. Before contact with the outside world changed this condition, the influence of the church in the community was scarcely less than that of the college.

THROUGH EYES OF OTHERS

CHAPTER VIII

THE growth of the College and the Colony from the year of their founding to the days of the Civil War was not viewed with satisfaction in all quarters. Doubtless back of all the criticism of college and colony was the definite declaration of the trustees of the College to receive Negro students and the endorsement by the Colony of this action. This at once earned the hatred of people south of the Mason and Dixon Line and the dislike in possibly less degree of intensity of many in the North.

There was a noticeable lack of endorsement on the part of many outside the immediate world of Oberlin of the wording of the Oberlin Covenant. The fact that those pioneers, who came here in the early days to help build college and colony, were drawn almost altogether by the missionary spirit accounted for an apparent coolness toward the project on the part of outsiders. There was a suspicion that the Oberlin of the early days felt itself a little better than communities founded by the laws of chance or of accepted enterprise. Those who may have desired to make their homes here in the early days, while the Covenant was in force, were frankly told that neither Colony nor College desired new citizens not in entire sympathy with the rules of conduct laid down in the Covenant. At this same time those outside the circle of college and colony felt that "Father" Shipherd had established a code which no people could follow to the letter. Time proved that this outside opinion held much of truth.

Enforced attendance on the part of students at religious services, a rule which maintained in principle for more than six decades, was supported very largely all this time by the sympathetic attitude of the residents of the village. Whatever may have been the merit of the rule against the use of tobacco, those living beyond the confines of Oberlin frankly regarded its enforcement for three-fourths of a century as the placing of emphasis by Oberlin on matters not of first importance. Other rules in the early days, which not only placed a ban on cards but forbade any member of the institution playing checkers, chess or any game of chance or skill, were construed in similar fashion by people of the outside world. The same feeling of wonder or mild exasperation was raised in the minds of the many not affected by such a regulation as that passed in 1859 by the college prohibiting students "from unnecessarily frequenting groceries, taverns, the railroad station, and other similar places of public resort." Such regulations, which were little modified prior to the death of President Charles Grandison Finney, reflected the spirit of "Father" Shipherd and of Mr. Finney. Mr. Shipherd was a man of fine character, but of limited formal education. Mr. Finney remains a great figure in the history not only of Oberlin College and Community but of the progress of religion both in America and abroad. Many who conceded to him this high place in the days of his almost unlimited power and influence in the college and the community held the view that he was inclined too greatly toward a policy of enforcing personal righteousness, as he saw it, to the detriment of a fair degree of responsible liberty to the students and the people in his charge.

It remains true, however, that the chief point of attack on Oberlin College and Community prior to the Civil War was the attitude of both with reference to slavery. This was made emphatic in the Wellington Rescue case, where arrests were made of men who had not participated in the affair, solely with the idea of punishing Oberlin. Discussing this feature President Fairchild says: "The people in neighboring towns were at the outset not in sympathy with Oberlin in its anti-slavery position. They agreed with the rest of the world in regarding it as unmitigated fanaticism. The feeling was often bitter and intense, and an Oberlin man going out from home in any direction was liable to be assailed with bitter words; and if he ventured to lecture upon the unpopular theme, he was fortunate if he encountered words only."

Less than four years prior to the incorporation of the village Honorable Josiah Harris, of Amherst, then a representative in

The Story of a Century

the State Legislature, discloses the attitude of some of the law-makers toward Oberlin in a letter to his wife in which he says: "You can have no conception of the opposition and prejudice existing against Oberlin College in the Legislature. This year it arises principally from the numerous petitions presented last year for the repeal of its charter and from a book, 'Oberlin Unmasked,'[1] passing around the House, and a thousand unfavorable rumors in relation to amalgamation, fanaticism, harboring fugitive slaves, etc., all founded upon rumor." Mr. Harris stoutly defended Oberlin and says that he advised his fellow law makers that, "Most or all of the rumors about the people there are unfounded." But for the support of Mr. Harris and other good friends Oberlin would have lost its charter by legislative enactment.

This feeling against both college and community grew largely out of the anti-slavery attitude of both. Politics was at the root of the discussion. Supplementing the revival meetings of the church Oberlin had in its first thirty years of existence opportunity to hear not only Mr. Finney and Mr. Mahan and others of the college faculty but visiting leaders of public thought as well discuss pertinent topics of the day. These talks were largely in keeping with the purpose of the founders of the community and the college and would in the main, in modern day, be regarded as a little heavy and tedious. Debates on questions of religion frequently turned to a discussion of the provisions of the Oberlin Covenant. This led naturally to the particular provision as to food and drink. President Fairchild says in his history: "The Covenant was measurably specific as to the use of strong drink and tobacco, and these indulgences were discarded. The use of tea and coffee was regarded as questionable, under the Covenant, but how far it was 'practicable' to dispense with them, was never perfectly ascertained. Simplicity of diet was at the beginning maintained on the ground of economy. . . . Mr. Stewart, the first manager of the college boarding hall, had

---

[1] A scurrilous pamphlet published by a former student after he had been dismissed from the college.

Oberlin Colony

very positive ideas on the subject. To diminish the cost of living without detriment to health or vigor was his constant aim. Mr. Finney brought with him ideas on diet set forth by Dr. Mussey, of Dartmouth, and such writers as Graham and Alcott. These views generally involved the use of animal food. . . . The facts were that after two years Mr. Stewart left the boarding hall and a steward was called from Boston who held radical views on a vegetable diet. . . . A table was still set for those who preferred a different diet. . . . Tea and coffee were not introduced into the college boarding house until 1842."

That these experiments in diet touched the life of the community is shown by a call for a meeting at the Chapel for consideration of this topic. The call reads: "Oberlin, Ohio, March 30, 1841. Believing that the Experiment has now been fairly tried, and the merits of a vegetable diet been sufficiently tried in the boarding house of the institution and that the health of many who board there is seriously injured and suffering not only in consequence of a sudden change of diet but also by the use of a diet which is inadequate to the demands of the human system has at present developed;

"We, the undersigned, invite those who believe with us to meet in the Chapel on . . . . afternoon next to express our views on this important subject." This notice bears the signatures of fifteen of the leading citizens of the community, including Lewis Holtslander, Dr. Alexander Steele, T. D. Eells, Deacon Thomas P. Turner, and Nathaniel Gerrish. The experiment in the community was similar to the one in the college. Many families discarded tea and coffee and adhered for years to a vegetable diet.

It was natural that the earnest attention given to spiritual matters in the community should lead in time to a discussion of "sanctification" or "Christian perfection." This had much attention at the hands of speakers, including President Mahan, and, in the language of President Fairchild, "To numbers it proved a lifelong elevation of soul. . . . It was inevitable that in such a movement there would be superficial imitations of the genuine experience." It is probable that the founding of the Oberlin Evangelist near the closing of 1838 logically followed this movement. Mr. Finney, Mr. Mahan, and Mr. Morgan of the faculty were chief contributors.

Thus in the consideration of topics largely touching the spiritual and political side of life, the community was actively engaged in its earlier years. There were no secular newspapers published in Oberlin prior to 1860. Public meetings were made open forums for passing upon questions of a political nature. The commitment of the community and college to anti-slavery at the outset meant with people of the temperament of the founders of Oberlin that this advocacy would grow with the years. Oberlin's attitude on slavery, together with the policy of the college of opening its doors to Negro students, determined for college and town in those days the prejudice and dislike which are born of opinions lacking a basis in sound logic. This feeling from outside served to strengthen the zeal of Oberlin people for freedom without regard to race. The Oberlin-Wellington Rescue was a natural result of a quarter of a century of belief in universal civil liberty and of hatred of oppression.

Comment on Oberlin and its ways was by no means all unfavorable. The Oberlin Evangelist in 1848 published a statement from a traveler from the outside world who says that he put up at the hotel on a visit here and was delighted to find no swearing, no drinking, and no noise which interfered with his comfort. He concludes his word of praise with this statement: "You have my prayers that the morality of your place may never suffer from the encroachments or clouds made by any of our great national or public thoroughfares, which are but so many broad highways of sin and iniquity."

The early fathers may have been dour at times and possibly too serious over matters frequently regarded as trivial in the world beyond the confines of the village and college, but they were unquestionably men of strength and sincerity, and it was out of these latter factors that Oberlin's splendid record of contribution to the Civil War was built.

HIGHER LAW INVOKED

CHAPTER IX

THE Oberlin-Wellington Rescue had its birth at least a century before its occurrence in the consciences of the New England ancestors of the men and women of Oberlin Community and Oberlin College. The love of freedom inherited from this ancestry was shared in more or less intensity by all the pioneer residents of the Connecticut Western Reserve. This veneration for the principles of the Declaration of Independence, even above and beyond a feeling of respect for the Constitution of the United States, was linked in Oberlin in 1858, the year of the rescue, with a definite hatred for human slavery, a passionate abhorrence of the Fugitive Slave Act as a thing "born of the devil," and with open espousal of abolition. This public view of a question which was to result within three years in the bloodshed of civil war, may of course be directly traced to the demand of "Father" John J. Shipherd in 1835 that the trustees of the Oberlin Collegiate Institute go on record as committing the college to education of colored students and, in a broader way, to the abolition of slavery.

Many in the North had resented the terms of the compromise of 1850 and in Oberlin in particular was there great resentment at the granting to the South by Webster, Clay, and their adherents in the national legislature of a new fugitive slave act replacing the enactment of 1793 and virtually attempting to require the northern people to join in the pursuit of escaping slaves. The passage of this compromise, seen in the light of history, was just another step leading to the settlement of the slavery issue on the field of battle. In lesser degree this may be said of the Oberlin-Wellington Rescue case and of John Brown's misguided but heroic effort at Harper's Ferry. Oberlin, with its teachings and traditions, aligned itself with William H. Seward and Salmon P. Chase. Seward, it will be remembered, declared in the Senate in the debate on the compromise act, "There is a higher law than the Constitution." In this viewpoint he was sustained by Chase, who was governor at the time of the Oberlin-Wellington Rescue trials. This doctrine had of course the hearty support of Wendell Phillips, Theodore Parker, and William Lloyd Garrison. Lincoln took the position that, while he was opposed to the principle of the fugitive slave enactment, it should be supported as a part of national law. Seward said on the floor of Congress, "We deem the principle of the law for the recapture of fugitives . . . unjust, unconstitutional, and immoral." This pronouncement was endorsed by the people of Oberlin, who almost as a unit sustained the conduct of those who had part in the rescue and honored them for their unquestioned courage and devotion to principle.

With this background of adherence to the doctrine of abolition and of firm belief in human freedom, it is not at all remarkable that Oberlin had, prior to the rescue case, a long record as a successfully operated station on the Underground Railroad. It is said that in one year alone three hundred and fifty slaves had been cared for in Oberlin and sent forward in safety to freedom in Canada. It was a further boast that no black man fleeing to Oberlin for safety was ever after returned to bondage and that no act of violence had ever accompanied any rescue case here. In view of this anti-slavery history, it was not at all surprising that numerous leading citizens of Oberlin, some of whom were connected with the faculty of the college, were suspected of having part in the rescue at Wellington.

John Price, a negro boy of eighteen, began his career as a figure in history when he came to Oberlin in January, 1856. He obtained employment and lived in peace and safety until the late summer of 1858, when Anderson Jennings, a personal friend of John G. Bacon, a citizen of Masontown, Kentucky, who claimed ownership in Price, arrived in Oberlin. Jennings recognized Price and wrote to Bacon for a power of attorney, saying that he would recover the Negro and return him to Kentucky. Early in September Richard P. Mitchell, an employee of Bacon, came to Oberlin with the requested power of attorney. Jennings then went to Columbus where he secured from the United States Commissioner a warrant for the apprehension of Price. This warrant was given to Jacob K. Lowe, who deputized Samuel Davis of Franklin County as an assistant, and the three returned to Oberlin.

In his stay in Oberlin at the Russia House Jennings had aroused the suspicion of citizens. It was known that he had communicated with Lewis W. Boynton, a farmer living north of Oberlin who was thought to be in sympathy with the Fugitive Slave Act. By the terms of the apparent arrangement between the two, Shakespeare Boynton, a boy of thirteen, son of Lewis W. Boynton, was engaged for the price of twenty dollars to decoy John Price into a ride out of town where he might be apprehended by the United States officers. This plan proved successful and John was arrested Monday, September 13, about two miles northeast of Oberlin by Lowe, Mitchell, and Davis. Jennings was not in the party. Tradition has it that the boy was lured to the place of capture by a statement that one of the farmers in the neighborhood desired his assistance in planting potatoes.

Following the arrest, the three men with the prisoner started to Wellington with the intention of taking Price to Columbus and later to Kentucky. It chanced that the three, in taking a diagonal road leading from Elyria to Wellington, passed two Oberlin young men at Pittsfield. These two hastened to Oberlin and spread the alarm. Among those informed of the capture, according to testimony at the trial later held, were Ralph Plumb, a leading attorney of the village, Reverend J. M. Fitch, bookseller, and Professor Henry E. Peck, a member of the faculty of the college, whose life was devoted in no small part to the interests of Oberlin Community. Within a short time after the two men reported the capture of Price a crowd of at least two hundred residents of Oberlin was on its way to Wellington. The officers had arrived with Price and had their prisoner at the village hotel, the Wadsworth House, where they were awaiting the arrival of a train to Columbus. When the Oberlin crowd appeared on the scene it was soon swollen to a number estimated at five hundred, although not all these were active in the attempt to rescue Price. One witness at the trial stated that in the

The Story of a Century

Oberlin party he saw fifteen or twenty guns, while one of the men who attempted to hold Price estimated the display of firearms at five hundred. History seems to agree that there was no threat on the part of the crowd to use weapons of this character to attain their ends. Many varying stories have been handed down by word of mouth and through public print as to the methods employed to rescue the negro. The one which seems to bear the appearance of truth is that the three officers on the approach of the party from Oberlin took Price to the third story of the Wadsworth House, where they held him in a small room. This room was invaded from time to time, and for a while by agreement of the officers, by rescuers in squads of three and four. Finally, despite the efforts of the officers to keep the room clear, a sufficient number had gathered to make it possible to push Price from the room and to convey him to an awaiting wagon. One of the officers complained at the trial that he had been struck on the head with some sort of weapon pushed through a stove-pipe opening near the door which he was guarding. No one was seriously injured in the argument. Price was returned to Oberlin, where he was kept in concealment for two or three days and was later conveyed to Canada.

In an address delivered in Oberlin in 1899 Reverend Richard Winsor, for thirty years in the mission service and enrolled in the Seminary here 1857-62, told of his participation in the rescue of John Price, who was a student in a Sunday School class conducted in a room on East College Street by Mr. Winsor. Mr. Winsor related the story of the rush in rigs of all kinds by Oberlin people to Wellington and told how he, with William E. Scrimgeour and one other, gained admission to the room where the deputy marshals were keeping Price. Mr. Winsor claimed that when the door was broken open by the crowd on the outside he rushed out, with Price holding on to him. Simeon Bushnell was waiting near the door of the hotel with a horse and buggy and the men drove to Oberlin with Price. The colored boy was concealed for a time in the attic of President Fairchild's home.

Oberlin Colony

At the same meeting at which Mr. Winsor related his experience Mrs. A. A. F. Johnston gave her recollection of this historic event. She had been teaching in the South and with her mother had traveled from Rochester to buy some books at James M. Fitch's book store. While she was in the store Simeon Bushnell and Professor Henry E. Peck came in greatly excited and consulted with Mr. Fitch in regard to the rescue of Price. Taking their horse and buggy, which was on the street, Mrs. Johnston and her mother joined in the crowd and drove to Wellington. On arriving in town they were met by a woman who had observed the gathering throngs and the display of guns, and inquired what it all meant. When an explanation was given, the woman exclaimed: "What are we coming to? A fire in the morning and war at night." There had been a destructive fire in Wellington the morning of the rescue.

At an informal meeting on the Oberlin public square that same night short talks were made by men who were later indicted for participation in the rescue. While the use of names was carefully avoided by the speakers, it was more or less apparent that the rescue was ably conducted by men who stood high in Oberlin Community.

This action of Oberlin people, in conjunction with a few from Wellington, raised the issue of support of the Fugitive Slave Act for conservative people and the issue of the enforcement of the Federal Statutes in the minds of some of high character who, it may be assumed, were moved by a sense of duty outside of any political consideration. It did not come as a great surprise when the Federal Grand Jury of the Circuit Court for the Northern District of Ohio was charged at Cleveland by Judge Willson to give consideration to reports of violation of federal law in the Oberlin-Wellington Rescue. After several weeks of labor this grand jury on December 7, 1858, returned true bills for violation of the law by rescuing or aiding and abetting the rescuing of John Price against the following residents of Oberlin and Wellington: John H. Scott, John Watson, Simeon Bushnell, Jacob R. Shipherd, Ansell W. Lyman, Henry Evans, Wilson

The Story of a Century

Evans, David Watson, William Scrimgeour, Henry E. Peck, James M. Fitch, William Watson, Thomas Gena, Oliver S. B. Wall, Walter Soules, William Sciples, Ralph Plumb, John Mandeville, Matthew DeWolfe, Franklin Lewis, John Hartwell, Abner Loveland, Lewis Hines, Matthew Gillett, Chauncey Goodyear, Lorin Wadsworth, Daniel Williams, Henry DiNiles, Eli Boies, Charles Langston, James Bartlett, Richard Winsor, William E. Lincoln, Jeremiah Fox, John Copeland, James H. Bartlett, Robert L. Cummings.

On the day of the return of these indictments the United States marshal came to Oberlin and was assisted by Professor Peck in making service. Fifteen of the twenty-one Oberlin men sought were found and arrested. They were released on their own recognizance on their promise of voluntary appearance in court the following day. When the fifteen left Oberlin by train for Cleveland the next day a great crowd gathered to cheer them at the station. A considerable number of prominent men of the village headed by Mayor Beecher volunteered to accompany them to Cleveland. On their arrival in Cleveland they were met by Honorable R. P. Spaulding, D. G. Riddle, and S. O. Griswold, who, as attorneys, volunteered their service to the defense without charge. The fifteen who thus reported were John H. Scott, Henry E. Peck, John Watson, William Watson, Henry Evans, Wilson Evans, David Watson, Ansell W. Lyman, James M. Fitch, Simeon Bushnell, James H. Shepard, Oliver S. B. Wall, William E. Scrimgeour, James Bartlett, and Ralph Plumb. While Mr. Plumb is given in the list reporting, he was allowed a few days in which to arrange business affairs before he made a formal plea. All the men when arraigned entered pleas of not guilty.

At the Palmer House in Oberlin, January 11, 1859, was held the "feast of felons" at which were present the thirty-seven Lorain County citizens indicted by the federal grand jury, together with their wives and a number of invited guests. Participating in the program were Reverend John Keep, Professor Henry E. Peck, John M. Langston, Ralph Plumb, J. M. Fitch, and others. Mayor A. N. Beecher of Oberlin referred to the indicted men as "men of true grit. May we never fall into worse company." A short talk was made by the editor of the Cleveland Leader.

While at the time of pleading the defendants asked for trial, postponement at the request of United States District Attorney was had until April 5, 1859. By the middle of May two convictions had been secured. The first was that of Simeon Bushnell, a white man, and the second that of Charles H. Langston, a colored man, both of Oberlin. Bushnell was sentenced to sixty days imprisonment and fined six hundred dollars and the cost of prosecution. Langston, when asked by the court if he had any statement to make before sentence was passed, presented very ably the attitude of the rescuers and the general attitude of abolitionists of the North toward the enforcement of the Fugitive Slave Act. In the course of a very eloquent address he said: "Being identified with that man by color, by race, by manhood, by sympathies such as God has implanted in us all, I felt it my duty to go and do what I could toward liberating him . . . But I stand here to say that if for doing what I did on that day in Wellington I am to go to jail, according to the Fugitive Slave Law, and such is the protection the laws of this country afford me, I must take upon myself the responsibility of self-protection; and when I come to be claimed as his slave, by some perjured wretch I shall never be taken into slavery, and as in that trying hour I would have others do to me, as I would call upon my friends to help me; as I would call upon you, your honor, to help me; as I would call upon you (to the district attorney) to help me; and upon you (to his counsel), so help me God! . . . I stand here to say that I will do all I can for any man thus seized and held. We have a common humanity. You would do so; your manhood would require it; and no matter what the loss might be you would honor yourself for doing it; your friends would honor you for doing it; your children through all generations would honor you for doing it; and every good and honest man would say you had done right." (Great and prolonged applause). Langston was fined one hundred dollars and sentenced to twenty days in jail.

The Story of a Century

After the trial of Langston several of the Wellington men indicted entered a plea of *nolle contendere* and were given a fine of twenty dollars and sentenced to one day in jail. Father Gillett, a Wellington pioneer, had to be coaxed to leave the jail and return to his home. It was otherwise with fourteen Oberlin men who had been held in jail since April 15. They continued in confinement upon what they considered a point of honor. At the beginning of the case they had been permitted to come and go upon their own recognizance. At the conclusion of Bushnell's trial these fourteen Oberlin men gave notice that they would dismiss their counsel, call no witnesses, and set up no defense. The district attorney then demanded of the court that these men be taken into custody. They refused to give bail and were placed in jail. This ruling was recalled and the men were offered freedom that they might again be at liberty upon their own recognizance, but they resented the action of the prosecutor and declined to take advantage of this offer. While they were held in confinement they were treated with consideration by the jailer and had the sympathy of the great body of the people of Cleveland.

While the Oberlin men were confined in the jail in Cleveland many meetings to consider their treatment and to voice appreciation of their public service were held throughout northern Ohio. The largest of these was on May 24, 1859, and was in response to a call for such a meeting signed by more than 500 Liberals of the Buckeye State. Several thousand paraded and gave the prisoners an ovation at the jail. Speeches were made by Joshua R. Giddings, Honorable Joseph R. Root, Governor Chase, and others. Responses were made by Mr. Plumb, Mr. Fitch, Mr. Peck, and other prisoners at the jail. Another gathering of significance was the visit to the jail of 400 Sunday School children of Mr. Fitch, who was superintendent of the Sunday School of the First Church in Oberlin. The children, headed by a band, were under the care of Professor John M. Ellis. Mr. Fitch in his talk to the children closed with the statement: "Nothing shall by any means harm you if ye be doers of that which is right."

Oberlin Colony

An unusual feature of the jail experience of the Oberlin men was the publication of the "Rescuer," which was printed by the prisoners in an issue of 5,000 copies. The editor's announcement says: "After the 'political prisoners' had remained in jail for seventy-five days they began to find themselves possessed of 'thoughts that breathed and words that burned.' We not only wished to utter them, but we wished to print them. Could the thing be done? We looked around for printers, and found among the 'prisoners' two rusty and dilapidated 'typos,' one of whom had not handled a 'stick' for fifteen years. Would the sheriff allow us a corner of the jail for a printing office? We asked him. Generous as ever, he replied—'Certainly, and I will help you too, if I can.' Where shall type be found, we next inquired? The generous purchasers of our old printing office responded by lending us a font of small pica, and the publishers of the Cleveland Daily Leader added more. For a 'plane' we used a carpenter's plane with the irons knocked out. A policeman's club answered for a mallet in 'taking proof,' and for other purposes we could select pounding instruments from a large pile of shackles which lay at our feet. A fellow prisoner supplied us with 'side sticks,' 'quoins' and reglet, made from a white-wood board. Another prisoner sawed up a fence board to make a 'rack.' For a 'shooting-stick,' we hewed out a piece of stave and the door stone answered for a "table.' " The paper contained advertisements of Fitch & Bushnell, Oberlin printers; Henry Evans & Brother, upholsterers; John H. Scott, harness maker; and James Bartlett, boots and shoes. All these advertisers were among the prisoners held in the jail.

Appeal was finally made to the Ohio Supreme Court on a writ of *habeas corpus* on behalf of Bushnell and Langston. The court, by a decision of three to two, declined to grant the release of the two sentenced men. The Oberlin men held in jail had counted with much confidence upon relief from this source.

It had been the privilege of Langston, child of a people held in servitude, to present in burning words the attitude of the rescuers and their sympathizers in the North generally toward the Fugitive Slave Act. On the presentment of the matter to the Supreme Court of the State of Ohio it became the solemn duty of Chief Justice Joseph R. Swan not only to give the final vote of determination against the convicted men but to state his reasons for his action in language which after seventy years makes appeal to all Americans who believe that democracy, despite apparent injustices and inequalities, best functions in liberty under the law. Chief Justice Swan was a Republican in politics and his abhorrence of slavery and its evils was admitted. These personal views were not allowed to interfere with his duty as a judge sworn to interpret the law as it is found in the constitution and the statutes. The court was divided and the chief justice cast the deciding vote.

In denying the writ of *habeas corpus,* which would have secured the release of the two imprisoned Oberlin men, Judge Swan said: "For myself, as a member of this court, I disclaim the judicial discretion of disturbing the settled construction of the Constitution of the United States; and I must refuse the experiment of initiating disorder and government collision, to establish order and even-handed justice.

"I do not repeat here the judicial arguments sustaining the power of congress which have been pronounced by some of the soundest and wisest judges that have adorned the American bench, for it is my deliberate and confident conviction that the question has by time, acquiescence and adjudication, passed beyond the reach of judicial consideration of preponderance of argument— certainly beyond the reach of question before this court.

"As a citizen, I would not deliberately violate the constitution or the law by interference with fugitives from service. But if a weary, frightened slave should appeal to me to protect him from his pursuers, it is possible I might momentarily forget my allegiance to the law and constitution, and give him a covert from those who are upon his track. There are no doubt many slave holders who would themselves follow the impulses of human sympathy. And if I did it, and were prosecuted, condemned and imprisoned, and brought by my counsel before this tribunal on a *habeas corpus,* and were permitted to pronounce judgment in my own case, I trust I should have the moral courage to say, before God and the country, as I am now compelled to say, under the solemn duties of a judge bound by my official oath to sustain the supremacy of the constitution and the law, *'The prisoner must be remanded.'* "

It should be noted in this connection that history charges Governor Chase and his adherents with responsibility for the defeat for renomination at the hands of the Republican state convention of Judge Swan for another term on the supreme bench. This convention was held soon after the decision was rendered. Chief Justice Swan promptly passed on the matter at issue prior to the convention, that the representatives of his party might have the opportunity of refusing him renomination, if they so desired. It will be agreed that Judge Swan in this particular action was greater than his party and that this upright jurist should share with the humble colored man who presented the views of the rescuers the respect accorded to the memory of men who have played a manly part in the game of life.

Despite the fact that conjecture has no place in the writing of history, it is interesting to wonder what might have happened if the influence of Chase and others of the extreme faction of the Republican party had resulted in the release of the prisoners by the Supreme Court of 'Ohio and in a consequent collision between the arms of the state and the federal government. It will be agreed that the cause of the black man and the cause of liberty would have suffered if a northern and not a southern state had been first by show of force to question the authority of the federal government. Chase, while an able man, lacked that final touch of greatness which was peculiarly the property of Abraham Lincoln, who saw clearly, where Chase did not, that the safety of the nation and the well-being of the slave lay in obedience to the constitution and to federal enactments. It was only when national authority had been upheld on the field of battle that Lincoln issued the Emancipation Proclamation.

The Story of a Century

While the fourteen Oberlin men remained in jail at Cleveland a movement was begun by men in Lorain County who held views similar to theirs as to the iniquitous features of the Fugitive Slave Act. As a result of their plans, the three men who had taken Price into custody were indicted in the courts of Lorain County on a charge of kidnaping. It was known that the prosecuting attorney, W. W. Boynton, and men of the grand jury called to act favored the rescuers and did not look with affection on the cause of slavery. The three indicted men were brought into court. The presiding judge called a special jury said to have been composed entirely of anti-slavery men. Counsel for the three indicted men then saw the light and a conference with the prosecuting forces in the federal court at Cleveland resulted in the release of the Oberlin prisoners and the quashing of the indictment brought against the three arresting officers.

The return of the prisoners on July 6, 1859, was marked by one of the greatest demonstrations in the history of the village. They were met at the railroad station by a vast throng and were formally welcomed home by Professor James Monroe, who greeted them as "Friends of liberty, who made no compromise with slavery . . . erect as God made you, you went into prison; erect as God made you, you have come out of prison." A band led the great procession to the First Church. The volunteer fire companies in uniform served as guard of honor. At the church addresses were made by "Father" Keep, Honorable Ralph Plumb, Professor H. E. Peck, J. M. Fitch, John Watson, Father Gillett, and others. A feature of the great meeting was the singing of hymns. The final prayer was made by Dr. Morgan. It was midnight before the vast audience dispersed.

The following resolution, introduced by Professor H. E. Fairchild at this meeting was acted upon by the Oberlin council at a meeting following soon after this gathering of welcome: "Resolved, that this meeting request the town council to enter the following minute upon the records of the village of Oberlin:—

"The citizens of Oberlin assembled in mass meeting to welcome home our faithful representatives, Messrs. Peck, Plumb, Fitch,

Oberlin Colony

W. Evans, Winsor, Lincoln, H. Evans, J. Watson, D. Watson, Bartlett, Lyman, and Scott who, rather than give the least countenance to the Fugitive Slave Act, have lain eighty-four days in Cleveland jail, under indictment for the rescue of a fugitive slave from the custody of a United States Marshal, give devout thanks to Almighty God for the courage which has enabled them patiently, faithfully, and firmly to maintain the contest against that impious enactment till the government has asked for quarter, and has volunteered the proposition to release the Lorain *criminals* under the Fugitive Act, on condition that Lorain would release the United States *executors* of the act.

"To our faithful friends we express our warmest gratitude and our commendation for the firmness, the wisdom, and the fidelity with which they have maintained our common cause.

"And finally, in view of all the consequences attendant upon this prosecution, and all the light shed upon the subject, we unanimously express our greatly increased abhorrence of the Fugitive Slave Act, and avow our determination that no fugitive slave shall ever be taken from Oberlin, either with or without a warrant, if we have power to prevent it." "Passed unanimously July 6, 1859."

A similar greeting in point of numbers and enthusiasm was given to Simeon Bushnell on July 11, when he returned to his home after having served the sentence imposed upon him by the court. Among the speakers was Joshua Giddings, well-known abolitionist.

These incidents, which have become a part of the history of America, are interwoven with matters more trivial, but possibly holding interest for the Oberlin of today. A communication to the Cleveland Leader under date of July 7, 1859, from an anonymous correspondent, gives the story of a reception of the released rescuers and touches on the attitude of E. F. Munson, the postmaster of Oberlin and one of the pioneer residents of the community. Mr. Munson was an ardent Democrat and was suspected of being out of sympathy with the attitude of Oberlin in the rescue case and in other matters. The correspondent says: "E.

The Story of a Century

F. Munson, the Oberlin postmaster—the man whose head was but recently as good as off and who stuck it on again by the work which he was able to do for the government and the intruders who have recently disturbed the quiet of our peaceful town,— stood motionless, green, dark and dreary, like a bald eagle on a rock, or a stork on a seashore. 'Poor fool,' said I, 'let him eat the fruit of his own doings, and be filled with his own devices.' "

Another minor echo of a great achievement is found in a letter to the Cleveland Leader dated Oberlin, February 20, 1860, and signed "Q." This communication tells of the departure from the village of A. P. Dayton, who served as deputy marshal to the Columbus officials in the rescue case. Dayton is condemned as a follower of Postmaster Munson and the story is told of his fleeing from the town the week previous with five active colored men on his heels. He was finally caught, but suffered no injury, as he agreed to leave Oberlin never to return and signed a confession in which he said that he had been informed by Mr. Munson that he, (Munson) and Chauncey Wack and Bela Farr had furnished the names of parties and of witnesses in the Oberlin-Wellington Rescue case. The article concludes with the reproving of Mr. Munson for "his endeavors to vex and harass Oberlin people with expensive suits and imprisonment."

WAR AND PEACE

THE INEVITABLE CONFLICT

CHAPTER X

MORE than twenty-five years before the slave power of the South determined to uphold its cause on the field of battle, Oberlin had gone on record as opposed to slavery and for its abolition. In those early days there was no thought in Oberlin that the question would have to be decided by force of arms. When that appeal to arms came Oberlin Community and College responded to the call of Lincoln with heartiness and enthusiasm and with firm belief in the justice of the cause. The history of the community and the college from the time of the adoption of the trustee resolution admitting colored students—an action which had, if not at that time, within a few years following, the support of the community—was one of steady growth in love of freedom and hatred of slavery. This station on the Underground Railroad was a refuge for many slaves seeking liberty in Canada. The Oberlin-Wellington Rescue, characterized by apparent resistance to federal authority, was marked as well by frank and wholesome opposition to oppression. The fugitive slave law was never popular in the North and had fewer friends in Oberlin than in other towns north of the Mason and Dixon line. Oberlin came in touch with the John Brown tragedy at Harper's Ferry. Brown's father had served the college as a trustee. Brown himself had had correspondence with college officials with reference to certain land interests of the institution. Two of the men who gave their lives in Brown's effort to free the slaves were Oberlin men. Newspapers of the country, north and south, that preached the cause of southern Democracy were frank in their condemnation of Oberlin's anti-slavery attitude, of her participation in the Oberlin-Wellington Rescue, and of what they conceived to be her encouragement of Brown in his attack on the South. A paper published at Philadelphia said at the time of the Harper's Ferry incident: "Oberlin is located in the very heart of what may be called 'John Brown tract' where people are born abolitionists and where abolitionism is taught as the 'chief end of

Oberlin Colony

man' and often put in practice . . . Oberlin is the nursery of just such men as John Brown and his followers . . . Here is where the younger Browns attain their conscientiousness in ultraisms, taught from the cradle up, so that while they rob slave holders of their property, or commit murder for the cause of freedom, they imagine they're doing God service."

While this comment fairly reflects the attitude of pro-southern or pro-slavery newspapers, it does not give an accurate picture of the feeling of the community and the college with reference to John Brown and his plans. The Oberlin Evangelist, a religious paper, was the only regular publication in the village at the time of the John Brown raid. The Evangelist, commenting on Brown's attempt at Harper's Ferry, said editorially: "We object to such intervention, not because the slave power has any rights which mankind, white or black, are bound to respect, and not, therefore, because it is properly a moral wrong to deliver the oppressed from the grasp of the oppressor; but entirely for other reasons. We long to see slavery abolished by peaceful means, and as a demand of conscience, under the law of righteousness, which is the law of God. Such a result would be at once glorious to Christianity and blessed to both slave holders and slaves. It is especially because an armed intervention frustrates this form of pacific, reformatory agency, that we disapprove and deplore it. Perhaps the day of hope in moral influence for the abolition of slavery is past already; we cannot tell. If so, it is a satisfaction to us to be conscious of not having unwisely precipitated its setting sun. If a mad infatuation has fallen upon southern minds, and they will not hear the demands of justice, nor the admonitions of kindness, let the responsibility rest where it belongs. We would not have it so. 'We have not desired the woeful day, O Lord, thou knowest.' "

The expression of this opinion in the style of the prophets of old may be taken fairly to represent the beliefs of the people of the college and the community. Oberlin of the late fifties was neither pacifist nor militant. It was strongly anti-slavery and strongly pro-Republican and had welcomed the formation of the new party known to be built about opposition to the extension of slavery and known to be opposed to the doctrines of the Democratic party, up to that time dominated by the slave interests of the South. Thus, while Oberlin was not in those days in a war-like frame of mind, neither was she obsessed by pacifism. When it became apparent that the South would secede rather than see slavery abolished and that the North would fight rather than see the Union destroyed, Oberlin was found ready and entirely willing to meet the issue.

There were leaders both north and south who saw in the Harper's Ferry tragedy the beginning of the end of compromise. In the South particularly this attempt of a handful of men to free a race was seen as the first step on the part of the North looking to the suppression of slavery by force of arms. Condemnation of Brown's methods by many northern newspapers and northern political leaders did not serve entirely to allay this feeling. Public utterances by such extremists in the cause of anti-slavery as Wendell Phillips, who openly praised Brown and condemned the State of Virginia for his execution, added to the fury of southern wrath. When within a few months following this "invasion" of Virginia it became apparent that the Republican party would name as its candidate for president in 1860 either an outstanding abolitionist leader, such as Seward or Chase, or a steadily growing figure of menace to injustice, Abraham Lincoln, those leaders of the South who were concerned for the maintenance and growth of slavery felt still further justification in the belief that there was a growing conspiracy in the North to do away with the "sacred institution." Here in Oberlin these fast moving changes of temper in the people both north and south were observed with intelligent interest. Oberlin did not drift with the tide but rather moved in the forefront of those thoughtful Americans who had become convinced that "a house divided against itself cannot stand."

The southern Democracy, frightened by Douglas' "Freeport doctrine" and further frightened by the John Brown raid, began, early in 1860, an agitation for congressional relief in behalf of slavery. Jefferson Davis, later president of the confederacy, championed their cause. The failure of Democratic delegates to make a nomination at Charleston, South Carolina, in April, and the withdrawal of the delegates from eight southern states following the adoption of a Douglas platform raised the hopes of opponents of slavery in the North. The Douglas delegates adjourned to meet in Baltimore and the southern faction arranged to meet at Richmond. Leaders of both wings of the party well understood that secession and war were now in sight. The Baltimore convention nominated Douglas and the southern voters put Breckenridge in the field. When Lincoln was chosen at the Chicago convention as the candidate of the Republican party, the storm began to break. Southern papers freely stated that the nomination of "The Rail-Splitter" was part of a wicked plan to free the slaves. There were many intimations and a few open statements that the South would not remain in the Union after Lincoln had been inaugurated. Through the summer of 1860 and the early fall there were still hopes in the South that Lincoln might be defeated. His election was followed by the secession of South Carolina and by treasonable speeches on the part of southern senators and representatives in the Congress of United States and by treasonable conduct on the part of members of the cabinet of President James Buchanan, who, if loyal to the interests of the nation, was more fitted for president of a sewing society than of a great country about to enter upon a civil war to maintain its existence.

Under the leadership of men like James Monroe, Oberlin had steadily grown in its adherence to the Republican party and the principles which, in those days, moved it. Mr. Monroe was a representative in the Ohio Legislature in the years from 1856 to 1860 and senator from 1860 to 1862. His career as a friend of liberty and an opponent of slavery reflected the opinion of his constituents in Oberlin. While at the outset sentiment here favored the nomination of Salmon P. Chase, Oberlin lent enthusiastic support to Lincoln in the 1860 campaign. The Lorain County News, Oberlin's first newspaper, was established early in

1860 and had an important part in the campaign for that year. A sound majority was given Mr. Lincoln and other candidates of the Republican party in 1860 and college and community actively supported the cause of the party and the new president. It was apparent soon after Lincoln's election that further attempts to compromise were useless. Lincoln's appeal to the South in his inaugural was without effect. Several southern states had seceded and war talk in the South, particularly in South Carolina, the hotbed of secession, was a promise of the strife to come. When Sumter was fired upon April 12, 1861, this definite act of warfare unified the North as well as the South. Oberlin was ready in answer to the call of the president for troops for the suppression of armed rebellion, and the part taken by community and college in those days makes a record of conspicuous patriotism and devotion to country.

1860

In this year when the nation was divided in politics and torn by disputes which would lead to warfare, Oberlin was carrying on its normal life while having a part in these larger contests. One of the early issues of the new Lorain County News tells of fame won by Alonzo Pease in the field of art. Mr. Pease was a son of Hiram A. Pease and a nephew of Peter Pindar Pease, Oberlin's first settler. He later served for a time as captain of a Company in the Forty-first O. V. I. While the Charleston Convention was making evident the growing division on slavery, Oberlin folk were interested also in the institution of the new Second Congregational Church. The forming of this new church and the organization a year or two prior of the Episcopal Church marked the end of a period in Oberlin significant for the dominating influence of the First Congregational Church in affairs both religious and civic. The organization of the Second Church was a result of a friendly agreement of a number of members of First Church to withdraw their membership on the ground that the First Church had grown a little large for efficient service. The new newspaper, reflecting from week to week the life of the community, has in one column a plea for Salmon P. Chase for President and in another an announcement from Marx Straus, one of the early business men of the village, that he is selling silks at 37 1-2 cents a yard. At this same time while the living were disturbed by a promise of national tragedy the dead were not forgotten, since the paper reports the building of a new fence around the cemetery. S. S. Calkins, who was conducting the Commercial Institute, was advertising for students, P. Weed and William Hovey were tinsmiths, James Bailey was a saddler, Straus & Kupfer were selling clothing, and J. Watson was in the grocery business.

Threat of war and desolation was very properly not allowed to interfere with the conduct of village affairs. At the April election in 1860 Samuel Hendry was chosen as mayor. Members of council elected included men who had been active for years in the life of Oberlin, who have left records of good citizenship. The new council was composed of Professor John M. Ellis, Ralph Plumb, William Johnson, M. Bronson, and A. N. Beecher. E. J. Goodrich, for more than half a century in the book business here, was elected recorder. William Hovey, a pioneer resident and father of Frank Hovey, was made treasurer. E. F. Munson was serving as postmaster. He was one of the very few Democrats in Oberlin at the time. In the month of June, 1860, when history was made by the nomination of Abraham Lincoln at Chicago, Oberlin was boasting of its building activity. In the year closed new structures included the Episcopal Church, forty-three dwellings, and seven stores. Proper pride was taken in the erection of a factory for the manufacture of artificial gas. The new Brokaw-Carpenter-Jarvis building had room for three stores and a public hall seating eight hundred. At about this time the Empire Hook and Ladder Company won a silver trumpet in Sandusky at a firemen's contest. This was first of several which they won. Jenkins & Haines built a new sawmill located on Water Street, west of the gas factory. In October C. H. Favel, for many years in the livery business here, bought a "new and splendid omnibus." The editor at this period offended a large number of his sub-

TAPPAN SQUARE, 1860

scribers by complaint of piles of fuel wood on the streets of the village. At the fall election in 1860 several ladies of the village demonstrated that Oberlin is always a step ahead of the procession by calling at the polls and urging their right to vote. While they were denied the ballot, they were only about sixty years ahead of the time in their demand.

1861

The year opened with ominous prospect for trouble. The editor of the News gravely asks, "Should the North arm itself?" That question was answered a few months later. Note is made of the secession of South Carolina and several other southern states prior to the inauguration of Lincoln in March. The appointment of G. F. H. Stevens as postmaster on March 26, 1861, and the naming of E. P. Johnson as his assistant are recorded in the issue containing as well the rather peculiar purchase by council from M. T. Gaston of a hearse for the village. Within less than a week Sumter was fired upon. This act of rebellion changed the course of living for the people of Oberlin, as it did for the people of the United States both north and south.

Reflecting the patriotic fervor of both community and college the one newspaper of the village, in its issue following Major Anderson's surrender, urges support of the government in the suppression of rebellion. It carries a proclamation calling for a meeting at First Church that 'Oberlin may go on record as loyal and willing. An editorial concludes: "Who knows but that the throes of mortal strife which began at Sumter are the signs of our country's regeneration?"

The call was not an academic matter as Oberlin viewed it. Editorials and speeches were supported by prompt enrollment. Excitement ran through both college and town and students and those outside college hurried to enlist for the defense of their country. Within two days after Mr. Lincoln's call for troops, following public meetings at First Church, a company of 100 volunteers, made up largely of students, was enrolled in Oberlin. On April 25 almost the entire population of the town escorted the company, then known as the Monroe Rifles, so named in honor of the Honorable James Monroe, then in the Ohio Legislature, to the railroad station where they entrained for Cleveland, where they went into Camp Taylor and became Company C of the Seventh Ohio Volunteer Infantry. G. W. Shurtleff was made captain of the company. He retired at the end of the war as a Brigadier General and was for many years an honored citizen of the community, serving for some time as treasurer of Oberlin College.

Both company and regiment saw hard service. The majority of the soldiers reënlisted at the end of the three-year period and some for the duration of the war. The company suffered severe losses at Cross Lanes, West Virginia. A number of officers and men were taken prisoners and spent many months in southern prisons. During the three months of the service of this first Oberlin company to enlist, its roll contained the names of one hundred and fifty students of Oberlin College. The company and regiment had part in the battles of Winchester, Port Republic, Cedar Mountain, Chancellorsville, Antietam, Gettysburg, Lookout Mountain, Ringgold, and Resaca.

Oberlin's enlistment did not, of course, cease with the formation of Company C. A company from Oberlin joined the Forty-first 'Ohio Volunteer Infantry and a number of students and citizens enrolled in the Second Ohio Cavalry. A. B. Nettleton, enlisted from Oberlin, rose from the rank of private to be commander of his company and was mustered out as a general officer. In 1862 an Oberlin company joined the 103rd Ohio Volunteer Infantry, under the captaincy of P. C. Hayes. In this same year, when Kirby Smith's army threatened Cincinnati, the "Squirrel Hunters" were called out and scores of men of the community and students of the college were enlisted and hurried to the threatened point. In the same year a company of "ninety-day men" went from Oberlin directly to the front and saw some service. Finally in 1864 Oberlin sent a second "Company C" to the 150th Regiment of Ohio Volunteers. In addition to these activities a number of students enrolled in the college returned to their homes and enlisted from the county of their residence. The most distinguished of these sons of Oberlin was Jacob Dolson Cox, who attained the rank of Major General and who served with high credit as Governor of Ohio after the close of the war. President Fairchild in his history of Oberlin estimates the number of students who enlisted at not less than 850. The annual attendance of students in the college was reduced from 1313 in 1860 to 859 in 1862. President Fairchild relates that "In the first excitement and anxiety of the war, the work of the classroom was maintained with some difficulty. The telegraph or newspaper often brought news so distracting that neither teachers nor pupils could give their full strength to the work of the hour; but at length all learned to possess their souls in patience. Still there were often sad interruptions when one who had fallen was brought back to be buried among us."

This same depth of feeling through the war days was manifested by citizens of the community. Recreation of students and of young men of the village took the form of military drill. A gymnasium built by voluntary contributors was deserted after the fall of Fort Sumter. One in every ten of those enlisted from Oberlin never returned. The Soldiers' Monument, erected in 1870 and still standing in 1933, near the southeast corner of West College and Professor Streets, bears the names of one hundred citizens and students who fell in battle or died in prison or in hospital.

J. F. Harmon, the editor of the Lorain County News, was among the first to enlist. V. A. Shankland took up his duties. In the list of members of Company C appears the name of Noah Huckins, for many years in the hardware business in Oberlin and prior to that time in business in Wellington. Professor G. F. Wright, distinguished scientist and professor in Oberlin College and a long-time resident of Oberlin, was one of the early volunteers but was forced out of the service by ill health.

While the boys of the college and community were enlisting for service, those at home unable to bear arms were manifesting their interest in other fashions. In June of 1861 a flag pole one hundred twenty-two feet high was placed on the campus square and the stars and stripes were raised and lowered each day. July wheat, in these stirring times, was selling at sixty cents a bushel. In mid-summer, while the nation was tightening its belt after the defeat at First Bull Run and the people of the North were gaining a realization of the magnitude of the task confronting them, here in Oberlin the Oberlin Cemetery Association was formed. At this time another link in the chain connecting the then present with the peaceful past was broken in the death of Lewis Holtslander, a pioneer resident of the community and the first mayor of Oberlin. He served in the years 1847-1848. He came to Oberlin in 1836. A few days following his death Deacon William Wheat, who united his fortunes with Oberlin in 1833, passed from life. In the fall of this same stirring year occurred the death of Peter Pindar Pease, Oberlin's first resident. All had lived to get a glimpse of a new world in the ferment of making and all had played a part in the building of a community, the character of which was to change more and more for better or for worse in the decades following their death.

In November of 1861, while James Preston was receiving from the Village Council his salary of $1.00 for services as marshal for the current month, Samuel Sedgwick, superintendent of schools, was reporting that the total attendance of pupils was 442. The annual receipts of the schools of the district were then $3,355.49. Mr. Sedgwick received $600 a year and seven "female" teachers $60 per month. The following month Simeon Bushnell, the first man convicted in the 'Oberlin-Wellington Rescue trials of 1859, died suddenly in the vestibule of the Second Church where he had been attending services. In this same month the Methodist Episcopal Church of Oberlin bought a lot on South Main Street for the purpose of erecting a church home. Retail prices included butter at 12 cents, corn at 20 cents, cheese at 5 cents and 6 cents, potatoes at 37 cents, dressed chickens at 5 cents.

Oberlin Colony

1862

Early this year H. E. Peck, of the college faculty, and J. B. T. Marsh, later treasurer of the college, took over the Lorain County News. In March P. R. Tobin, father of Frank W. Tobin, was advertising his saddle and harness business. Complaint was made that people pastured horses and cows in the village streets. The Goodrich store was advertising among new books "Agnes of Sorrento" and "Tom Brown at Oxford." Note is made of the heart-warming fact that Captain John W. Steele, later Colonel Steele and Judge Steele, led a brilliant charge on a Confederate battery at the battle of Pittsburgh Landing. In the spring of this year council paid E. M. Leonard $9.00 for cleaning snow from the sidewalks in the winter of 1861-62. In June, 1862, Captain Shurtleff writes of prison life at Charlestown, South Carolina. He tells of the crowding of sixty-six men in a room 40x70. Shortly after this the Seven Days Battles are noted and the editor remarks with profound dejection that McClellan is "unequal to the task of high command." Independence day was celebrated with a fine parade in which five soldiers on leave had part. They were H. L. Hendry, G. F. H. Stevens, A. Ingersoll, D. P. Reamer, and J. E. Davis.

Oberlin was loyal to Lincoln, but the community and college were in tune with many other people of the North in attempting to press the question of emancipation faster than in Mr. Lincoln's judgment it could be successfully promoted. "Father" Keep, then eighty, preached a sermon on the state of the country in which he pleaded for support for the cause of the North. A little later in August of 1862, at a chapel meeting at which Mayor J. M. Ellis presided, resolutions were passed asking for immediate emancipation. This action anticipated the Emancipation Proclamation issued by Lincoln soon after the battle of Antietam, fought in September of this year. At this time Oberlin had sent more than two hundred soldiers into the field.

That war has its effect on customs and habits of people is shown by an editorial comment in the News of September 3, 1862.

The Story of a Century

With much feeling the editor says: "The vile and repulsive practice of smoking is gaining foothold in our village." A week later a matter of possibly greater importance received attention in the statement that Oberlin had sent her quota of "Squirrel Hunters" to Cincinnati to repel General Kirby Smith. Captain W. M. Ampt was in command of a full company of 120 men. In October of this year, with the country rejoicing over the Emancipation Proclamation and victory at Antietam, R. H. Birge, a veteran business man, added to the hilarity at Oberlin with an advertisement which said: "Abraham Lincoln has liberated 3,000,000 slaves and R. H. Birge has just received a splendid stock of fresh groceries." With the nation's life at stake, politics was a serious and often a bitter concern in those war days. The News notes in October that the vote of Russia Township stood 513 Republicans to 78 "Secesh." This reference to the Democratic party was followed with the short and more direct statement that: "Vallandigham, the cowardly Secessionist, has been elected to stay at home."

In the early fall of 1862 all business houses in Oberlin closed an hour each day to allow military drill. Rejoicing over the result of Antietam and the Proclamation of Emancipation was followed by discouragement in the late fall over the lack of Union victories. "There is no hope in McClellan," said the News editor. Note was made in November of the promotion from Sergeant to Lieutenant of Henry W. Lincoln, of Pittsfield, in whose honor Henry Lincoln Post, Grand Army of the Republic, was named. He died of a disease contracted in the service before the close of the war. Men too old for active duty were busy in the late fall husking corn for women whose fathers or sons or brothers or husbands were in the Union ranks. A further echo of Oberlin's pioneer past is found in a notice of the suspension of publication of the Oberlin Evangelist, established in 1838. Scarcity of silver, due to the stress of war, is manifested in a decision of Oberlin business men to issue currency checks of ten, twenty-five, and fifty cents. These were made payable in current sums in S. Plumb's bank. The editor attempts to sustain the morale of the people with the statement: "Business good, money plenty. What fools croakers are!"

1863

Early in January a mass meeting at the Chapel rejoiced over the Emancipation Proclamation. In March of this year Jacob J. Safford died. He came to Oberlin from Royalton, Vermont, in 1833, when only the Peter Pindar Pease log cabin stood here. He was one of sixteen who lodged in its garret and helped to clear the forests. The attendance at college was reduced to 525, with 200 students in war service, of whom thirty held commissions. In April the population of Oberlin was 2061, Elyria 2658, Columbus 17,867. The village annual expense for general purposes at this time was $678.53, with a road fund of $229.76. Despite distractions of war, improvements went forward in the village. Samuel Plumb heads a stock subscription for a new bank with $20,000. Ground was broken in May for the new chapel of the First Church. In July J. B. T. Marsh, city editor, was commissioned as Lieutenant and resigned from the village paper. Report of the victories at Vicksburg and Gettysburg was received with enthusiastic acclaim.

1864

The Ohio Legislature in 1864 passed a law giving soldiers the right to vote in the field. At a dinner given in 1927 to the few surviving comrades of Henry Lincoln Post Alfred E. May, for many years an employee of the college and a valued citizen of Oberlin, told of the first election held in his regiment. He held back from the ballot box while the other soldiers were voting. His captain said to him: "Why don't you come and vote?" This was in the second Lincoln campaign. The young soldier said that he was only seventeen and not entitled to vote. The captain responded with emphasis that if he was old enough to risk his life on the field of battle he was old enough to vote. He voted. In this month fourteen Oberlin colored men joined the 54th

The Story of a Century

Massachusetts regiment made up of Negroes. Three of these were fugitives and three were emancipated slaves. In this time of heroic endeavor and national uplift Artemus Ward delivered a lecture here, "Evidently," says the editor, "in an uncongenial atmosphere." The Hook and Ladder Company won another prize of $75 at Toledo by running ninety-seven rods, erecting a ladder and sending a man to the top in one and one-fourth minutes. L. A. Whitney was foreman and the members included A. N. Wood, E. S. Lyman, Hiram Bedortha, H. E. Worcester, and Charles T. Beckwith. In the midst of war's alarms the News notes that Oberlin factories include the flour mill of L. M. Hall & Company, the door and sash factory of Waterman & Peek, steel sawmill of Haines & Swift, cabinet factories of H. Evans & Company and S. Bedortha, the chair factory of J. B. Davidson, the gas works of Samuel Plumb, the tin and sheet iron plants of Weed & Beckwith and T. S. Fuller, the saddle and harness factories of James Bailey, P. R. Tobin, and J. H. Scott, and the monument and mantel shop of Hayes & Company.

The effect of three years of war was reflected in prices. Wool had gone to the then unprecedented figure of 65 cents to 70 cents and wheat, which was selling at 60 cents at the outbreak of the war and for a time thereafter, had gone to $1.25. Butter was selling at 22 cents, cheese 12 cents, eggs 18 cents, and smoked ham 10 cents. Citizens and students gathered at the new cemetery June 8 of this year to help in the work of clearing it. The name Westwood was selected on motion of James M. Fitch, veteran bookseller and honored Oberlin citizen. Women of the community served dinner to the workers at noon. "Soldiers Rest" was at this time set off in the center of the grounds as a place of burial for soldiers of the Civil War.

The tract, finally known as Westwood Cemetery, included a little more than 27 acres and was bought in April, 1863, for $1400. Westwood Cemetery was dedicated as a permanent place of burial on July 16, 1864. The dedicatory address was delivered by Professor James H. Fairchild. Professor C. H. Churchill and President Finney had part in the exercises. The first burial at the new cemetery was of the body of Samuel W. Montgomery on August 20, 1863. President Fairchild served as president of the association from 1861 to 1867. Other presidents have been James Dascomb, John M. Ellis, A. A. Wright, A. Z. Tillotson, and Garrett Newell. J. N. Stone was clerk for the period from 1902 to 1927. A. P. Behr, who was elected clerk in 1927, was still serving in 1933.

At the November election "Father" Keep, then 83, voted for Lincoln. He prepared this brief and pointed written statement, which was read at the polls: "Palsied be the tongue which now wags for treason." Colonel Giles W. Shurtleff, who was home from the front because of wounds received in action, openly wept when the crowd at the polls cheered him as he cast his ballot for Lincoln. At this same election Ebenezer Penfield, 92, Oberlin's oldest resident, voted for Lincoln. In this year the Village Council grew conservative and passed an ordinance limiting the speed of teams in the village to four miles per hour. The automobile speed limit in 1933 was 35 miles an hour and was occasionally observed. J. F. Harmon, back from the war, buys the interest of V. A. Shankland in the News.

1865

Early this year George Kinney, of the firm of Kinney & Reamer, was made treasurer of Oberlin College. In March, Professor H. E. Peck, of the college faculty and long a valued citizen of Oberlin, was named consul general to Haiti. He died in the public service there. In this same month J. F. Harmon was appointed postmaster, an action definitely marking the prestige and strength of Civil War veterans in public affairs, a strength which was carried forward through the Grand Army of the Republic and which was a dominant factor in American politics to the end of the nineteenth century. The report of the school board for the year ending in March shows the receipts for school purposes were $4,547.67. Teachers' salaries were $2,185.33. Seven teachers were employed. At this time, near the end of four years of warfare, prices had hit their peak. Butter was 25 cents to 30 cents, corn 50 cents, eggs 25 cents, wool 95 cents to $1.00, smoked hams 20 cents, potatoes $1.00, and wheat $1.75 to $2.00. D. W. Jones, of Galway, New York, showed his faith in Oberlin by establishing a plant for the manufacture of corn planters. In March of this year gold was 156 1-2 and falling. The high mark for gold was 276, touched in July, 1864.

In this month, with the war drawing to a close, a sword was presented to Captain A. B. Wall, Oberlin's first colored commissioned officer. It was the gift of Oberlin friends. In April many bodies were removed from the old cemetery at South Main and Morgan to Westwood. News of the taking of Richmond was coincident with the naming of a committee to act in the matter of securing funds to erect a soldiers' monument. The surrender of Lee was reported in the News in its issue of April 12. The assassination of President Lincoln was recorded one week later. A service was held at the chapel the day following the death of Lincoln and a resolution passed pledged Oberlin to "Every worthy effort to conquer the rebellion and bring its authors to condign punishment." Many from Oberlin journeyed to Cleveland to attend the service held there for President Lincoln as his body paused on its journey to his old home in Illinois. The grand review of the Armies of the Republic at Washington closed the Civil War. Oberlin's part in the conflict was in every respect inspiring.

PEACE COMES AGAIN

CHAPTER XI

THE years immediately following the close of the Civil War were lacking in that indefinable exaltation of community spirit which precedes and accompanies the settlement on the field of battle of issues vital to the nation. For a decade prior to the outbreak of the war Oberlin had been busied with the issue of freedom for the colored race. In the years of the war town and college alike made untold sacrifices in support of the Union cause. Interest in public affairs after Lee's surrender did not lag, but it was an interest lacking the burning zeal that marked discussions during the war and immediately preceding the war. For almost a decade after the coming of peace both college and town were busied in an effort to gather up the wreckage which always follows civil strife. College attendance in all departments in 1860 totaled 1311, the highest record in the school's history up to that time. The enlistment of many students and the disruption of business generally, such as accompanies warfare, resulted in a drop in one year to 1071 and in 1864 to 901. In 1865 the attendance was 1020 and it did not return to the high mark of 1860 until the year 1873.

Community life was of course affected by lessened college attendance and by other factors growing out of the losses incident to prolonged warfare. Returned soldiers took up their usual vocations. Many students whose college work had been interrupted by war service resumed their studies where they had dropped them. Citizens who had been absent for years in army service again went back to the duties of civil life.

Less than a month following peace the usual town caucus was held in the college chapel for the choosing of delegates to a Republican county convention. At this convention, held at Elyria, Samuel Plumb, banker and capitalist, and Professor John M. Ellis, of the college faculty, were chosen as delegates to the Republican state convention which nominated General Jacob Dolson Cox, distinguished Oberlin graduate and later an Oberlin resi-

The Story of a Century

dent, for Governor of Ohio. A month later a mass meeting of citizens passed a resolution favoring the amendment which gave the ballot to the Negro. At an alumni celebration held in August General Cox made an eloquent plea for funds for the Soldiers' Monument. Subscriptions amounting to $500 were added to the fund which had been started shortly before this time. This same month saw the resignation of President Charles Grandison Finney, one of the notable figures of Oberlin College and Community and a preacher of international fame, accepted by the Board of Trustees of the college. Mr. Finney assigned ill health as the reason for his action. He continued his work as the pastor of First Church until 1872. He was succeeded in the presidency of the college by James Harris Fairchild, a student in the college at its founding and honored as one of the outstanding executives of the school and as one of the most valued citizens of the community. This period was marked by an effort for subscriptions in aid of the construction of a railroad directly from Elyria to Oberlin.

While these activities were in progress Carpenter's Block, the Oberlin Hall of the old days, received a new front. Peaches were selling at $2.00 a bushel and table board in the college halls was from $3.00 to $3.50 per week. That the war had not bankrupted all people is shown by the record in September of this year of seventy residents of Russia Township who paid an income tax as having incomes in excess of $600 per year. The highest income recorded in the township was that of I. M. Johnson, well known merchant, who paid on $2990. M. Straus, merchant, was second with an income of $2820. The total tax rate at this time in Oberlin was 19.7 mills.

In October, 1865, J. F. Harmon, who had a fine record in the service in the Civil War, sold his interest in the Lorain County News to J. B. T. Marsh, later treasurer of Oberlin College. Mr. Harmon had received appointment as postmaster at Oberlin. The editor of the News makes proud record of the fact that Deacon D. B. Kinney's sorghum mill was running full time. In

Oberlin Colony

the fall of this year the county voted for an infirmary which was soon after built. Elyria at that time had a population of 3,000. That the farmer's condition was much better in those days than in 1933 is shown by a note that J. W. Worcester of Pittsfield had cleared $1366 on his sheep in one year. At about this same time gold at New York was 144. Some Oberlin market prices then were: ham 15 cents, potatoes 50 cents, wool 60 cents, wheat $1.50 to $1.75.

The question of liquor selling in Oberlin had become a serious one and a meeting of citizens was held in the chapel to consider remedies. E. H. Fairchild was made chairman of a vigilance committee. In November of this year the members of the Oberlin Volunteer Fire Department created consternation by resigning as a body. They had a good record for efficiency and resented the failure of the Council to heed their request for the purchase of a new steam fire engine. The Council called a public meeting for consideration of these complaints and steps were taken looking to the buying of improved equipment.

That editors in those days had courage, if not discretion, is shown by an editorial appearing in a November issue of the News in which the writer pleads for "chastity of taste" in the dress of Christian ladies of Oberlin. While the writer was not entirely specific in his selection of styles for the gentler sex, he unqualifiedly condemned what he described as "disgusting waterfalls, furbelows, bugles, and tinseled brass." It is not of record that any definite change was brought about in feminine styles as a result.

About this time the village committee on temperance reported that two drug stores and one saloon were in operation, selling cider and ale. The News is authority for the statement that in the fall of this year Professor James Monroe declined the presidency of Oberlin College which had been "informally" offered him, returning to his consular work at Rio de Janeiro. As indicating the march of progress and the growing wealth of the community, note is made of the sale for $1,000 of a building lot which brought only $30 about thirty years previous.

The Story of a Century

1866

The first of the year saw a stiffening in all prices such as usually follows war. Wool stood at 60 cents, with ham 22 cents, lard 18 cents, and wheat $1.75. Accompanying a notice that the township trustees would receive bids at T. D. Fuller's store for the keeping of the town poor for the coming year—three persons in all—the editor of the town paper condemns the indecency of this practice of caring for community indigents and makes a plea for a better system. Oberlin College and Community took a stand against the reconstruction policy of President Johnson at a public meeting at the Chapel on February 28, 1866. The call for the meeting was signed by such representative citizens as James H. Fairchild, William Hovey, Homer Johnson, A. H. Johnson, Samuel Plumb, J. B. T. Marsh, E. H. Fairchild, C. H. Churchill, E. Follett, S. S. Calkins, C. P. Griffin, and I. M. Johnson. Judge John W. Steele was one of the speakers.

In March there was not a vacant house to be found in Oberlin. The school report at this time showed 834 of school age in the district. There were one superintendent and eight teachers. Receipts for the year were $4,000 and expenditures $3,200. These figures are an unusual record in view of the 1932 budget of the schools amounting to $129,000. In April S. W. Lincoln was made the first health officer of the village. The town continued to grow and the extension of West Street was opened south from West College to Forest Street.

That times had changed in the thirty odd years since the founding of the community is shown by the fact that livery stable proprietors reported that between the demand of ministers and Sabbath school teachers who lived out of town, Sunday was the busiest day of the week with them. The News editor inquires if that is just the thing for a "day of rest." Travel on Sunday was frowned upon in the pioneer days of school and colony. In the midst of the heat of summer a melancholy record is made of the fact that no one was delivering ice in the village. The college offered $2500 toward the building of a hotel, if the village would raise the balance needed. Samuel Plumb gave $500 and the improvement was soon under way. In the fall of 1866 the war measure taxing incomes was still in force and some of the returns from Oberlin were: J. M. Fitch $2257, Charles G. Finney $2235, E. J. Goodrich $1694, William Hovey $1600, I. M. Johnson $3140, E. P. Johnson $1725, Marx Straus $5330, Dr. J. F. Siddall $1660.

In September the college trustees adopted a new salary schedule by the terms of which the president received $1600, the professors in the department of Theology $1200, and college professors $1000. The new depot was being finished "in fine style, with Gothic windows." At the state election in October Oberlin gave a Republican majority of 635. It may be mentioned that since the year 1858, when James Monroe was a candidate on the Republican ticket, 'Oberlin has given Republican majorities at all general elections, excepting that of 1912, when a majority was given the Progressive ticket headed by Roosevelt. These have not varied greatly in their overwhelming percentage.

In November the new steam fire engine arrived and twenty-seven men drew it from the depot through the mud of Main Street. A demand for modern methods in the construction of sidewalks was made. At this time community leaders insisted on a sidewalk tax. It had been the custom for property owners to provide only the material for new walks in front of their property. A change in some degree in the character of the community is shown by an editorial in the News of December 12, 1866, in which the editor says: "No man can deny that theaters and balls are responsible for a fearful amount of intemperance and immorality." This comment is coincident with a warm defense of parlor socials and ballads and sleigh rides, which had apparently earned the opposition of the more straight-laced residents of Oberlin. The year closes with rejoicing on the part of citizens generally in the streets "so excellently lighted with gas lamps."

The Story of a Century

1867

That the village committee on temperance had secured results is shown by the announcement in January, 1867, that Oberlin had no grog shops. Satisfaction was expressed in the fact that it was without billiard halls and bowling alleys. To offset these shortcomings it was pointed out that the community contained 150 pianos, more than any town of its size in the state. In this year John M. Langston, Oberlin colored attorney, was admitted to practice in the Supreme Court of the United States on motion of James A. Garfield, later president. Langston was the first colored lawyer in the country to gain this privilege.

This was a period of what in those days was known as a "revival in religion." Mr. Finney conducted a series of special services in First Church and several hundred "came forward." A conspicuous feature of this series of meetings was the interest taken by business men. Many business men's prayer meetings were held for several months following the close of the special meetings. These were conducted three times a week by men in business, the leaders in the work changing from meeting to meeting. In February a note in the News says: "The revival continues; the work is manifestly one of divine power." Noting the fact that 500 in all had claimed "conversion" the News says: "The winter has been memorable for a glorious work of grace. Profane swearing is rare and the use of tobacco has declined."

In the early summer of 1867 Dr. Alexander Steele, pioneer resident, was the first to begin sidewalk reform by replacing a plank walk with a flagstone pavement eight feet wide. Deacon W. W. Wright set out seventy-five elm trees along Forest Street. Old Colonial Hall was sold at auction for $200. The summer marked the death of J. M. Fitch, a chief figure in the prosecutions following the Oberlin-Wellington Rescue case. He had come to Oberlin in 1835. He had conducted a book store here for many years and was highly esteemed. In June occurred the death of Professor H. E. Peck, in Haiti, where he was United States minister. He had been a member of the Oberlin faculty from 1851

Oberlin Colony

and was a recognized leader in the community, doing especially good work in aid of soldiers in the war time. The late summer saw the retirement of J. B. T. Marsh as editor of the News. He sold his interest to Albert W. Clarke. In September ground was broken for the Second Church Building.

At the height of the revival in religion in Oberlin this year was organized Oberlin Lodge of Free Masons with L. B. Wilcox as Master. Heretofore members of the fraternity living in Oberlin had largely held membership in Elyria. An echo of this action was heard in October when Mr. Finney preached in First Church the initial sermon delivered here by him devoted entirely to a setting forth of the evils of fraternal organizations, and of Masonary in particular. Second Church suspended its service for the day and many from other towns came to hear Mr. Finney's discourse. Two services were held, occupying a length of five hours.

The News editor in his comment says that Mr. Finney came to a positive conclusion against Masonry, but reached no conclusion as to whether Masons should be excluded from the church. The editor states that many church members who were then among the strongest pillars and most beloved members of the church were likewise members of the Masonic fraternity. In an editorial answering derisive comment by the Cleveland Plain Dealer on the question, the News says: "Two or three months ago some young men applied for admission to one of the Oberlin churches and were questioned as to views on secret societies. One or two avowed themselves Masons. Soon afterward the question came up in the First Church and the First and Second Churches appointed a joint committee to consider and report. The committee named took the stand that Masonry was unfavorable, but not necessarily fatal, to piety. Professor John Morgan was asked to prepare a statement and he presented an essay strong against Masonary on account of 'its blasphemous oaths, puerile ceremonies, and its murderous history.' President Finney, in an address later, reached the same conclusion and no doubt he carried the minds of the great mass of his hearers with him."

The Story of a Century

Near the close of the year the controversy had grown in heat. Extra meetings were held in both churches, once and sometimes twice a week for two months. Frequently the entire day of preaching was devoted to the subject. Mr. Finney took the ground that the Masonic institution was antagonistic to Christianity. He said he had been a Mason, but had abandoned Masonry and tobacco on conversion. He finally concluded that the duty of the church was clear to refuse membership to active members in the lodges. He held that an intelligent and sincere Mason cannot be a Christian. At Christmas time in this year the Second Church reached a final decision that "If a candidate, after due time has been taken to enlighten him, seems to endorse Masonry we hold he cannot give requisite evidence of piety and so cannot be admitted to church fellowship." The First Church holding was that "If a candidate for admission is a Mason we will try to convince him of his error; if he desires to continue active in the fraternity we cannot bid him 'God speed' by giving him the right hand of fellowship." These two actions represented the final determination of the two churches and were effective, in letter at least, until the assumption of the pastorate of First Church by the Reverend Dr. Bradshaw. The controversy was further marked by the presentation of the supposed first three degrees of Masonry under Mr. Finney's direction at First Church. At this time Mr. Finney's influence was such that he controlled the situation in his own church and in Second Church. As a result of this attitude of the two leading churches of the community the Masonic lodge, while it retained its charter, did not grow to any extent in this period and for some years following. The only public protest made at the time seems to have been one filed by members of First Church who were in no way connected with the Masonic fraternity. This protest attempted no defense of the institution of Masonry, but gravely questioned the wisdom of the action taken by First Church. It was signed by a number of Oberlin citizens prominent in the work of the churches of the town. The signers included C. H. Penfield, L. Herrick, C. H. Churchill, G. F. H. Stevens, E. J.

Oberlin Colony

Goodrich, R. H. Birge, Horace Crosby, William Hovey, A. C. Comings, C. J. Ryder, Hiram A. Pease, J. F. Harmon, Edward Gardner, E. Follett, and "many others." The editor of the News says by way of final comment: "By common consent the question of Masonry is to be dropped in Oberlin churches for the present that the Gospel may receive some attention at least on the Sabbath."

1868

This year the practice continued of removing bodies from the original village cemetery at South Main and Morgan Streets to Westwood. Records show that of fifty-nine burials for the year ended March 1, 1868, thirty-one were of bodies originally interred in the old cemetery. Oberlin was interested in a report at this time that Elisha Gray, once a student here, had received $500,000 from the Western Union for a right to use his self-adjusting relay in telegraphy. The steadily growing influence of the Civil War veterans in public affairs was shown by the election in April of General G. W. Shurtleff as mayor. Price quotations at the first of April showed butter 30 cents, corn 60 cents, and wheat at a maximum price of $2.25. Dressed turkeys at 14 cents were selling one cent a pound less than chickens. Oats brought 75 cents. These prices meant prosperity for the farmer.

The editor of the News blames the spread of neuralgia to the change on the part of the ladies from bonnets to pasteboard hats on the top of the head. Council in May, following a public meeting, decided to proceed with definite arrangements for a new town hall. Oberlin adherence to conservative Republican doctrine was made manifest by resolutions passed at a town meeting held at the chapel favoring the impeachment of President Johnson. S. Plumb was chairman of the gathering and the resolutions were signed by J. M. Langston, G. W. Shurtleff, and others. A chapel meeting held in May ratified the nomination of Grant at Chicago. Among the signers of the resolution endorsing the Republican candidate and the platform were E. J. Goodrich and Dr. James Dascomb.

OBERLIN—BIRDS-EYE VIEW

Oberlin Colony

In June Deacon T. P. Turner, a pioneer who aided in clearing the ground here and in erecting the first buildings, moved to Chicago. In July occurred the death of William Hovey, the Republican nominee for county treasurer and for several years prominent in business and in public affairs in Oberlin. The march of progress is shown by a statement in August that the rattle of the town pump, near the college chapel, is heard no more. It had been replaced by a suction pump. A month later the walls of the Second Church and of the First Baptist Church were about completed. This summer the Hook and Ladder Company won its third trumpet at Sandusky, worth $125. The company drew its wagon forty-eight rods, stacked a thirty-foot ladder, and put a man on the top round in fifty-two seconds. Lack of railroad transportation curtailed the use of coal in Oberlin and purchases of wood were estimated at $20,000 a year. At a Republican rally here in October 5,000 people were present. Colonel John W. Steele was in charge of a drill of the Grant Boys in Blue, made up of Civil War veterans. The members were given a free supper at the hotel. At the fall election Republicans of Russia Township cast 809 votes to 95 for the Democrats.

1869

Early in January a committee waited on Council to ask action to prevent the sale of ale and beer and to suppress the playing of billiards in the village. Public sentiment was making itself felt and one grocer who had been selling tobacco "on the sly" put sixteen pounds of tobacco, his remaining stock, in the stove and burned it. An anti-tobacco pledge was being "leisurely circulated." President Finney, in an eloquent sermon decides that billiards or ten pins "can not be sanctified."

In May an anti-secret society organization was formed at a chapel meeting. Professor John Morgan was made president. The village council had a menace to contend with in the matter of the riding of velocipedes on the sidewalks. The college fell in line with a resolution prohibiting their use on the plank walk or the ground west of it or on the paths around Tappan Square.

The Story of a Century

These three-wheel affairs were apparently as plentiful as were bicycles in the early years of the twentieth century. School records show E. F. Moulton superintendent with the following teachers: Julia C. Jump, Mrs. M. J. Hubbard, May C. Gaston, Hattie M. Holtslander, Olivia Cramer, Mary Castle. Late in summer Council passed an ordinance against the use of billiard tables in the village. Public welcome was accorded the Empire Hook and Ladder Company on their return from Wooster where they had won another first prize. The mayor and Council headed the welcoming body of citizens. In November died Pringle Hamilton, 68, one of the last of the Oberlin settlers who came here in 1833. Mr. Hamilton came from Westford, Vermont. His was the third family on the ground. Hamilton Street was named in his honor.

1870

An echo of the Civil War is found in the Oberlin News of January in reference to the death of Edwin M. Stanton, the great war secretary, who is referred to as "one of our nation's greatest and best of men." Current prices in Oberlin began to fall from the high level of the year preceding, with butter selling at 25 cents, chickens 12 cents, corn 40 cents, eggs 25 cents, potatoes 25 cents, wheat $1.00, and wool 40 cents. The decided drop in potatoes, wheat, and wool meant serious loss to the farmer of Northern Ohio. These prices made plain the hard times and the scarcity of money of which public complaint was made in the village. A plea was made for a reduction of taxes, which were high in view of the need of paying for the cost of the Civil War. Oberlin continued to move forward as evidenced by a public plea for the numbering of houses in the village. The proposed cost was ten cents per house.

In February "Father" Keep died at the age of 89. He was responsible for the decision of the college to accept colored students, having cast the vote as trustee which broke a tie in the board. He was a trustee of the college from 1834 to the time of his death. He had never been confined to his bed by sickness at any time in his life, with the exception of the day of his death. At about this time occurred the death at Olivet, Michigan, of William Hosford, 78. He came to Oberlin in 1833, having sold his Vermont farm, in response to the pleading of John J. Shipherd. He lived here for ten years and went with Shipherd to Olivet in 1844, together with about forty other Oberlin residents who had part in the founding of the Michigan college.

Early in this year the Methodist Episcopal Congregation bought a lot on South Main Street for the building of a church. The report of Superintendent Moulton of the public schools for the year ended March 1, 1870, showed 660 pupils entered during that period with a record of 900 of school age. Under the leadership of Mrs. Marianne P. Dascomb, principal of the Female Department of the College 1835-36 and 1852-70, 140 married women of Lorain County filed protest against the movement for equal suffrage. A resolution adopted said: "We are content that our fathers, brothers, husbands and sons represent us in the corn field, the battlefield and at the ballot box, and we them in the school room, at the fireside and at the cradle." This opposition to a right finally granted the women of America was logical then on the part of refined gentlewomen who could not forsee the economic changes to come in less than half a century. While they did not take women to the battlefield and the cornfield, they took them by hundreds of thousands to the offices, the mills, the shops, and small business of every character.

Early in the year appeal was made for the teaching of music in the public schools of the village, thus forecasting the excellent work done in recent years largely through the influence of Professor Karl W. Gehrkens, present head of the Department of School Music in the 'Oberlin Conservatory of Music. The Oberlin Agricultural Society, formed in the early days of the village and college, was still active in this year and held regular meetings. At this time the state law making the term of the mayor and members of the council two years instead of one became effective. The Oberlin News speaks of "the secret order of farmers known as Grangers" and gravely asks "what is it

The Story of a Century

for?" The Grange, in the last six decades, has done good work for farmers through this section of Ohio. Appeal was made to the Ohio Legislature to pass a law which would be effective in suppressing the liquor traffic in Oberlin. Several arrests were made and several convictions were set aside before City Solicitor Webster finally drafted an ordinance which proved effective. President Fairchild delivered a lecture in Chapel in opposition to voting by women.

On Memorial Day ground was broken for the Soldiers' Monument which was dedicated one year later. The Memorial Day addresses were delivered by President Fairchild and General G. W. Shurtleff. Attention was called to the fact that Oberlin never sent a drafted soldier into the Civil War. All government calls were filled by volunteer recruits.

The movement for the building of the Second Church, started in war days, saw its completion this year. The cost was about $30,000. Seats to the number of 1065 were made by Peck & Colburn in their Oberlin factory. Addresses were delivered by President Fairchild, Charles G. Finney, and Professor John Morgan. That baseball was an all-day sport in the old days is indicated by the score of 54-26 in a game between the Forest City Nine of Cleveland and an Oberlin team. The home team had the lesser score, which would in modern time be sufficient to win about a half a dozen games. Reports of assessors showed that the personal property valuation in Oberlin was $286,934. In a storm on July 4 the flag pole, put up in the first Lincoln Campaign, was broken and fell to the street, doing some damage. During the war days the flag was swung to the top for a Union victory and placed at half mast for defeats. A great rally was held around the flag pole when the news came of the surrender of Lee.

In August Bradstreet Stevens, 83, died. He was listed as the last survivor of 'Oberlin colonists who came here in the fall of 1833. He aided in building the first college hall and built the first frame dwelling house in town. He did not agree with other colonists in their adherence to vegetable diet and his home was a

One hundred twenty-three

resort for students who repaired to it when nature craved a more substantial bill of fare. When Stevens built his frame house there were only four log houses in the town, with no school. He was a cousin of Thaddeus Stevens, famous Abolitionist legislator.

The total value of Oberlin realty was $597,055. Property exempt from taxation was: college $97,400, churches $73,800, public buildings $28,800. This year pay of township school teachers ranged from $20 per month for women to $37.50 for men. Gas lights for streets cost $267.14 for eight months. This street lighting charge was for the year 1932 more than $8000. Prices at the end of the year showed an upward trend, with wheat selling at $1.30, potatoes 75 cents, corn 50 cents, chickens 10 cents. The population of the village was 2940.

1871

The new year was ushered in with a destructive fire on January 6, which caused a loss of $10,000. Buildings destroyed or damaged were located on South Main Street near the College Street intersection. They included Munson Brothers' restaurant, Mead's bakery, Morris & Haylor meat store, and buildings belonging to Deacon Burrell, V. Hebebrand, Charles Ryder, and John Broadwell. The firm of Johnson, Whitney & Cole was succeeded by I. M. Johnson & Son. A farm wagon sank to the hubs while trying to travel along South Main Street. School reports showed a total operating cost for the year closed of $5,223.97. The average enrollment of pupils was 523. A mass meeting of voters of the town held in May went on record as against the construction of a new school house. This action was later reversed.

The chief community event of 1871 was the dedication on Memorial Day of the Soldiers' Monument still standing, although in dilapidated condition, in the year 1933, at the southeast corner of College and Professor Streets on ground given for the purpose by Oberlin College. The address at the afternoon service held at the monument was made by Professor Judson Smith of the faculty of the college. At a special service held at

The Story of a Century

First Church in the evening the chief address was made by Honorable James Monroe. Short talks were made by Professor J. M. Ellis and General G. W. Shurtleff. In the course of his address Mr. Monroe said: "This monument has a heavenly presence. It is not as high as the Pyramids of Egypt. It is not on account of its magnificence nor its beauty, though it is beautiful, but because it stands to tell of noble deeds and acts of heroism as lofty and great as those of the old heroes that we rejoice in it. Those brave young men! We almost envy them their resting place.

"These young men went out from their homes and college classes, in which were cherished associations, and gave their lives —not for reward, not for fame, not for position, not for pleasure, not to have their names proudly shouted among the children of men; neither did they rush to battle for any doubtful movement, but they gave their lives to fulfill simple duty.

"You recall the meetings we held here long ago to denounce war as sinful. It is said that life is the most valuable of all possessions, but is not honor more than life? How many men are there when they come to the alternative that do not hesitate at all to pitch life and everything overboard for the sake of great principles? These young friends of ours went forth to battle because God had called, their country had called, their friends had called. They loved peace but they were not so devoted to her shrine as to be insensible to the agonizing cry of the nation. We are asked by a few if their monument may not be baneful in lending countenance to the spirit of war, but it is too late to ask that now. Our war for the Union was a righteous war. It is the object of the war which makes it either noble or degrading."

The monument was built of Amherst sandstone in Gothic effect. Its total cost was about $5,000. Oberlin citizens contributed $1500, students $1300, and Mr. Clough, the contractor, donated $1400 towards its cost. When this monument was dedicated, six years after the close of the Civil War, there were surviving several hundred veterans who had gone from Oberlin College and Oberlin Community in answer to their country's call.

At present (1933) George H. Houghton is the sole resident survivor of Henry Lincoln Post, Grand Army of the Republic, which in the old days was one of the strongest posts in Northern Ohio.

As has always been the case in Oberlin in time of human distress, the people of the village responded to the cry for help following the great Chicago fire in October of this year. Mayor Backus made a special trip to Chicago, taking a car load of food and clothing and $450 to relieve the sufferings of the people of the city.

1872

In March Reverend Charles Grandison Finney for the third time tendered his resignation as pastor of First Church. On the two previous occasions the congregation declined to accept a severance of the pastoral relation. Mr. Finney's health had failed and his resignation was this time accepted. Dr. Alexander Steele, father of Judge John W. Steele and the first practicing physician in Oberlin, died April 6, 1872. He came to Oberlin with his family in 1836.

A town caucus in July accepted the college offer of $5500 for the public school building, later known as Cabinet Hall. The vote was 83 to 36. This was a preliminary step toward the building of a new school house on South Main Street on a lot purchased from George W. Ells and Jasper Hill for $5,000. The purchase of the lot was determined at a second town meeting by a vote of 113 to 65. The trustees of the Second Methodist Church bought a lot on Water Street between Groveland and Mill Street for $125 as the site of a church.

An element of the dramatic appeared in the national campaign this year between General Grant and Horace Greeley when Asa Mahan, first president of the college, at that time a resident in the West, came to Oberlin by invitation to speak. Signers of the invitation claimed that Mr. Mahan was brought here in the belief that he would speak in behalf of Grant. They charged no duplicity on Mr. Mahan's part, but claimed a lack of frankness on the part of managers of the campaign. President Mahan, who spoke in aid of Greeley, in the course of his talk referred to General Grant as one of the most ignorant mortals that ever led an army. That his speech had little value for Greeley in Oberlin was shown by a canvass of college students made later which recorded 113 votes for Grant to 6 for Greeley. In the state election the Republicans carried Russia Township by a majority of 590 and the county by a majority of 2219.

In October the College Chapel bell was first used as a town clock. By hand operation the bell struck the hours during the course of the day and early evening. This ante-dated by several decades the present modern electrically-operated mechanism which strikes the hour with an accuracy which justifies the setting of village timepieces by it. In October John Watson, colored, member of the Oberlin-Wellington Rescue party, died. He and his wife came to Oberlin about 1840 from slavery in the south. He kept a grocery for many years and had a fine reputation for integrity and good citizenship.

1873

Early in the year Council passed an ordinance providing for numbering of houses in the village. It was said of Deacon Horace Crosby, who came to Oberlin in 1835, walking from his home in Massachusetts, and who died in March of this year, that: "He was free not only from the vices but from the frivolities of youth." The public schools were operated at a cost of $7,659.95. The average enrollment was 629. It was found necessary to remove horsesheds from the First Church lot because of their nearness to the construction work of Council Hall. These had stood for many years. Only twenty-four votes were cast against the bond issue for a new school building on South Main Street. The discouraging condition of Oberlin streets was manifested in this statement: "A man was seen riding a mule up Main Street a few days ago. This was ascertained to be a fact by a view of a hat and a pair of ears as they occasionally appeared above the surface of the street." L. B. Kinney's brick yard furnished 800,000

Oberlin Colony

bricks for the new school house which was begun in June. It also furnished half a million bricks for Council Hall on which work was in progress. At a public meeting, held in June at First Church to consider the wants of the college, President Fairchild said that the work of the college could not be done by the college alone; members of the community, not connected with the college, who furnished homes for students performed a part in the education of the young people quite as important as that accomplished in the recitation room; not even the discipline of the college could be maintained without the continuance of good order in the community and the mutual confidence of the people of the town and officials of the college. Mr. Fairchild further said that the college authorities would always welcome suggestions about their work from any persons in the community; mistakes had doubtless been made, but the college authorities would endeavor to correct them whenever they were pointed out. Mr. Fairchild told his audience that the college faced, in a period of very hard times, a serious condition in view of the fact that the annual expenses of the institution had grown from $6,000 in 1850 to $24,000 in 1873. In 1932 the annual budget of the college was in excess of $1,000,000.

Community residents began a campaign for storm sewers in July of this year. The town had but one storm sewer and that was an open ditch. The mayor, council members, and citizens generally, with a brass band for good measure, met the Empire Hook and Ladder Company on their triumphant return from Mansfield where they had won first prize in a state contest. This was the sixth prize the "Empire Hooks," as they were known, had taken. They ran with their equipment forty rods and put Frank Hovey at the top of a thirty foot ladder in 36 1-4 seconds. This time was 2 1-2 seconds better than that of their closest competitor. A formal speech was delivered on this occasion by Professor J. M. Ellis.

Deacon Theodore S. Ingersoll, one of the 1833 Oberlin pioneers, died at Berea and was buried here. His journey to

Oberlin with his family from New York took two months to make. He covered only two miles on the last day, being forced to cut his way through brush and timber to reach his destination. The First Methodist Episcopal Church on South Main Street was completed this year. The congregation was organized in 1858. County expenses in 1873 were $208,000—about one-sixth of the county budget in 1932. In August Edwin Regal bought the Fairchild book store. H. O. Swift became owner of the sawmill, taking over the interest of Reuben Stone. The school census this year showed 820 white children of school age and 232 colored. T. R. Mayhew sold his livery business. In November the Reverend James Brand was installed as pastor of First Church. At the close of the year the Lorain County News was sold by J. N. Brown and J. H. Lang to Pratt & Battle, who changed the name to the Oberlin News.

1874

Oberlin was one of the centers in this and following years of the state fight on the part of temperance advocates on the proposed licensing of saloons. Reverend James Brand was chairman of a committee that reported at a public meeting that the liquor traffic in the three drug stores of the village was at the rate of sixty-eight barrels a year. Marx Straus, leading dry goods merchant, announced that he would take dried apples in exchange for goods. At the April election Montraville Stone was chosen as mayor and Aaron Bacon, George S. Pay, and W. T. Henderson were elected to the council. The first number of the Oberlin College Review was issued. In August Council Hall was completed and formally dedicated. A month later the cornerstone of the Second M. E. Church, on Water Street, was laid. In November the new school, built on South Main Street, now owned by Oberlin College and used for class room purposes, was opened for school uses. It was built at a cost of $37,000.

Oberlin Colony

1875

With the death of Charles Grandison Finney, former president of 'Oberlin College and former pastor of First Church, in August, 1875, there passed from the scene in Oberlin the man most responsible for the ideals and practices of both college and community in the forty years of his living here. The impress of his character was such that for years after his death both college and community were largely guided in their conduct by vivid memories of their profound respect for the things for which in his life he stood. Primarily an evangelist, and interested first and possibly last in the spiritual, rather than the material growth, of the college and community, Mr. Finney's reputation will always rest on his career as a preacher rather than on his work as a college executive. He came to Oberlin in 1835. He was Professor of Systematic Theology from that period until 1858 and Professor of Pastoral Theology from 1835 until the time of his death. He was a member of the Board of Trustees 1846-51 and was elected president of the college in August, 1851. He resigned this office in 1865. President Fairchild says of Finney: "He belongs to the world, and not to 'Oberlin alone." Mr. Finney was 83 at the time of his death and continued active in his preaching work until the year 1874. In this same year died Deacon T. P. Turner, Oberlin pioneer, who as a carpenter had part in the early building program of the college. In August of this year J. B. T. Marsh was elected treasurer of Oberlin College to succeed George W. Kinney resigned.

1876

Early this year T. H. Rowland and W. B. Bedortha were leaders of an effort to establish a free library and reading room in Oberlin. This operated for a time under financial difficulty. It was ultimately supplanted by an arrangement with Oberlin College for the use of the college library on the part of community residents. This practice continues.

Hard times, which were at their peak in the panic of 1873, had not yet vanished. Oberlin citizens were complaining of high taxes and seeking frantically for relief. Among suggestions made was one of the substitution of coal oil street lamps for gas. Other citizens thought that the small police force of the village should serve without pay. Another suggestion was that $100 could be saved in salaries by cutting the remuneration of the mayor and clerk. The salary of the mayor was at that time $100 per year; that of the clerk was a little more. At the same time there were those who took a more hopeful view and insisted that good times were "just around the corner." The public schools and their operation had consideration. Objections were made to an annual cost per pupil of $15, which in 1932 would have been welcomed by any well conducted school. The salary of the superintendent, $1700, was finally cut to $1300. The salary of teachers was $600. The levy for school purposes was but seven mills.

The first Mock Republican Convention conducted by the college was held in June. The students nominated James G. Blaine to head the ticket. In this year Blaine was defeated in the convention and Rutherford B. Hayes, of Ohio, was named as a dark horse. A cooperative meat market was forced to suspend for lack of patronage after two months of experiment.

1877

In February a social was held at the Park House for "all interested in cultivating friendly feeling among community residents." The call for this gathering was signed by M. Straus, W. B. Durand, R. H. Birge, O. F. Carter, A. R. Williams, and M. Day, Jr. That there is nothing new under the sun is demonstrated by the fact that there was much complaint of loafing on the three corners of the public square. Committees were named and theoretically they were still seeking a remedy in 1933. When the temperance agitation was at its height, in the spring of this year, the Cleveland Herald published an article on Oberlin which reflected in some degree the outside views of people who were probably unable to see beneath the surface in a study of the college and the community. The editor speaks of Oberlin as horrible in winter because of lack of roads and sidewalks and deals roughly with Oberlin views and methods. He says of the people: "They are good, very good, and are not afraid to let others know it. Some of them are holy—that makes us feel uncomfortable."

In July W. B. Bedortha, at that time a printer employed by the Oberlin News and later one of the leading attorneys in this section of Ohio, began the work of compiling a street directory of Oberlin, the first in the history of the village. In October the Sheridan & Hilman Telegraph School resumed after a short suspension. James Sheridan, who conducted one of the largest schools in the country here for several years and who was a pioneer in this work, was still living in Oberlin in 1933.

The fall of this year saw Oberlin participate in an effort to build a railroad from Lorain to the coal fields in Perry County. Those active were Professor J. M. Ellis, General G. W. Shurtleff, E. J. Goodrich, Judge John W. Steele, O. F. Carter, and W. B. Durand. It was urged that the proposed line would bring cheap fuel and cheap lumber to Oberlin and then nothing could interfere with Oberlin becoming a manufacturing town. In December of this year W. H. Pearce became editor of the Oberlin News.

1878

In March William B. Bedortha had been admitted to the bar and made his first plea in Common Pleas Court with Judge Steele as his associate counsel. Mr. Bedortha and Judge Steele were close friends and associates for almost thirty years. Private telephones, put up by a Cleveland man, were in operation at the homes and offices of W. B. Durand, Attorney I. A. Webster, and O. F. Carter. A report of the clerk of the Board of Trustees of Westwood Cemetery showed that burials in the cemetery from 1863 to 1877 made a total of 632. A poll tax was in operation and residents talked of combining to resist its enforcement. The tax was $1.00 a year.

In May, S. Royce began work on a new block to be built at the corner of West College Street and College Place. It was

WEST COLLEGE STREET, 1878

described as to be of brick two stories high, 75 feet deep, with a small office room fronting on College Place. This is the present home of the Comings book store.

At First Church in June was given by Professor Churchill, of Oberlin College, and Professor Elisha Gray, of Chicago, an exhibition of the telephone, then in the process of perfection, and of the Edison Phonograph, which had been invented a short time before. Mr. Gray anticipated the evils and blessings of radio with a hookup through his telephone with the Western Union Telegraph Company instruments in Cleveland and the audience listened to the playing of Yankee Doodle and several other selections by performers located in the Cleveland office. Phonographs were still so scarce that one promised the exhibitors was not delivered in time for the lecture. A large wooden model made by Professor Churchill was shown instead.

The early summer of this year saw the opening, near the railroad depot, of a billiard hall and pop stand. This at once aroused the opposition of the community and gave rise to several public meetings before the proprietor was persuaded to quit. Crusade methods were adopted at the outset and it was reported that the "Christian people of Oberlin have made the billiard hall a constant place of visitation for a week." Needless to say these visits on the part of both men and women were not for the purpose of playing billiards or drinking pop. The callers were there in an effort to persuade the owner to close his place. It was announced that four hundred ladies had reported to the committee their willingness to visit the billiard parlors in furtherance of the crusade effort. Picketing of the establishment was done for a number of days. This method has been frequently employed by organized labor for the settlement of arguments where non-union labor had been employed in the case of strikes. An incident at one of the gatherings gave rise to severe criticism outside of Oberlin of what were assumed to be Oberlin views. C. M. Tambling, as leader of the regular temperance prayer meeting, announced that in conversation with the proprietor of the billiard hall the ladies engaged in crusade work and others have been met with the statement that it is no worse to play billiards than to play croquet. "As a great many of the good people of Oberlin are of the opinion that croquet should be abandoned" said the speaker, "I propose that the meeting take up croquet playing as the subject for discussion." He had been in the habit of playing croquet but he had played his last game. His objections were stated at some length. A few detailed were the temptation to lie and cheat and become excited, so that time is devoted to this which could be employed to a better purpose. In this he had some support, but General G. W. Shurtleff opposed such action, saying that there were matters of too grave importance, such as getting rid of the billiard and pop stand and promoting temperance, to warrant consideration of Mr. Tambling's problem. At this same meeting P. G. Akers said he thought that the temperance cause frequently suffered by excessive zeal against tobacco. The committee and the crusaders finally succeeded in persuading the billiard hall proprietor to close his place. The public agitation against the billiard hall had its basis in the fear that such a place would develop into a saloon for the selling of liquor. There was justification for such a fear, in view of what had occurred in other towns.

Announcement was made in August of the anonymous ·gift of $25,000 for the chair of Sacred Rhetoric of the College. This was at that time the largest donation received by the college from any one person. School expenses had increased to $16,047.98, but this included $6,792.34 interest and retirement of bonds issued for the new school building. The total enrollment was 797. The tax rate in Oberlin was 19.4 mills.

1879

In January died Fay Hopkins, Oberlin pioneer, who came from Vermont in 1834. He was one of the organizers of the First Church and had seen service in the war of 1812.

In this year Oberlin College had received the full effect of the hard times which began in the early 70's and which had reached their culmination here. In 1873 college attendance was

1371. In 1879 it had dropped to 949. The college had an endowment of about $175,000, with an annual expense of $33,000. A meeting of citizens of Oberlin was held at the chapel to consider possible ways of aiding the college in this emergency. President Fairchild outlined the situation and asked Oberlin people to give such aid as they could. Mr. Fairchild, in the course of his remarks, said that there might be some criticism due to the fact that he and other members of the faculty lived in large houses. He was obliged by circumstances to do this and informed his hearers that his large house was not built from his small salary, but grew out of the sale of his cow pasture. President Fairchild for many years kept a cow and himself led her to and from the pasture. Despite the hard times the citizens of the community responded to the appeal with aid for the college.

In April Frank Hovey, still an honored citizen of Oberlin in 1933, was made chief engineer of the fire department. Oberlin residents attempted to secure the building of the proposed new court house here and the transfer of the county seat to Oberlin. This was not successful. E. J. Goodrich was chairman of a meeting to consider a proposal for the building of the Lorain, Wooster and Perry County Railroad in an effort to bring Oberlin in direct contact with Ohio coal fields. Daniel Kinsey, who came to Oberlin from Vermont in June, 1834, died at the age of 75. When Kinsey arrived here the first two log cabins built in the colony stood near the site of the Historic Elm, end to end, with space between. Kinsey obtained permission to board up the space between the two and lived with his family in this improvised cabin for a year and a half. Mr. Kinsey served several terms in the Ohio Legislature.

An echo of the anti-secret society battle in Oberlin in the late 60's came when the corner stone of the new court house was laid at Elyria in November by the Grand Lodge of Ohio Masons. Honorable Heman Ely, of Elyria, delivered a brief address and read the protest of 35 Oberlin citizens against the laying of the corner stone by "a secret and oath-bound" order. Mr. Ely stated that it was not possible to comply with the protest, but that the protest with the signatures would be filed in the copper box placed in the corner stone with other articles, including newspapers, names of early settlers, and lists of church organizations.

In December Mrs. Esther J. Shipherd, widow of Reverend John J. Shipherd, died in Cleveland.

1880

In January a statement of the First National Bank showed total resources of $176,624.52. The total resources of the Oberlin Savings Bank Company and the Peoples Banking Company at a corresponding date in 1932 were about $2,500,000.

At an anti-tobacco meeting, held in First Church, Professor J. M. Ellis stated that sales of tobacco in Oberlin in the year closed amounted to $12,000, and that the use in public places was growing. The town had one tobacco store and another was soon to be opened. Mr. Ellis said children had no trouble in getting tobacco. A committee was named to devise means to end the sale here and many persons signed a pledge not to use tobacco.

In February of this year A. J. Frederick & Company bought the M. Straus store. In April died Dr. James Dascomb, whose wife, Mrs. Marianne P. Dascomb, had died the year previous. They came to Oberlin in 1834 and until the arrival of Dr. Alexander Steele in 1836 Dr. Dascomb, who was a faculty member, was the only physician in the village. President Fairchild, in preaching the funeral sermon of Dr. Dascomb, credited him with the movement which resulted in the planting of hundreds of shade trees in Oberlin. Dr. Dascomb also had a leading part in the work of buying and establishing Westwood Cemetery. He had much to do with the building of First Church and was properly regarded as one of the most valuable citizens of the community. He had served as mayor of the village.

The personal property return for Oberlin in this year was $311,141. In July Evan J. Phillips was chosen postmaster to succeed William Allen, deceased. This action was taken at a public

Oberlin Colony

election and was confirmed by the recommendation of Honorable James Monroe, member of Congress. The census this year showed Oberlin's population to be 3242. Elyria had a population of 4748 and Wellington of 2383. The Oberlin tax rate was 17.8 mills, while that of Elyria was only 14 mills. The Oberlin tax rate in 1932 was 20.4 mills.

The change in the attitude of party members toward party victories and party leaders in the past half century is shown by the action of Oberlin Republicans following the election of Garfield in November. When the news of Garfield's success was finally confirmed the day following election a spontaneous demonstration broke out in which faculty, students, and townspeople took part with hearty joy. College students left their classes, the public schools were dismissed, and business was suspended. Horns, sleigh bells, and all forms of noisemakers were used in a parade in which almost the entire community had part. One hundred young women were in the line of march. Professor James Monroe made the address of the day. General G. W. Shurtleff, of the college faculty, sensing the fact that the large crowd was not entirely content with results attained, arranged for a special train to take the Oberlin celebrators to Mentor that they might congratulate Mr. Garfield. The train was ready soon after noon and nine cars were loaded with students, faculty, and citizens of the community. The Oberlin band accompanied the crowd and President James H. Fairchild headed the procession of 600 people from the train at Mentor to the Garfield home. This delegation was the first to call upon Garfield and he expressed his warm appreciation in his response to the address made by President Fairchild.

At the close of the year people of Oberlin were clamoring for telephone service between Elyria and Oberlin. The invention of the telephone, credited to Alexander Graham Bell, had preceded this demand by only four years. There were in 1880 very few exchanges in the country and there was but little long distance service.

The Story of a Century

1881

In May occurred the death of Alonzo Pease, artist. He was a son of Hiram A. Pease, Oberlin pioneer, and accompanied his uncle, Peter Pindar Pease, when Oberlin's first citizen brought his family from Brownhelm to Oberlin. In view of Oberlin's splendid Civil War record other communities were disturbed and distressed by the fact that Oberlin, for the first time since the war, did not formally observe Memorial Day. The only explanation offered was that there was no one to take charge and arrange the service. In July P. R. Tobin, father of Frank W. Tobin, veteran druggist and in 1933 purchasing agent for Oberlin College, was elected marshal of Oberlin at a salary of $15 per month.

At this time a franchise for a telephone exchange was granted to Young & Arnold, who, near the end of the year, opened an exchange with 15 subscribers. Included in the list were T. H. Rowland, E. J. Goodrich, and W. B. Durand. Public explanation was made of the method of operating an exchange and assurance was given subscribers that they would have the use of the same sort of instruments then employed in the big cities of the country.

An effort to establish a saloon in Oberlin was responsible for a mass meeting on temperance at which it was reported that liquor was sold at four places in town. Five hundred people signed a pledge to abstain. Druggists finally agreed over their signatures not to sell liquor for any purpose. At that time it was legal to sell for medicinal and mechanical purposes. Temperance advocates figured there was too much sickness and too much mechanical activity in the community for the good of its morals. After this pledge had been signed by the druggists, one of the number was found to have sold Hostetter's Bitters. A committee called upon the offender who reported that the sale was an oversight and agreed that the offense would not be repeated. These several actions were opening ones in a temperance war in Oberlin which covered a period of several years.

One hundred thirty-nine

Oberlin Colony

Public schools and the college were closed at the time of the death of President Garfield in September. Memorial addresses were delivered at community meetings at the chapel by Professor James Monroe, Professor J. M. Ellis, and General Shurtleff. Public note was made in the fall of an exhibit of original works of art in the study of F. A. Dart in the Park House block. Great praise was given a portrait of Professor Hiram Mead painted by Mr. Dart. Mr. Dart was still living in 'Oberlin in 1933 and had at his home on East College Street an interesting showing of his work in art and of valuable antiques.

Prices at the close of the year showed signs of stiffening and indicated that the period of hard times was about over. Butter was selling at 26 cents, steak 14 cents, coffee 30 cents, cheese 16 cents, ham 14 cents, sugar 10 cents, and wheat $1.30.

1882

The year saw active resumption of the liquor controversy. T. H. Rowland had sold his drug store to Frank Bronson of Elyria and it was charged that Bronson was violating the agreement of druggists not to sell liquor. At a public meeting $260,000 was pledged, in event of need, to put down the liquor traffic. Crusaders visited the Bronson store and a committee which called on Bronson was said to have been forced to leave when the proprietor of the store put a shovelful of cayenne pepper on the fire. Bronson finally appealed to the mayor and the sheriff for protection from the crowd who had called at his store and remained there for hours at a time. The mayor appointed thirty deputies, many of whom were men who had been on the crusading team. Two of the officers were assigned to the store during business hours. The culmination of the argument came some months later when, as a result of a sermon preached by Dr. Brand at First Church, Bronson filed suit in the Cuyahoga County Courts for $30,000 damages for defamation of character. The controversy continued for some time. Two trials were held and in both cases the jury disagreed. Finally the suit was dismissed.

The Story of a Century

March 6 of this year was the date of one of the two most destructive fires in the history of Oberlin. The fire was discovered in a two-story frame building at 7 East College Street. The Tuttle & Farr meat market, two frame houses on East College and the skating rink on East College were destroyed. To the west of the original blaze the fire took the George W. Ells house, caught a frame building near the Carter & Wood hardware building on South Main, and spread throughout the Ells block to the Goodrich block on the corner of East College and South Main. This block included the Goodrich book store, the Platt photograph gallery, Bacon's omnibus office, and the new telephone exchange. Going south on Main the flames caught the two-story drug store of J. M. Gardner and the Bronson drug store, south of Gardner's. Before the fire was under control, the whole corner east and south was ablaze. The Carter & Wood hardware store and the harness store of P. R. Tobin to the south were destroyed. The brick wall of the Westervelt building to the south saved this building and the Munson market. Virtually the whole town turned out to fight the flames. The loss was over $60,000. The fire was thought to be of incendiary origin. Within a day or two following the fire the Goodrich store and the Gardner drug store were temporarily housed in a hastily constructed building placed on the campus.

This same corner was destroyed by fire in 1848. Losers in the early fire were the W. H. Plumb book store, E. F. Munson, who was postmaster then, and James Fitch. The Goodrich block, which was burned in 1882, was built in 1849. Mr. Goodrich opened his book store there in 1856, buying the building two years later. The Ells block, destroyed in 1882, was built in 1849, and the Carter & Wood block in 1850. In December, 1864, all the buildings on the east side of Main Street, from the south line of the 1882 burned district to the Union school house on the south, were destroyed by fire.

In June the Citizens National Bank succeeded the First National Bank which had been established in September, 1863. In this same month a petition signed by 500 people asked Council to pass an ordinance against smoking within ten feet of a church one-half hour before or one half hour after services. No action was taken. At a special session of Council Judge John W. Steele submitted a report on the water supply of Oberlin. The recent fire had made it plain that the large cisterns known as reservoirs afforded no adequate fire protection in time of greatest need. This marked the first step in the building of a modern water works, which came about through the efforts of Judge Steele.

1883

At the outset of the jubilee celebration of college and community in 1883 Oberlin property was valued for taxes at $1,066,-330. The only outstanding bonds were school bonds in the amount of $8800, a part of the cost of the new high school building. The county debt was at the time $57,000. The proposal for better water service took the form of public approval of a drilled well at the suggestion of Mayor Clarke. The well finally produced a quantity of gas, but no water. This project seems to have marked the beginning of the development of shallow wells for household use here. There are scores of such wells in Oberlin.

In April E. P. Ralston had charge of the New Era mills. He was a Civil War veteran and was for 40 years a resident of Oberlin. Chester F. Ralston is his son. The event of the year was the observance of the fiftieth anniversary of the college. This was largely historical in character. Uriah McKee, father of O. C. McKee, cashier of the Oberlin Savings Bank Company, leased rooms in the town hall for the carrying on of his writing school. E. E. Lyon was running a steam engine to grind material for blackboard slating which he sold for many years. He was the father of Doren E. Lyon, superintendent of buildings and grounds of Oberlin College. Near the close of the year Deacon W. W. Wright, who came to Oberlin in 1835, died here. He was engaged in the nursery business and was largely concerned in the physical development of the western section of Oberlin, a greater part of which he had at one time owned.

THE THIRD QUARTER-CENTURY

AN ERA OF IMPROVEMENTS

CHAPTER XII

THE year 1883 marked the close of the first fifty years of the life of the community and the college. The years since the close of the Civil War were influenced by the thought and character of James Harris Fairchild, who in 1866 became president of the college. College and community were still in those days so closely related that Mr. Fairchild's influence was felt almost as largely in the latter as in the former. While his presidency lasted until his resignation in 1889, his record in the semicentennial year had been such as to fix firmly his place in the college and community. In a recent address on Oberlin's first one hundred years Dr. W. F. Bohn, assistant to the president of Oberlin College, said of Mr. Fairchild: "He was a magnificent figure, comparable, perhaps, on the intellectual side to the great Gladstone. In the past century, doubtless, Fairchild was the greatest educational force on the Oberlin Campus."

Thus the spiritual and educational growth of college and town were advanced in the years following the Civil War under Mr. Fairchild's direction. The natural growth of the college was retarded by the hard times following the war and by those of the decade beginning about 1870. There was, however, in 1883 certain promise of improvement in this regard. These quiet times were reflected in the life of the community. The invention, in the late 70's, of the telephone, the talking machine, the incandescent lamp, the arc lamp, and the gasoline motor, while not yet followed by any general use in small communities such as Oberlin, served to emphasize the fact that the end of the first fifty years of college and town marked a looking toward a world which would be different in many respects from that of the half century preceding.

The next twenty-five years in the history of community and college would see a steady expansion of the school and a steady modernizing of the community in the matter of public utilities and the agencies of public service. These changes on the community side would include a modern water plant, a modern system of sewerage, improved streets and sidewalks, free mail delivery, the erection of two new school buildings, and the general expansion and betterment of the public schools.

1884

Oberlin College and Community began the second half century with a promise of growth in the building of Warner Hall, one of the first of the modern buildings on the Campus. The corner stone for this building was laid January 23. In April C. A. Metcalf was elected mayor. An echo of the pioneer days was found in the removal of a house located at 19 East College Street to a site on South Pleasant Street. The house was built by William Hosford in 1838.

This summer the Gibson Hose Company, known as Reliable Number Two, won a $100 prize in a match at Tiffin. The Oberlin time was 32 1-4 seconds as against 33 3-4 for Shelby, its closest competitor. This was the best time on record. Mayor Metcalf and citizens in general tendered the company a reception on their return. George Gibson was foreman. Other members were Edward Hopkins, Walter Spaulding, George Shanks, Edward A. Miller, Harry Brinsmaid, Eben Hopkinson, Bert Stewart, Mell Tobin, Edward Lyman, P. E. Gulick, Will Colburn, Watson Little, Garrett Newell, Jay Penfield, P. E. Clarke, James Stone, Henry Braithwaite, John Vaughn, Albert Bassett, Pett Gilman.

In September was laid the corner stone of Spear Library.

1885

The Supreme Court of Ohio held unconstitutional an ordinance passed by Council prohibiting the sale of intoxicating liquor. At this date there was no adequate state law covering the sale of liquor. C. T. Beckwith found a gas well on his premises. This followed the gas well which came in when the town drilled for water. In February Mark Twain and George W. Cable spoke in the U. L. A. Lecture Course. This visit of Twain's to Oberlin gave rise to the report that *The Man That Corrupted Hadley-burg* was based on an Oberlin experience and that its writing had a basis in Twain's inability to smoke in uninterrupted comfort and to his dislike for the opening of his meeting with prayer.

Oberlin thermometers on March 19 showed nine below zero. In April Tappan Hall was demolished. It was built in 1835-36. In May an election for postmaster was held. Mr. Wack, a veteran Democrat, received 163 votes, with no votes against him. When the appointment was finally made it was given to F. A. Hart. The election was not binding upon the appointing power. At a meeting at the chapel a flag, purchased by the women of Oberlin, was given to Henry Lincoln Post, Grand Army of the Republic. At the same time a portrait of Henry W. Lincoln, for whom the post was named, was given the organization by Lieutenant Lincoln's mother. Henry Lincoln Relief Corps was organized with Mrs. J. F. Harmon as president.

1886

In January Ladies' Hall burned, with a loss of $20,000. Reverend R. G. Hutchins was called from Minneapolis, Minnesota, to the pastorate of Second Church.

In March a bill passed the Ohio Legislature to permit Oberlin to borrow to build a water works plant. This was one of the final results of several years of effort on the part of Judge John W. Steele and others to improve by modern methods the fire and water situation here in Oberlin. Judge Steele prepared for the public at this time a carefully drawn statement expressing the purpose of the measures and urging citizens to support a bond issue. He pointed out recent fire losses and the scarcity of water. He stated that the system had probably saved few if any buildings and had only prevented the spread of the flames in the disastrous fire of 1882. Lorain had installed a water works system in 1885. Judge Steele called attention to the fact that Lorain at that time was one-third smaller than Oberlin and one-third poorer in financial resources. Oberlin College agreed to pay a fair share of the cost of construction. The statement of Judge Steele called attention to the fact that the duplicate in 1860 was $379,454 and that in 1885 it had increased to $1,144,756. Judge Steele estimated that this duplicate would double in the following 25 years, which it did. Despite this excellent setting forth of the need of the community for modern fire protection and adequate water for household use, communications in the public prints favored the "bucket brigade" as more efficient than the high-pressure system with fire hydrants.

At the April election the Prohibitionists, then coming into activity in Oberlin, nominated Lyman B. Hall for mayor and Uriah McKee for clerk. Mr. Metcalf was re-elected on the Republican ticket.

Within a week after the election of water works trustees Oberlin had its second costly fire. The blaze started in the Henry G. Carpenter block in the A. Straus store at Main and West College. Within two hours it had destroyed business buildings south from the Straus corner to the Gilchrist block on South Main and west to the J. D. Carpenter three-story block on West College Street. The flames took all the buildings for 100 feet south on Main Street and for a distance of 170 feet on West College Street. The buildings destroyed included the Henry G. Carpenter block, built in 1852. It was occupied until 1856 by George Kinney and Mr. Carpenter with a dry goods store. For a time the firm was Kinney & Reamer. Mr. Straus established his business there in 1880. The Commercial block on South Main was built in 1852. It was a two-story frame. South of this the fire took G. S. Pay's meat market, conducted in a two-story frame building which formerly stood in the rear of old Oberlin Hall as a college barn. This was erected in 1834. The final point south was reached by the flames when they destroyed the Wynn building, a one-story frame structure. West of the H. G. Carpenter building was a two-story frame owned by Mrs. J. M. Fitch and occupied by E. H. Holter, jeweler, and Judge John W. Steele, attorney. It was built by James M. Fitch for a book store in 1859. The last building to the west to burn was a three-story frame owned by John D. Carpenter. This was old

The Story of a Century

Oberlin Hall, built by the college in 1833, the first college building erected. The flames did some damage to the new Goodrich block, built on the corner of East College and Main following the fire of 1882. In the old Oberlin Hall were a candy store, a meat market, and a grocery conducted by J. A. Barnard. Tenants who suffered loss in the destruction of buildings on South Main Street were P. R. Tobin, harness maker; B. H. Brice, clothing store; James Cameron, barber shop; I. A. Webster, attorney-at-law; T. J. Elliott, harness store. The loss on all the buildings was probably in excess of $50,000.

At the April election an issue of $50,000 for a water works plant was carried by a vote of 437 to 100. This favorable vote was due in very large degree to the untiring effort of Judge Steele. At a special caucus to choose three trustees for the water works Judge Steele was chosen by acclamation. Edwin Regal and Professor A. A. Wright were the other two elected. To Mr. Wright goes a great share of the credit for the successful completion of the plant.

This year died Henry R. Johnson, colored, said to have been 115 years old. He was born in slavery and claimed he remembered the burning of the theater in Richmond in 1811. He was reported as a man grown at the time of the battle of New Orleans, when he was said to have held the horse of General Jackson.

A charter was secured for a street railway to connect Oberlin, Wellington, and Amherst. W. B. Bedortha was attorney for those applying. This action anticipated by about a quarter of a century the building of the Cleveland Southwestern and Columbus traction lines. Council took advantage of the provision of the new Dow liquor law and passed an ordinance prohibiting the sale in Oberlin.

August 19 one of the final steps in the construction of the water works was reached when Judge Steele and Engineer Dunham, after an all day expedition, discovered that the bed of the Vermilion River, three-fourths of a mile south of Kipton, is 47 feet higher than Plum Creek at South Main. This investigation was one of several made by Judge Steele and others in an effort to find a certain water supply for the village. This was the final selection made.

In September the Gibson Hose Company won the national firemen's tournament at Norwalk. They took their hook and ladder outfit for two runs of forty rods each in the average time of thirty-six seconds, winning a belt and $100 in cash. This prize belt was first given in Chicago in 1878. The winning time on that occasion was 48 1-2 seconds. At a tournament a few weeks later at Cincinnati the Gibson's won two firsts and $250 in money. They were given the usual reception on their return.

In November a contract was let for the construction of the new water works plant. In December was given the 28th production of the Messiah in Oberlin.

1887

At the April election Frank Hovey was made a member of Council. O. F. Carter was president of a company to prospect for natural gas. Encouraged by the experience with the water works, Mayor Charles A. Metcalf recommended to Council the construction of sewers and modern paving. This summer saw the removal of the Oberlin telephone exchange except as to toll service. It was stated that the cost of Oberlin service was such that patrons could not afford to install telephones.

Nathaniel Gerrish, then living at 47 East College, father of W. B. Gerrish, for several years city engineer of Oberlin and in 1933 still in business here, had reached on August 31 the fiftieth anniversary of his marriage. The ceremony was performed by "Father" Shipherd. Mr. Gerrish had lived all of that time in the same home on East College Street, erected on land bought from Peter Pindar Pease, the first resident of Oberlin. Captain L. L. Munson, for many years in business here, was in charge of a parade of the Oberlin Fire Patrol, an independent company serving without pay. In November Council investigated the possibility of electric lights for Oberlin. At the election in December Stephen M. Cole, a business man in Oberlin for forty years, was made Commander of Henry Lincoln Post. George H. Houghton, last surviving member of Henry Lincoln Post, was at that time elected Junior Vice-commander. Reverend Howard H. Russell was in charge of a committee to secure local option laws in Ohio. This anticipated by several years the organization of the Anti-Saloon League, which was formed here in Oberlin.

This year two new school houses were completed. One was erected on Prospect Street to take care of most of the grade school pupils on the west side of the town, and the other on Pleasant Street to render a like service for pupils in the eastern half of the village. Each of these buildings was a two story brick containing four classrooms and an office for a principal. The cost of each was about $8,000. An interesting comparison of construction costs is found in the statement that in 1910 a four-room addition was built to the Pleasant Street School and the following year a similar addition to the Prospect Street School. These additions each cost $11,000.

1888

In January occurred the death of Samuel Royce, who first came to Oberlin in 1838. He had been a resident in the village since 1853. His family was still represented here in 1933 by Mrs. Andrew G. Comings, a daughter. Thomas Waite died on his farm in Pittsfield, aged 88. He with his brother, Jerry Waite, were the first permanent settlers of Pittsfield Township. Thomas built the second log cabin in the township and spent his life on the fifty acres which were given him in 1821 for clearing land and opening the township to residents.

In March the water works plant was completed and in operation. It was described at the time as Oberlin's greatest public improvement. Arden Dale was elected mayor at the April election. Herbert Kenaston Camp, Sons of Veterans, was organized. It was named for Lieutenant Herbert Kenaston, who was killed in the battle of Gettysburg. E. J. Phillips was commander and B. O. Durand first lieutenant. A Republican caucus endorsed

Oberlin Colony

O. F. Carter for county treasurer. The 'Oberlin delegates to the convention, which failed to nominate Carter, included James Monroe, W. H. Pearce, John W. Steele, Thomas Mayhew, J. F. Peck, W. L. Tenney, H. H. Barnard, L. P. Chapman, H. C. Wangerien, and George Bailey.

In May the Soldiers' Monument was in need of repairs. O. F. Carter requested of Council that the village take charge of the monument and keep it in condition. Council later made a request of the township trustees to look after this duty. In 1932 the monument was fast going to pieces and the question of whose duty it was to care for it came up, after almost fifty years, another time. Early in 1933 the problem had not been solved.

M. G. Dick was making improvements this year in a store which he bought from E. S. Earle. Mr. Dick was in business here for a quarter of a century. He served on the Village Council and was active in church work. Postmaster E. G. Dick is a son, as is also Frank J. Dick, now of Coconut Grove, Florida, but for a number of years in the grocery business in Oberlin. Miss Mary I. Dick, a daughter, is employed by Oberlin College.

Students of Oberlin College held the usual Mock Republican Convention in May and nominated Walter Q. Greshem for president. The Republican Party this year nominated Benjamin Harrison for president. At a meeting June 12 of students and citizens $5,000 was pledged toward a $50,000 fund to establish the James H. Fairchild Professorship. In July a petition was circulated for free delivery in Oberlin. The post office receipts for the year closed were $10,298.79. In 1932 the receipts were about four times this amount.

Charles K. Whitney, son of L. T. Whitney, veteran Oberlin merchant, was this year secretary of the Harrison and Morton Club. This was the initial appearance in town and county politics of Mr. Whitney, who for almost forty years was a factor in Republican counsels in the county and state. He was associated with his father in business and later was senior member of the clothing firm of Whitney & Hill. In 1925 he sold his interest in the store to J. V. Hill, the present owner, and was early in 1933 making his home in Cleveland. In the same year of his entry into politics Mr. Whitney became associated as a partner with his father, L. T. Whitney, who had prior to that time for many years been a member of the firm of Johnson & Whitney. This year Mr. Johnson and Mr. Whitney dissolved partnership, Mr. Johnson taking the dry goods business and Mr. Whitney the clothing business. This deal was closed July 23.

The town was very proud of the section of paving on North Main Street from the town hall to the Lorain Street intersection. It was made up of large stone slabs eight inches in thickness. John D. Carpenter put up a brick block on the site west of that occupied by A. Straus before the fire of 1886. Among those listed who voted for William Henry Harrison in 1840 and for his grandson Benjamin Harrison in 1888 were E. Denis Horton, Lyndon Freeman, Amzi West, Luther Broadwell, and S. W. Rowland.

This was a period of experimenting with silos which began to come into general use among farmers in the county. One hundred fish horns figured in a rally over the Harrison election at Finney Chapel. Speeches were made by General Shurtleff, Professor Monroe, and Professor Ellis. A band furnished music and the meeting was opened with prayer.

1889

In January O. F. Carter bought the interest of his partner, R. Hatch, in the hardware store, which they had been conducting on South Main Street. Oberlin Camp, Sons of Veterans, chose R. T. Paden as captain. Mr. Paden was village marshal for several years. Henry Braithwaite was given praise for his work as engineer at the water plant. Braithwaite and Judge Steele were busy at this time beautifying the grounds around the pumping station. Sage Brothers and G. H. Houghton were among exhibitors at the Oberlin poultry show given in February. Council decides to open Elm Street from West Street to Prospect. Oberlin Council, Royal Arcanum, was organized in March, with Honorable A. G. Comings as president. At this time the village had 300 rods of solid stone roadway, exclusive of 160 rods from the intersection of Main and College Streets to the depot on South Main Street. More than 300 rods were laid in the summer of this year. L. P. Chapman was named as chief of the fire department to succeed C. H. McChesney, who resigned because he was leaving town.

In April the Oberlin News carried a modest note, without heading, of the granting of a patent to Charles M. Hall, of Oberlin, for a certain process with reference to the commercial manufacturing use of aluminum. Note was made of the fact that Mr. Hall was a son of Reverend and Mrs. H. B. Hall of Oberlin, and a graduate in the class of 1885. Mr. Hall was then engaged in a small way in the promotion of this and other aluminum processes at Pittsburgh. There was no knowledge at this time, of course, of the revolutionizing effect of Mr. Hall's discovery both on Oberlin College and Community and on the business world at large.

The Oberlin Bank Company began business in May of this year. F. L. Fuller was cashier and A. M. Loveland was employed in the bank. Portraits of Mr. and Mrs. Peter Pindar Pease were given to the college by their son, Professor Fred Pease, of Ypsilanti, Michigan. These were still on display in Carnegie Library in 1933. Oberlin people gave with their usual generosity to the sufferers in the flood at Johnstown, Pennsylvania, in June. Council was agitated over private use of the public watering trough and passed legislation to correct the abuse. In 1932 there were no public troughs and few horses in the village. In June of this year contributions completed the $50,000 fund for the James Harris Fairchild Professorship in the college. Charles Weeks and Fred Wright were among the star pupils of the Manual Training School. The name of Mill Street, one of the original streets of the village, was changed to Vine Street. In September died Hiram A. Pease, brother of Peter Pindar Pease, at the age of 92.

In October free mail delivery was established in Oberlin. This was brought about solely on the basis of total receipts for the office, which at the end of the fiscal year July 1, 1889, were in excess of the minimum of $10,000. The first mail carriers named were L. P. Chapman, A. J. Monroe, and A. S. Glenn. Substitutes were Fred E. Chauncey and G. C. Cahill. The work of the office grew rapidly and within a short time Chauncey was made a regular carrier—four in all serving in this work. The college campus at this time was not as well kept as in later years. Notice was given that no more auctions of old furniture would be held on the campus, as it was the intention to renew the lawn and give it better care. Oberlin's first Credit Association was organized in 'October with O. F. Carter, president and A. G. Comings, secretary. In the fall A. Z. Tillotson moved to Ridgeville with his family to take up his duties as superintendent of schools. Mr. Tillotson was practicing law in Oberlin in 1933 and was one of the veterans of the Lorain County Bar.

The public had generally reached the conclusion that the board sidewalk had had its day and pressure was brought to bear on Council asking for action looking toward the laying of sawed stone walks. This agitation continued for a period of ten years. Board sidewalks had almost disappeared at the beginning of the twentieth century. In November there was discussion with regard to gas and gasoline public lighting. Judge John W. Steele and Professor A. A. Wright were among the few who thought that electric street lights were too expensive for the town. It is characteristic that Judge Steele had made an investigation a year previous on his own initiative and spoke with knowledge of the probable cost of such a change. Even at that early day there was a strong feeling that if a change were made to electric lights that the city should build its own plant.

ENTER THE GAY NINETIES

CHAPTER XIII

BOTH college and community felt in the decade beginning with 1890 the effects of a changing world. The small measure of economic prosperity, which had followed the depression beginning almost twenty years before, had about run its course. The hard times which reached their peak midway in this period of ten years were on their way in 1890. The immediate presence of economic depression accounted in great measure for the election of Grover Cleveland in 1892. His inauguration the following spring took place in the midst of a period of industrial quiet which was forecast by such incidents as the Homestead strike the summer previous. The tinsel glow of the world's fair at Chicago in 1893 did not altogether serve to make the people of the country forget their economic troubles. The war between China and Japan the following year had little effect, save as it increased in small measure the price of wheat. The same year saw the nation-wide strike of coal miners, followed by a strike of Pullman employees and the resulting calling out of national troops by President Cleveland to suppress riots in Chicago. When the Cuban Revolution broke out in 1895 there was no general feeling that this development would touch the interests of the United States. The Klondike gold rush in 1897 was scarcely noted here in Oberlin, despite its wide-spread effect in putting aside, at least for a generation, any further serious plea for the free coinage of silver. The year previous had seen the election of William McKinley as president after an intensive campaign in the course of which William Jennings Bryan gave the conservative element of the country a severe attack of the jitters. Two years later, when the battleship Maine was blown up in Havana Harbor, it was apparent that war with Spain must come. There were few enlistments in Oberlin, and while the victories of Schley and of Dewey were celebrated with enthusiasm, the war itself did not immediately touch the town. Its results, of course, had permanent effect, not alone on college and community but on the nation itself. The acquisition of the Philippines by America placed the nation on the road to a program of expansion through what Senator Albert J. Beveridge called "manifest destiny." It is probable that the state of mind created by the Spanish War and the change in international outlook on the part of the country had much to do with the participation of America in the World War.

While national and world events were thus changing the course of history, Oberlin was moving along in even tenor, although the change in college and community apparent at the close of the Civil War continued. The vacancy in the presidency of the school caused by the resignation of Mr. Fairchild was filled in January, 1891, by the election of William Gay Ballantine, who had been Professor of Old Testament Language and Rhetoric in the School of Theology and who had been acting as chairman of the faculty since the resignation of Mr. Fairchild in 1889. Mr. Ballantine resigned in June, 1896. He was succeeded in 1898 by President John Henry Barrows, who served until his death in 1902. Near the end of the decade the college planned an unusual effort to increase its endowment. This bore fruit at the alumni reunion in 1900 when endowment and scholarship pledges to the extent of $82,000 were received. These gifts made plain the fact that the "good times," which were promised in the McKinley campaign of 1896, had about reached their peak.

Two actions taken by the college early in this decade were significant of the changes slowly affecting both school and community. One modified the ruling which had existed since the founding of the institution requiring students to attend church service twice each Sunday. This was amended to make only one attendance obligatory. At the same time the ban placed on card playing was lifted. A modification of rules, regarded as strict for the time, was the granting of permission to men of the school to leave town without formal report unless they expected to be absent over night.

Oberlin Colony

1890

In the village the year was ushered in with a more or less definite movement for the lighting of streets by electricity. In February the light committee of Council recommended electricity for street lights and the establishment of a plant owned by the village on the ground that this would be more economical. The committee said that street and community lighting could be taken care of at an initial cost of $15,000, and urged that the proposed municipal lighting plant could be coupled with the water plant as to management and employees. In its recommendation for village ownership the committee said: "Being thus under public control all danger of extortionate charges to public and private consumers would be avoided." At this date the annual cost of lighting the streets by gas and gasoline was about $1500.

Note was made in the Oberlin News of the cutting down of two village trees which had been set out by Brewster Pelton, Oberlin pioneer, on his premises at the corner of East Lorain and North Pleasant Streets, forty years before. Early in this year the "Ram's Horn" a religious paper was started at Indianapolis by Elijah Brown, a coverted infidel who in 1870 was editor of the Oberlin News. The "Ram's Horn" for several years enjoyed support and popularity. Among the contributing editors was Robert Burdette, noted Baptist minister. Brown is said to have left Oberlin because his beliefs at that time made the village an uncomfortable place in which to live.

In February died Dr. Homer Johnson, practicing physician here since 1846. He was 76 and had practiced his profession for forty-four years. At the April election Arden Dale was elected mayor for a second term. The college appealed to the Court of Common Pleas for permission to sell the Oberlin Society Cemetery. This was the pioneer cemetery on the site between Main and Professor Streets at the Morgan Street intersection. The greater portion of the bodies buried there had been removed to Westwood Cemetery almost a quarter of a century before the making of the application.

The Story of a Century

This was the era of the bicycle. Wheelmen protested against restrictive legislation drawn to exclude bicycle riders from sidewalks of the village. The wheelmen put up the argument that the bicycle had come to stay. General G. W. Shurtleff was supported by Oberlin as a candidate for Congress in the twentieth district. E. G. Johnson of Elyria was also a candidate. V. A. Taylor was nominated. In this year 'Oberlin's population by the 1890 census was 4330, of whom 650 were colored. Realty in Oberlin was valued at $733,990. College property exempt from taxation totaled $253,300 and village school property so exempt totaled $82,000.

In September was laid the cornerstone of Sacred Heart Catholic Church at Groveland and South Pleasant Streets. Ten priests had part in the ceremony. On the platform were seated President James H. Fairchild, Professor J. M. Ellis, and Reverend O. Badgley, pastor of the First Methodist Episcopal Church. In November great interest was created in a phonograph on exhibition at Quick's jewelry store. It was described as a wonderful invention.

1891

In January J. L. Edwards, successor to A. B. Johnson in the grocery business, was making a number of improvements in his store. In this same month Ridgeville Township voted dry under the state law. At that time Amherst had eight saloons, Avon four, Lorain twenty, and Elyria nineteen. W. J. Fuller bought the Favel livery business. In April was held at the college chapel a mass meeting of citizens generally for consideration of the topic "How to make Oberlin a Model Home." At the April election A. M. Loveland was chosen as clerk, E. L. Burge, marshal, S. M. Cole, C. B. Glenn, and Dr. H. G. Husted, councilmen; G. C. Prince and Professor A. A. Wright, water works trustees. Arden Dale, who was finishing his second term as mayor, was defeated by Attorney A. Z. Tillotson for Justice of the Peace.

Oberlin Colony

1892

In April A. G. Comings was elected mayor on the Republican ticket. In August of this year Reverend Willard Burr died while attending a prayer service at First Church, at the age of 81. He came to Oberlin as a student in 1836. After a quarter of a century in the service of the ministry he returned to Oberlin to make his home in 1864.

1893

Again the new year was ushered in with further discussion of the question of municipal lighting. Judge Steele, although not a member of the Council, was named by Mayor Comings to act with the light committee in a preliminary investigation covering not alone the need for better street lighting service but as well the question of municipal ownership. Colonel Steele reached the conclusion, after investigation, that a municipally owned plant would not, at that time, be economical for 'Oberlin taxpayers. He was supported in this view by W. B. Gerrish. Steele's characteristic fairness is shown in a report a few weeks later in which he points out that actual lamp costs were less in municipally owned plants than in those privately operated. The Oberlin Gas & Electric Company, to which a franchise was ultimately granted, estimated the price per street lamp at $50 per year. Judge Steele's investigation disclosed a cost to municipalities of $36.80 a year in publicly owned plants.

Reverend George Thompson died in February at the age of 75. He came to Oberlin in 1835 and worked on the building of Cincinnati Hall. He was employed, as were other students, at four hours a day at a rate of six cents an hour. Board at that time could be obtained at fifty cents a week. In April there was much public discussion of the question of the use of standard time as compared to "sun" time, which had been in use. The state had adopted standard time and recommended it generally. There were in the village conservative citizens who felt that this change was brought about by railroads for some devious and unexplained motive. Council finally recommended by resolution the use of the new time, which gradually became common in the village.

At the April election Council submitted to the voters two questions. One was for the establishment of a municipal electric lighting plant. This proposal fell just six votes short of the necessary two-thirds majority. A second proposal for a bond issue of $5,000 for the erection of a standpipe at the water works plant was carried. In May, following the failure of an effort to establish a municipal plant, Council voted a franchise to the Oberlin Gas & Electric Company for lighting of the streets with thirty-nine arc lights. At this time the tax levy for corporation purposes alone was 10.8 mills.

At Spear Library, May 24, was formed a temperance organization which was later known as the Anti-Saloon League. The initial organization was made up of a committee from the churches of Oberlin representing the Oberlin Temperance Alliance. The forming of the new league was suggested by Howard H. Russell, for many years a leader in temperance work in America and in 1933 a resident of Westerville. Those present on this historic occasion were A. G. Comings, J. T. Henderson, Professor A. S. Root, Reverend James Brand, Reverend Henry M. Tenney, Dr. H. G. Husted, Albert Deming, W. H. Pearce, Professor F. F. Jewett, General G. W. Shurtleff, J. B. Hart, Richard Hicks, George W. Waite, and Dr. J. F. Siddall. Mr. Henderson and Dr. Russell are the only two survivors of this original organization. The Anti-Saloon League, largely under the guidance of Wayne B. Wheeler, graduate of Oberlin College, was mainly responsible for the adoption of the prohibition amendment to the Constitution.

The Merchants Exchange, a three-story frame business block on North Main Street, was burned June 1. The building had a frontage of seventy-four feet and was one hundred feet in depth. It was occupied at the time of the fire by Weed & Edwards, then owners of a hardware store; Samuel Squire, clothing; J. A. Keyes, novelties; and J. M. Jackson, meats. The brick block of M. G. Dick, which was north of the Exchange, was damaged, as was also the brick block of the Citizens National Bank on the south. The Exchange had its start in frame buildings put up in the late thirties by Brewster Pelton. Additions had been made from time to time and in 1856 the structure was the central business place of the community. After the fire Weed & Edwards sold their hardware store to Carter & Huckins and retired. The firm was then the oldest in the town, having been established in 1866. Philo Weed, the senior member, had been in business in Oberlin for fifty years. He had been associated with Brewster Pelton, pioneer resident. Following the fire Behr Brothers and Samuel Squire & Son began promptly the building of a two-story brick block to replace the burned Exchange.

In July a contract was let by Council for the building of sanitary and storm sewers. This marked the beginning of a modern system of sewers in Oberlin and followed a complete investigation made by Council and by Judge Steele, who had been appointed by the mayor to give assistance. W. B. Gerrish was engineer. In the summer of this year one hundred men were employed on the project. The college agreed to pay one-eighth of the cost of the trunk sewer.

A. D. Booth of Greensburg bought a half interest in the R. B. Ransom undertaking establishment. Mrs. Theodore Ingersoll, who came to Oberlin with her husband in 1833, died at Berea at the age of 101. The hardest of the hard times of the first half of the nineties had been reached in this year. The needed sewer improvements went forward despite this fact, but citizens and council members generally agreed that for the time being there should be less work in the way of new sidewalks. Enumeration made by B. O. Durand showed 1307 children of school age in the village.

The work of excavating for the sewer on South Main Street from Plum Creek to College Street was in progress in September. Cuts made by the workmen showed the various stages of road making in 'Oberlin from the early days until that time. At a distance of from four to six feet the old corduroy road made of rocks laid crosswise was found. Above that was a roadway made of small blocks of stone. Above the second was the roadway then in use, made of small block stone. The Oberlin News said in commenting: "The next generation will perhaps use brick or some other material that will be an improvement over the sandstone." Inside of ten years from that date two or three of the main streets of Oberlin were paved with brick.

In September Henry F. Smith opened the Gem Pharmacy in the corner room in the H. G. Carpenter block vacated by F. E. Burgess. Mr. Smith had served as clerk in two drug stores here before establishing his own business, which proved very successful. He was one of the leading citizens of Oberlin in 1933. He had been then for a number of years vice-president of the Peoples Banking Company and had served several terms on the Council and as mayor of Oberlin.

September 28 of this year saw the first use of the electric street lights in Oberlin. The current was turned on by Mayor Comings. It was noted that "the new lights gave the village a pleasing and somewhat city air." In December the use of electricity by citizens began. The first to install the service in his home was C. T. Beckwith. Other early users were O. F. Carter and F. B. Rice.

1894

The Oberlin fire department got a new hose wagon, "The George S. Pay," this year, and June 1 a parade of members of the department, headed by a brass band and under the direction of Chief L. L. Munson, was held. The new wagon was conspicuous in the line.

W. D. Hobbs purchased a half interest in the Preston bakery and restaurant on East College Street. After some years Mr. Hobbs went into business on East College Street for himself, building a handsome brick block. He was for several years manager of the Oberlin Inn, retiring from this position in the fall of 1932. Mr. Hobbs rendered fine service as trustee of the water works and as a member of Council. He was in 1933 still a valued resident of Oberlin.

Oberlin Colony

A. L. Jones, who in 1892 had succeeded his father in the monument business here, was married January 8 to Miss Julia Rothgery of Cleveland. Mr. Jones' father was one of the early business men of 'Oberlin. Samuel M. Wilkinson and M. J. Watson opened a new hardware store in the J. D. Carpenter block at 12 South Main Street. It is significant that in the midst of agitation for a traction line from Lorain to 'Oberlin, H. G. Redington of Amherst wrote to Judge Steele asking for his opinion. V. E. Rice, East Lorain Street greenhouse owner, was anticipating an active business of a quarter of a century later when he grew mushrooms for the market. On the occasion of the retirement of Colonel Steele as a postmaster he was given a cane by the post office employees, who were A. J. Monroe, L. P. Chapman, F. E. Chauncey, A. S. Glenn, A. E. Griffin, John Woodruff, and F. C. Leesman. The presentation was made by J. F. Randolph, one of the owners of the Oberlin News.

Charles Farrar died in February. He came to Oberlin from Vermont in 1834 and had been a member of First Church 56 years. In March James R. Severance was named treasurer of the college to succeed General Giles W. Shurtleff, who had resigned. An appeal was made by Oberlin citizens for congressional support for George H. Ely of Elyria. The list of signers, amounting to a roll call of Republican leaders in the community at the time, included A. G. Comings, John W. Steele, O. F. Carter, Noah Huckins, S. G. Wright, E. J. Goodrich, W. B. Bedortha, F. L. Fuller, W. J. Fuller, M. V. Rowley, E. L. Disbro, L. T. Whitney, George E. Smith, George C. Prince, C. T. Beckwith, A. H. Johnson, and Alfred Fauver.

Oberlin this year began to feel the need for electric railway connection with other towns and Colonel John W. Steele came to the front in preliminary investigations. He was assisted by W. B. Gerrish in surveying for a proposed line between Oberlin and Wellington and Steele himself wrote many letters to traction line men seeking information and aid. Numerous proposals were made before the final building of the road from Elyria to Oberlin and later from Oberlin to Wellington.

The Story of a Century

In March occurred the death of Professor John M. Ellis at Chicago. He was enroute home from the West, where he had gone for the benefit of his health. Professor Ellis was for many years a member of the college faculty and was active and helpful as a citizen of the community. Mr. Ellis had served as mayor and chief of the fire department and was a member of the board of sewer commissioners when forced to resign because of ill health.

The location at this time of the Johnson steel plant in Lorain aroused enthusiastic interest here in Oberlin. In April Council passed an ordinance for the renumbering of the houses of the village on the basis of the assignment of house numbers at stated street intervals regardless of whether or not the lot was occupied. In the spring of the year plans began for the construction of brick pavements in Oberlin. In May was formed the Edward A. Ellis Camp, Sons of Veterans, with H. N. Clark, captain, A. P. Behr, lieutenant, W. L. Persons, sergeant, and O. C. May, quartermaster sergeant. Engineer Gerrish explained the operation of the sewage disposal plant. It was built largely from designs prepared by Mr. Gerrish and Judge Steele.

Pansy Chapter, Order of the Eastern Star, was organized in June. The building of the Mt. Zion Baptist Church was completed this year. In May Oberlin Lodge Knights of Pythias was organized. In August A. H. Redington died at Omaha, Nebraska. He was a son of Captain E. Redington, agent for Street and Hughes, from whom the site of 'Oberlin was secured. He helped Peter Pindar Pease build his log cabin on the campus. The steady growth of the popularity of the bicycle in Oberlin is shown by the fact that this summer Oberlin riders won five firsts in eight contests in Elyria. Praise was given E. H. Bacon's management of the Park House. Mr. Bacon came to Oberlin from Brownhelm and was the father of Mrs. J. V. Hill, Miss Edith Bacon, and Mrs. Elizabeth Deuble of Oberlin.

In October T. J. Rice bought the Upton photograph gallery, located in the Royce block on West College Street. He had his studio in the same location in 1933 and in addition was engaged in the real estate business.

Oberlin Colony

The Oberlin Kindergarten Training School was organized. It was conducted for several years under financial difficulties, but eventually was placed upon a paying basis and acquired considerable property of value. In 1932 its property was bought by Oberlin College. Miss Clara May was superintendent at the time the sale was made. The work of the school finally terminated in 1933. The New Era Mills on South Water Street burned December 16, with a loss of about $10,000. The building was put up in 1846. The contractor was Lyman A. Hill.

1895

Early this year the Oberlin Business College Company was incorporated, with J. T. Henderson as president and J. D. Yocom as secretary. Agitation for traction service continued in Oberlin and the Lorain and Wellington Electric Line was incorporated, with J. W. Steele and O. F. Carter of Oberlin in the list of promoters. William Behr, Oberlin business man, who came here to live in 1885, died while on a visit to his relatives in Germany. In February was organized the Oberlin Board of Commerce. Officers were O. F. Carter, president; M. G. Dick and Alfred Fauver, vice-presidents; F. L. Fuller, secretary; H. J. Clark, treasurer.

At the caucus in March Mrs. Alice Swing was nominated by Oberlin Republicans as a member of the school board and was elected in April. She was the first woman to hold this office in Oberlin and one of the first women in the state to hold an elective office. Fifty women attended the caucus and 253 women voted at the school election in April. Mrs. Martha A. Brown of North Main Street, claimed to be the first woman in the village to exercise her voting right. She was at the polls in her precinct two minutes before they opened at 5:30 A. M.

G. J. Peake retired as ticket agent at Oberlin. He later opened a telegraph school here. For some time there had been a movement looking to the establishing of a telephone exchange in Oberlin. At a meeting of the Board of Commerce in April Judge Steele submitted a report with reference to preliminary investigations. At this same meeting the Board of Commerce recommended a brick pavement for East College Street. F. F. Beckwith, in 1933 assistant postmaster of Oberlin, was engaged in the jewelry business. A. B. Spear was made clerk of the Board of Education to succeed W. B. Durand, who had held the position for a number of years. Council gave approval to the paving with brick of East Lorain Street from Main to Pleasant.

Judge Steele was chairman of a committee of the Board of Commerce appointed to have in charge arrangements for a cinder walk, eight feet in width, suitable for pedestrians and open to wheelmen, to be built on all four sides of the college campus. The college gave its consent, and, with more than four hundred wheelmen in Oberlin, the net sum of $400 was contributed, either in cash or labor, and the work was completed in October. It was dedicated when one hundred wheelmen, led by Mayor A. G. Comings, rode around the campus on bicycles decorated with college colors.

In response to the cry for telephone service in the village the Oberlin Telephone Company was incorporated by W. H. Pearce, E. P. Johnson, A. G. Comings, W. B. Bedortha, and F. L. Fuller. At a meeting at the college chapel the Oberlin Cinder Path Association was organized for the purpose of building a cinder path to the lake and to other points in nearby counties. Officers were: President, J. F. Randolph; vice-president, C. W. Savage; secretary, C. P. Doolittle; executive committee, John W. Steele, A. G. Comings, C. P. Doolittle, Elmer Whitlock, and E. A. Siebert.

On the night of July 4, Wellington appealed to the Oberlin fire department for help in fighting a fire which finally destroyed $50,000 worth of property. Members of the department started to Wellington with the old steamer, no longer in use here. Road conditions were such that relays of eight teams were needed to pull the steamer. The trip, which could be made in 1933 over modern roads by automobile in ten minutes, required one hour and forty-five minutes. When the Oberlin firemen reached Wellington and attempted to put the steamer in use it was discovered that it had been disabled and it was impossible to throw a stream of water. T. H. Rowland's chestnut mare, Contention, won first money in the 2:35 trot and his horse, Riley Wilkes, took first in the 2:20 pace at Toledo. Mr. Rowland had refused an offer of $1500 for Contention. Sidney Bedortha, 82, a resident here for fifty years, died in August. Colonel Steele, O. F. Carter, and L. L. Munson were a committee which arranged for the Board of Commerce a series of visits by Oberlin business men to other towns of the county. The first trip was taken September 4. Thirty-five men went in rigs decorated with flags. A publication distributed on this trip, "Oberlin Today," giving a printed list of the various forms of business in the community at the time, shows that Oberlin had then two banks, three dry goods stores, four hardware stores, three book stores, twelve groceries, five drug stores, three jewelry stores, three clothing stores, two harness stores, two furniture stores, two planing mills, one grist mill, one machine shop, four blacksmith shops, two carriage shops, four millinery stores, three coal dealers, three livery stables, six barber shops, five meat markets, three hack lines, two florists, four draymen, two hotels, one fruit store, four bakeries, five restaurants, two dentists, four insurance offices, three laundries, two marble shops, one notion store, three photograph galleries, three printing offices, six shoe dealers, two tailor shops, one architect, six newspapers and periodicals, one telegraph school, ten physicians, one business college, three lawyers, and three real estate agents.

When A. M. Loveland resigned as village clerk Charles Seth Brown was named to the vacancy. In October M. Straus gave the Park Hotel block to the college. The estimated value of the lot and building was then $50,000. The corner on which the hotel still stood in 1933 had been used for hotel purposes since the founding of the village in 1833. The original hotel building there was destroyed by fire and the building given to the college by Mr. Straus was built by Henry Viets in 1868. The east wing of the building was constructed later by A. J. Dyer.

The Story of a Century

Lewis F. West, in the fall, bought a lot on South Main Street for the building of a blacksmith shop. He was the last man in this business in Oberlin, having been forced to give up his work about thirty years later because of the supplanting of the horse by the tractor and the automobile. The new Beckwith block, built by C. T. Beckwith, on South Main Street, was completed at the close of the year and on December 5 the post office was moved into quarters on the first floor, built especially for post office use. Post Office Inspector Fleming was quoted as calling the post office "the handsomest in the United States." The upper floor of the building has been used since that time by the the Oberlin School of Commerce, then known as the Oberlin Business College.

At the close of the year the new reservoir at the water works plant was about complete. It had a capacity of 17,000,000 gallons. Judge Steele and Engineer Gerrish had given much time and personal attention to the work of construction.

1896

In January Council granted a franchise for the use of East College Street in Oberlin in possible construction of a line from Elyria to Oberlin. W. G. Sharp and A. L. Garford, Elyria capitalists, were among the incorporators of the company. The Citizens National Bank elected A. H. Johnson, president; C. T. Beckwith, vice-president; and Albert M. Johnson, cashier. O. F. Carter sold his interest in the hardware firm of Carter & Huckins and the new firm was Huckins & Huckins, Howard Huckins associating himself with his father, Noah Huckins. In January J. L. Edwards opened an insurance and real estate office. Officers of the newly formed 'Oberlin Telephone Company were: President, E. P. Johnson; vice-president, A. G. Comings; secretary, W. H. Pearce; treasurer, John H. Wood. Mrs. Eliza McRoberts, representative of a family well known in Oberlin, and a resident of Pittsfield since 1832, died at the age of 92. The merits of centralized schools and the cost of public conveyances, known in more modern days as "kid wagons," to carry pupils, were discussed in Oberlin. Judge Steele and O. F. Carter had secured consents from sufficient property owners for a traction line from Oberlin to Wellington. In February B. F. Shuart shipped fourteen of his road graders in one week. He preceded the Ohio Road Machinery Company and made money in a business which was finally killed largely by modern hard surfaced roads. In March of this year O. F. Carter was nominated by acclamation as a Republican county candidate for treasurer. He was elected in the fall and served two terms in the office.

Professor A. S. Root, librarian for many years and a member of the Oberlin School Board, was this year named as the Prohibition candidate for Probate Judge. Mr. Root was in later years, with the decline in activity of the Prohibition party, a staunch Republican. He was a leader in college circles and was respected for intelligent citizenship and for his interest in community affairs. In the spring of this year the Board of Commerce renewed the request for a new railroad depot in Oberlin. At the March caucus Republicans named Alfred Fauver for mayor, G. C. Prince for treasurer, Charles Seth Brown for clerk, A. A. Wright for trustee of the water works, and A. G. Comings and Henry Churchill King for the school board. A. R. Champney, in the coal business in Oberlin in 1933, was the Democratic candidate for mayor. The Republican ticket was elected. This same month A. M. Loveland was elected cashier of the Oberlin Bank Company. He served with conspicuous success in this position until ill health brought about his resignation in 1918.

When H. G. Martin, owner of a section of the First Ladies Hall, built here in 1835, which had been placed on his lot on West College Street in 1865 when the new Ladies Hall was built, this year tore down this historic building to make room for a modern house, it was noted that Deacon W. W. Wright was a student for many years in the old Hall and that former Governor Jacob Dolson Cox, closely identified with Oberlin College and Oberlin interests, once served as college baker there. The contract was let in May for the Tank Home for children, which was built on East College Street at a cost of $15,000.

In June the college Mock Republican Convention nominated William McKinley for president. This same action was taken by the Republican National Convention. Following the national convention Oberlin held a mass meeting, at which Honorable James Monroe pledged community and college to the support of McKinley and the gold standard.

The Oberlin Telephone Company opened its exchange on Friday, July 17. Miss Edith Andrews was the first operator employed. W. C. Benschotten was manager. The company began with 82 patrons. Dr. G. C. Jameson, still a leading physician in Oberlin in 1933, had a patient this month suffering from too long exposure to X-ray. This is the first mention of the modern treatment in Oberlin. In September Frank Hovey and H. C. Tuck, still well-known residents of Oberlin, were listed as painters and paper hangers who had been kept busy during the season. In the early fall Oberlin formed a McKinley Club. Colonel Steele was president; A. G. Comings, secretary; and C. K. Whitney, treasurer. The Alexander Brothers sold their photograph gallery to L. W. Upton and A. B. Johnson. In the early fall twenty-four new hitching posts were put in around the business section under the direction of the Board of Commerce. This was the day of the horse. There were in 1933 no hitching posts and few horses in Oberlin. Resumption of sidewalk building began in the fall and sidewalks of sawed stone had grown common. They were all laid to an established grade.

Oberlin Republicans made a pilgrimage to Canton to visit Governor McKinley on September 11. Two hundred from the village, including twenty-five women, helped to make up two sections, one of thirteen cars and one of nine cars, bearing Republicans from Lorain County. An Oberlin resident, then a very young man, now prominent in business here, remembers vividly his introduction to Mr. McKinley by Judge Steele and McKinley's earnest statement that he was glad to know any man who was a friend of Colonel Steele. The Windecker Dry Goods

Store was opened in September. That the change to better times was slow in coming is indicated by Oberlin prices at this time. Butter was selling at 18 cents, potatoes at 40 cents, and beef 3 cents to 3¾ cents a pound live weight.

Judge Steele had made a careful canvass of the stores in Oberlin and in the course of a political talk made the estimate that farm produce bought by Oberlin business people and Oberlin citizens amounted yearly to $211,254. A straw vote at chapel in October was McKinley 765, Bryan 95. The Oberlin football team beat Ohio State 16 to 0. This was the fifth successive defeat sustained by State in games with Oberlin. The total score in the five years was Oberlin 166 to 16 for State. The team this year had such stars as Chez, "Bill" Mosher, and Clayton Fauver. Wheat, by late fall, had increased in price to 72 cents, compared to 51 cents the previous year. Frank Foster was elected Chancellor Commander of Oberlin Lodge, Knights of Pythias. A. C. Burgess opened a piano store. He was still in business in 1933.

1897

In January Hose Company No. 1 elected W. H. Spencer, foreman; Charles Edwards, treasurer; Orlen C. May, secretary. General Giles W. Shurtleff was elected president of the Oberlin Board of Commerce, and Professor A. S. Root, secretary. Congressman Kerr advised Oberlin people that he would not have an election in Oberlin for postmaster, since he had determined to appoint Judge John W. Steele. Mr. Kerr explained that he would consent to determination by election in case all candidates agreed. He spoke in praise of the records of Charles T. Beckwith and H. H. Barnard, who were candidates against Judge Steele, but stated that he felt that Colonel Steele was the man for the place. M. J. Watson, hardware dealer, talked to the village Y. M. C. A. on "Thoughts on the Life of Daniel." Harry Wood of Oberlin won a six-day bicycle race at Cleveland. He rode in all 728 miles. Sabram Cox, born in slavery, died at the age of 80. He claimed to have lived at Alton, Illinois, in

The Story of a Century

1837, when Lovejoy was killed by a mob that dismantled his plant and buried his presses in the river. Cox, then a drayman, hauled the presses from the river back to the office. He came to Oberlin in 1839 and for a time attended public school here.

A movement began this summer for abandoning the caucus which had been a feature of Oberlin life almost from the founding of the village. The initial plea was made by H. J. Clark. In April Dr. H. W. Pyle opened an office over the Gem Pharmacy. A franchise was granted for the use of Oberlin streets to the Elyria, Oberlin and Wellington Electric Railway Company. W. H. Spencer was elected chief of the fire department. Fire wardens named by the mayor were F. E. Sherrill, Frank Hovey, L. L. Munson, C. K. Whitney, H. H. Barnard, A. G. Comings, and R. R. Stetson. C. T. Beckwith was president of the Board of Education. Reverend C. N. Pond, for many years a resident of Oberlin, made a plea for the annexation of Hawaii. Mrs. Ann Haylor died in May. She was the mother of William H. Haylor, in business here for several years as a member of the firm of Allen & Haylor. In June the G. W. Gibson livery barn was burned. Eight horses were lost. At the high school commencement one of the graduates was Morton A. Houghton, later postmaster of Oberlin, who read an essay on "trusts."

The presidency of Oberlin College was tendered to William Frederick Slocum of Colorado College, but declined. The Village Council and the Board of Commerce united with the college in the invitation to Dr. Slocum. Mr. Slocum wrote the Board of Commerce a letter of appreciation.

Shortly before midnight December 31 fire was discovered in the Worcester block, known also as the Gilchrist block, at 26-28 South Main Street. The fire was discovered by Ira West, pioneer moving picture owner in Oberlin, in 1933 a resident of Florida. The block was wrecked before the fire could be extinguished. Four firemen were disabled from fighting the flames in zero weather. The block was built by Joseph G. Worcester in 1874. Among the losers were Ransom & Booth, furniture and undertaking; Oberlin Lodge of Masons, whose records were destroyed; and Oberlin Lodge, Knights of Pythias. The total loss was $20,000.

The Loyal Temperance Legion, through Helen Cook, secretary, sent a bouquet to Frances E. Willard, president of the Woman's Christian Temperance Union, the flowers having been picked from her old home at 54 North Pleasant Street. Miss Willard came with her parents, Mr. and Mrs. Josiah F. Willard, from New York in 1841, when a child of three. The family lived here until 1846. They first leased a home at 123 North Main Street and then moved to the North Pleasant Street home which Mr. Willard built.

In July it was noted that grading of the traction line from Elyria to Oberlin was about complete. Relics on public exhibition here included a piece of plaster an inch and a quarter thick, a part of a section estimated to weigh half a ton which fell from the ceiling of Second Church, April 17, 1877, about ten minutes after the congregation had dispersed. Judge Steele and four council members were named to inspect various grades of brick before the town should proceed with the brick pavements on East College and East Lorain Streets. Wheat in August had gone to $1.05. Ex-Governor Jacob Dolson Cox came to Oberlin this fall to live, giving his valuable library to the college. John S. Peck, for thirty years a deacon in Second Church, opposed individual communion cups as against the spirit of Finney. Professor Frank F. Jewett, long a member of the faculty and a loyal citizen of the community, giving especially good service on the water board, created consternation by a report that root beer made by him and permitted to stand for three weeks showed alcoholic content of 3.3 per cent. The U. L. A. lecturers for the season included Charles Emory Smith and Professor Woodrow Wilson, then a member of the faculty of Princeton University.

Lamps and chimneys were still selling well, despite the operations of the Oberlin Gas & Electric Company. Dress shoes for ladies were advertised at $1.25. Muskrat traps were selling at

11 cents, overalls and jumpers at 21 cents, and working pants at 49 cents. Morris Brothers rebuilt their slaughter house south of town. In 1933 there was little or no independent butchering of cattle in Oberlin and vicinity. Provisions were brought by retailers from Chicago and other cities.

The Elyria-Oberlin traction line was opened December 14. The round trip fare was 25 cents between the two cities. There may be no significance in the fact that the first traction car to arrive at Main Street at 10:10 A. M., December 14, 1897, was No. 13. A crowd of 100 people gathered and gave it three cheers. A. Straus, who established his clothing business here in 1860, was advertising "An elegant all wool suit" for $5.00.

1898

In January Mrs. Annie E. Gibson, widow of Orrin Gibson and mother of George W. Gibson, died at the age of 82. She had been a resident of Russia Township since 1825 and descendants of the family were still living here in 1933. Samuel Wildman Rowland, 88, died January 7. He was the father of T. H. Rowland, well known Oberlin business man, and had resided in Ohio since 1818. He came to Oberlin to live in 1867.

At the annual meeting of the Board of Commerce Mrs. A. A. F. Johnston, dean of women of Oberlin College, made a short talk in which she said: "There is no prosperity for college or town that does not grow out of a happy union of the two. I congratulate you that the college is here and I congratulate the college that you are here." Mrs. Johnston had a long and useful career with the college and was of great value to the community as a citizen. She was principal of the woman's department 1870-94 and dean of the department 1894-1900. She was the first woman to be elected as a member of the board of trustees, serving in that capacity 1901-02.

Retiring Postmaster F. A. Hart made personal delivery in January to Colonel Steele of a letter containing the latter's commission for a second appointment as postmaster. The sinking of the battleship Maine, in Havana Harbor, February 15, made

Oberlin Colony

fairly evident the resulting war with Spain. The second livery barn fire within a few months came when the barn of Henry Lee burned February 16 with a loss of fourteen head of horses. In April Alfred Fauver was again elected mayor. Fred H. Maddock, conducting a news agency, was appointed local agent for the Cleveland-Berea-Elyria and Oberlin traction line. The bond issue for the Children's Home was approved by the voters of the county. Oberlin citizens were appealed to by college students to help improve the Arboretum, known also as Ladies Grove. Dr. Dudley Allen, who had been practicing medicine here since 1865, died in April.

A state of war with Spain began April 20. John (Pat) Miller, in 1933 employed on a Cleveland newspaper, was the first to enlist from Oberlin. Dewey's victory in May was celebrated with the firing of cannon, a bonfire, and band music. War had forced the price of wheat to $1.50.

Council voted to pave North Main with brick from College Street to Union Street. George R. Worcester was appointed fire chief to succeed W. H. Spencer, resigned. A movement was begun in June to secure the location here of the Lorain County Children's Home. Largely through the efforts of Judge Steele this was brought about. Colonel Steele suggested action through the Board of Commerce. Professor A. S. Root and Noah Huckins were other members of the committee of which Judge Steele was chairman. In June Louis E. Burgner, still active in business in 1933, bought the insurance and real estate business of Charles Seth Brown.

Recruits for service in the Spanish War included E. G. Dick, Howard Dick, Anson Cheney, Henry Miller, and Ernest McRoberts. Honorable James Monroe, a sketch of whose life and service will be found in another part of this volume, died July 6. In the fall a new Gilchrist block replaced the one burned in the early morning of New Years Day. E. J. Goodrich bought the W. H. Rollins book store. T. H. Rowland was Democratic candidate for county treasurer.

The Story of a Century

Mrs. Eliza Branch Clark died in August. She was the first teacher of the primary school here, serving for the college, and was the last resident survivor of adults who signed the Oberlin Covenant and the last survivor of the original members of First Church. She was born in Vermont in 1808 and came to Oberlin in November, 1833. At that time there were sixty-three in the village. She worked for her board in the Shipherd household and taught for a wage of $2.25 per week. Her pupils were children of colonists here and included Charles Fairchild, a brother of President Fairchild, and Dwight and Harriet Ingersoll, whose father kept the first dry goods store in Oberlin. The primary department was dropped by the college at the close of the term. Mr. and Mrs. Clark came to Oberlin to make their home in 1845.

In August was held the first Lorain County Firemen's convention at Amherst. L. L. Munson of Oberlin was elected president. H. L. Bassett, in later years prominent in the banking business in Oberlin, was with the Schubert Glee Club. Mr. Bassett's ancestors were pioneer residents of Russia Township. Before his retirement he was vice-president of the Oberlin Savings Bank Company. With the Children's Home near completion Judge John W. Steele was supported by Oberlin as a trustee and was appointed by the county commissioners. Oberlin College beat Wesleyan 48 to 0 near the close of a second successful season. Star players included Morton Houghton, the late Fred Hatch, and the Fauver twins. Oberlin this year won the state championship.

In November Dr. John Henry Barrows was called to the presidency of Oberlin College. At the close of this year A. J. Frederick & Company, who had for a number of years conducted the largest dry goods store in the county, at a location on West College Street, closed out their business and moved to Wooster. This change was attributed to the opening of the traction line, which took buyers away from Oberlin. This year, as was the case in the preceding year, closed with an expensive fire when the Royce block on West College Street was destroyed. It was occupied by W. J. Stone, shoe dealer; Marie DeFrance, milliner; J. F. Harmon, druggist; E. C. Shallies, grocery; T. J. Rice, photographer; J. L. Edwards; The Owl Printing Office; R. P. Hodge, and Dr. J. F. Siddall. Damage was done to the Comings book store on the west and the Westervelt block on the east. The loss was about $20,000.

1899

In January J. F. Harmon, who with V. A. Shankland, established the Oberlin News in 1860, sold the drug store which he had conducted for twenty-four years to Charles W. Persons. In this year 105 saloons in Lorain County paid the Dow tax. Albert J. Gilchrist died early in the year at the age of 83. He had been a resident of Oberlin since 1864 and was reputed to be the wealthiest man in the village. He gave liberally in support of the poor. He made a gift of $5,000 to Oberlin College, with the provision that the return on this sum be used to buy coal for indigent people of Oberlin for a long period of years. J. L. Edwards and E. C. Shallies formed a partnership in the grocery business at 21 West College Street. Mr. Shallies died in April of this year and Mr. Edwards continued the business.

In an address before the Oberlin Board of Commerce President Barrows said that no college owed so much to the community as did Oberlin. Professor H. C. King objected to the separation of citizens and faculty members. He stated that he wished to be regarded as a citizen of the community in which he lived. Samuel Squire retired this spring from the firm of Squire & Son. At the April election Henry Churchill King and A. G. Comings were chosen members of the school board, L. E. Burgner was elected Justice of the Peace, and A. B. Spear, clerk. The annual budget for the Rust M. E. Church was $592.04. The pastor's salary was $273.16. E. A. Miller was serving his second year as principal of the schools at Webster, South Dakota. Mr. Miller was connected with Oberlin College from 1903 to 1932, when he retired. At his retirement he was Professor of

Education. He had given excellent service as superintendent of the Oberlin Public Schools. W. R. Moore bought the interest of E. M. Ransom in the furniture store of Ransom & Booth. Mr. Ransom went from Oberlin to Lorain and returned again to Oberlin to take charge of the store, which was once the property of his father. H. J. Clark made a report of the use of anti-toxin in diphtheria. This remedy was then first coming into the general practice of physicians.

Reverend James Brand, pastor of First Church for twenty-six years, died April 11. Mr. Brand was a minister of unusual power and ability. He was a veteran of the Civil War and was generally regarded as a worthy successor of Mr. Finney, whom he succeeded in the pastorate of the church here. In April Oberlin College received a donation of $50,000 from Louis H. Severance for the construction of a chemical laboratory. A special election was held May 1 to vote on the question of a one mill levy for certain improvements to school buildings. Only 47 votes were cast. The proposal had 33 votes, one more than needed to carry it.

In May the candidacy of Honorable A. G. Comings for representative in the Ohio General Assembly was announced. At a Republican caucus it was agreed that Mr. Comings should have the privilege of naming his own delegates and alternates. This list, given herewith, is a very comprehensive roll call of the leading Republicans active in party politics at the time: W. B. Bedortha, E. H. Holter, George C. Prince, J. B. Hart, M. M. Squire, J. W. Steele, W. J. Fuller, T. H. Mumford, J. L. Kinney, G. W. Turner, H. J. Clark, E. L. Disbro, O. F. Carter, Alfred Fauver, J. F. Harmon, George S. Pay, E. P. Johnson, C. K. Whitney, M. J. Watson, M. G. Dick, E. L. Burge, Henry Morris, W. H. Cooley, A. B. Spear, C. H. Glenn, M. Sherburne, J. L. Edwards, S. B. Dudley, James Kelley, C. D. Herrick, John Berg, Charles Barnhart, James Worcester, F. H. Maddock, Dr. F. E. Leonard, T. N. Carver, Rev. A. B. Allen, A. B. Johnson, George C. Jameson, P. G. Worcester, J. N. Stone, Dr. C. H. Browning, A. M. Loveland, R. P. Jameson, and George M. Jones. Mr. Comings was nominated and was elected in the fall. C. K. Whitney and Colonel J. W. Steele were Oberlin delegates to the State Convention.

Jonathan Hobbs, night policeman, received praise for dignity and avoirdupois. Mr. Hobbs, the father of W. D. Hobbs and Stanton Hobbs, well-known business men, and a Civil War veteran, was six feet three inches in height and weighed 240 pounds. Officers of the Oberlin Cinder Path Association were: L. P. Chapman, president; L. E. Burgner, vice-president; C. P. Doolittle, treasurer. The prudential board included President Barrows, Dr. Edward I. Bosworth, and twelve other faculty men, in addition to a dozen of the leading business men of the village.

Henry Lee, born in slavery, died May 31 of injuries sustained when crushed by part of a building he was moving. He came to Oberlin in 1860. He was best known as a hack driver, but was a preacher and lecturer as well. He was given to controversy and his arguments with rival hack drivers got him into the courts on several occasions. One of his cases growing out of such a dispute was carried to the Supreme Court of the State. By the end of the year Council had virtually abandoned the recognizing in resolutions of the use of board sidewalks. Sidewalk construction for several years had been leaning toward sawed stone and concrete.

At the inaugural of President Barrows in June announcement was made of the appointment as secretary of Oberlin College of George M. Jones, who was then described in the public prints as "a gentleman of enterprise, energy, and business capacity." Mr. Jones was still serving as secretary in 1933. In addition to his work for the college Mr. Jones has made a fine record of public service, definitely as a member of the Board of Trustees of the water works and generally by a showing of sympathetic interest in community affairs.

In the summer of this year four teams were needed to haul to Westwood Cemetery the largest single granite block in any

The Story of a Century

monument then there. It weighed 16,500 pounds and was for the grave of Mr. and Mrs. John Smith, "who once lived on the main road south of Oberlin." Henry M. Platt, who was born on a farm near Oberlin in 1835, died in June in Toledo, where he had moved from Oberlin in 1873. He was a pioneer photographer here.

The Oberlin News in its issue of July 7 said: "Capitalists seem to look upon the horseless carriage or automobile as the coming vehicle, judging from the amount of money being invested in their manufacture. A bicycle company at Lorain has increased its capital stock for the purpose of engaging in the making of automobiles." In August note was made that the automobile, in those days a rare sight, had made its appearance in Oberlin. Two passed through the village on Wednesday, August 16, from east to west along College Street. Both cars were Wintons, and the curious of the village, without regard to occupation or pride of family, gathered on the sidewalk to watch them. Dr. H. W. Pyle owned the first car operated in Oberlin.

In September the initial step looking to the extension of the traction line from Oberlin to Wellington was taken when a franchise for the use of Main Street from the College Street intersection to the corporation line was granted to the Cleveland-Berea-Elyria and Oberlin Company. In the fall the total enrollment in the public schools was 752. Attendance in the high school was 144. In October the Oberlin Videttes, an independent military company, were formed, with Claude Rhinehart, captain; Eugene Dick, lieutenant; R. M. Gove, second lieutenant. It had been planned to enter the Ohio National Guard. The company had fifty members.

An appeal made in October to save the Historic Elm by building a fence around it struck a responsive chord and C. T. Beckwith went to Cleveland to consult an architect for the preparing of plans and specifications to bring this about. At the annual meeting of the Oberlin Society held October 10, a resolution passed that officials take steps to transfer property to First Church and that the Oberlin Society, which was formed in 1834, be abolished.

The second annual meeting of the Lorain County Firemen's Association held at Elyria August 23, 1899, was marked by the winning of a banner by the Oberlin firemen as having the best drilled department in the parade, in which seven departments in this and adjoining counties participated. The Cleveland veterans were in line with their old hand engine. Seven hundred and fifty Oberlin people were present.

This occasion gave warrant to the publication in the 'Oberlin News of a list of the triumphs of the Oberlin fire department covering a period of more than forty years. Displayed in the H. F. Smith drug store were a number of the prizes won by the boys at different contests throughout the country. There were other prizes in the hands of families of former chiefs of the department who had moved from Oberlin. Those on exhibition were:

A solid silver trumpet won by the hook and ladder company September 2, 1858, at Cleveland, time prize.

A solid silver trumpet won in Tiffin, 1869, time prize. A solid gold badge presented by the president of the Northwestern Volunteer Firemen's Association in 1884, time prize.

A silver water pipe won by the Gibson Hose Company at Wapakoneta in 1885 for the best appearing company. A solid silver belt, which cost $500, won at Norwalk, September, 1886, by the Gibson Hose Company, a time prize, bearing with it the championship of the United States. Professor E. A. Miller was a member of the team.

A fine silken banner bearing the words "Lorain County Fire Association." The banner cost $50 and was awarded to Oberlin at the Elyria meeting in 1899.

Also shown in the window was a silver trumpet presented to Luther L. Munson in appreciation of his work as fire chief, and a gold band ring presented by the firemen in 1899 to Chief B. O. Durand.

The Story of a Century

In addition to the trophies enumerated, the department had won numerous money prizes. These included $100 in gold at Tiffin, 1884; a like sum in gold in Elmore, 1885; a like sum in gold in Norwalk, 1886; $375 in gold at Cincinnati, 1886; $100 in gold in Elmore, 1886.

At the Elyria meeting this year President Luther L. Munson read a paper giving a comprehensive report of the condition of the fire departments at Oberlin, Vermilion, Wellington, Lorain, North Amherst, Elyria, LaGrange, and Grafton. Those who knew Mr. Munson will find a hearty echo of the past in this quotation from his report: "I had the pleasure and honor of commanding the Oberlin department four years, and I know it from the hydrant to the nozzle. When I came in the boys were making horses of themselves pulling through unpaved streets heavy apparatus, some of which was fitted for horses. But there was no money to hire horses with, so the boys gladly did the work. You will generally find that when a lot of firemen are willing to turn themselves into horses, every councilman will gladly vote them the thanks of the municipality."

Mr. Munson read a statement of annual expenses for fire departments in the villages listed, showing per capita expense ranged from fourteen cents in Wellington to forty cents in Grafton. Oberlin's expense was midway between the high and low at twenty-three cents. He pointed out that "Lorain County folks get cheaper fire protection per capita." Rates for other cities in the state reached a point as high as $1.30 in Cincinnati. The former chief, who made a record as an excellent fire fighter, made strong plea for better fire protection and as a result lower insurance rates.

Mr. Munson closed his address in this characteristic fashion: "This is what usually happens when a fire occurs in a small town. Every one turns out and every man yells his loudest. The strongest lunged man in the crowd takes command. He never saw but two fires, one a barn struck by lightning and one a six-story brick in Cleveland the day of the excursion. He had often told how the Cleveland firemen went to work on that fire and the boys submitted to his orders, because if he didn't know how to handle this fire, who did? There are perhaps two or three small chemicals in the town which are brought out and turned loose with surprising good effect, but are soon empty. No one has ever charged the machines since the agent sold them, so the machines are thrown aside while the fire burns on. If there is a stock of goods in danger, the owner opens his doors and calls on his neighbors to help him get his property to a place of safety. Before that night there was only one man in that community ever suspected of stealing. The next morning the owner knows that there must have been fifty thieves helping to carry out the stock. Everything good there is to eat, drink, smoke or chew was raided, until what may have been a value of $100 is now $10, a loss no insurance company will ever pay."

Albert H. Johnson, Oberlin capitalist, was instantly killed December 4 in a railroad collision in Colorado. His son, Albert M., sustained a broken back, but was still living in 1933 and prospering in business in the West. Albert H. was a son of I. M. Johnson, one of the early business men of Oberlin. He was president of the Citizen's National Bank, The Oberlin Gas and Electric Company, and the Arkansas Midland Railroad Company. He was a trustee of Oberlin College at the time of his death. The Johnson home on South Professor Street, now the property of Oberlin College, is one of the show places of the village.

W. H. Haylor was elected master of Oberlin Lodge, F. & A. M. E. J. Goodrich, veteran book seller, advertised holiday literature at the close of the season, listing Janice Meredith, Richard Carvel, and When Knighthood was in Flower.

1900

Reverend Walter Scott of Bristol, Ind., succeeds Reverend W. H. G. Lewis as rector of Christ Episcopal church. Hiram B. Thurston, who had been U. L. A. librarian for several years, was employed as assistant in the treasurer's office. He became assistant treasurer in 1909 and treasurer in 1916. Mr. Thurston

The Story of a Century

was still holding this office in 1933. He rendered good service as a member of the Village Council and was a director of the Oberlin Savings Bank Company.

The opening of the interurban line had made, for small business in Oberlin, a problem in out-of-town buying which grew in intensity when the automobile came into general use a few years later. This problem was fully recognized by President Barrows in an address before the annual meeting of the Oberlin Board of Commerce. In the course of his talk Mr. Barrows said: "The town and the college go together in mutual dependence. The college may be the eye, but the town is the hand, and the eye cannot say to the hand 'I have no need of thee.' It is a foolish and suicidal mistake for citizens not to support the trade of their own town. It is a bad habit, showing a lack of municipal patriotism and good sense, for people to go away from Oberlin to buy. Our family experience has taught us that we can do just as well in Oberlin, in almost all cases. If a thousand families living here spend $300 apiece a year in groceries, books, clothing, etc., in other cities, when the year is over we have the things and the other cities have $300,000. If these families spend their money in Oberlin, when the year is over, we have the things and $300,-000 besides. Professor Carver may not think this is good political economy, but it appeals to my common sense and I believe it. We are bound by every law of municipal patriotic feeling and good neighborliness to support our own trades-people. Even if it costs us a little more, which it does not usually, we ought to stand by each other, the college by the town, and the town by the college."

C. T. Beckwith was made president of the Citizen's National Bank to fill the vacancy made by the death of Albert H. Johnson. Daniel P. Reamer, veteran business man, died. He began business in Oberlin in 1859 with George W. Kinney. For a few years following 1872 he had lived in Kansas, but finally returned to Oberlin to make his home. Jabez L. Burrell, charter member of the Board of Trustees of Oberlin College, died January 25, at the age of 93. On the same date occurred the death of J. J. Martin, 89, who had called to inquire as to Mr. Burrell's health just an hour before he himself died. Martin had lived in Oberlin thirty years and was reputed to be worth $150,000. Burrell had been a resident here since 1845. Lord Cottage was virtually destroyed by fire January 30 with a loss of about $20,000. Although the fire broke out at 1:45 A. M., forty young women students were rescued without injury. On the recommendation of Councilman M. G. Dick, Council voted to buy a team of horses for the use of the volunteer fire department. Up to this date livery barns had been patronized and on many occasions the apparatus was dragged to fires by hand. Mrs. Martha Royce, mother of Mrs. A. G. Comings, died in February. She had lived here forty-seven years.

The Oberlin W. C. T. U. made formal protest against the nomination of Attorney E. G. Johnson of Elyria for Congress because "he is an avowed champion of the liquor interests." This action was followed by a citizens meeting at Second Church under the auspices of the Oberlin Temperance Alliance. General Shurtleff spoke in opposition to Johnson on the ground that the Elyria man was an advocate of the open saloon and of machine politics. Professors H. C. King and E. I. Bosworth pleaded for a congressman friendly to the temperance cause. Despite this opposition on the part of a number of leaders of public thought in Oberlin, Mr. Johnson received the support of Lorain County and had a solid delegation from Oberlin. He had the support of Judge J. W. Steele, who was not at all friendly to wet interests but was friendly to Johnson himself. The Elyria man failed of nomination after a deadlock which lasted several days. Judge Steele was a member of the committee to confer with Johnson, who was permitted by the county convention to select his own delegates. Oberlin delegates included W. B. Bedortha, C. K. Whitney, M. G. Dick, and H. H. Barnard. No nomination was reached at Wellington in April after 1357 ballots. At Norwalk in May W. W. Skiles, of Shelby, was nominated on the 2,101st ballot.

H. F. Smith, in February, began his service as member of Council, succeeding E. H. Holter, who had resigned. Edward A.

The Story of a Century

Miller, Oberlin College '97, was elected superintendent of the Oberlin public schools. G. W. Waite retired after sixteen years of service. Oberlin College received a gift of $50,000 from Lucien C. Warner for a men's gymnasium. Mrs. Adelia A. F. Johnston resigned as dean of the woman's department after thirty years in the position. She continued to teach. Dr. C. H. A. Wager, in 1933 one of the outstanding members of the college faculty, began this year his work as Professor of English. A petition was presented to the Board of Education asking the board to make a levy of not to exceed one mill in support of the Oberlin Kindergarten Training School, which had been established in 1894 and which was supported by voluntary contributions. The suggestion was discussed in the school board and in the Board of Commerce, but strong opposition was based on the ground of the danger arising from any further increase in taxes, and no action was taken by the Board of Education. The Republican caucus nominated Mayor Alfred Fauver for a third term. Other nominations were clerk, C. H. Snyder; treasurer, J. N. Stone; trustee of the water works, Charles McChesney; township clerk, Carl W. Kinney. The name of Attorney A. Z. Tillotson was submitted to the caucus, but Mr. Fauver's excellent record gave him the victory. The first rural free delivery mail route in the county was established this year, extending from Elyria to Ridgeville. Henry C. Wangerien, in 1933 president of the Oberlin Savings Bank Company and for several terms prior to that date member of the Council, was this year elected County Commissioner. Chauncey Wack died in May, aged 85. He came to Oberlin in 1840 and, although a staunch Democrat, had served on the Village Council. W. D. Hobbs installed an electric fan in his restaurant on East College Street, the first to be put into use in the village.

Citizens had a part in the 1900 reunion of the college, which was a great success. Addresses of welcome were delivered by Mayor Fauver and Mrs. A. A. F. Johnston. A significant incident of the celebration was the dedication of the bronze tablet placed upon the Historic Elm largely through the efforts of C. T. Beckwith, who raised funds for the building of a permanent enclosure around the tree. The formal address of the occasion on Sunday, June 24, was given by Reverend William E. Barton. The inscription on the tablet reads: "Near this tree the logs were laid for the first dwelling in Oberlin, April 16, 1833." In the course of his talk Mr. Barton stated that it was known without question that the Historic Elm stood at the southeast corner of the campus when "Father" Shipherd and Philo P. Stewart first visited the site in 1832. He called attention to the testimony of Mrs. Williams, daughter of Peter Pindar Pease, that her father had spared the tree in his door yard because of its beauty. It was the recollection of President Fairchild that the tree was five inches in diameter when he first saw it in 1834. Mr. Barton called attention to the fact that the Elm had witnessed all the changes in Oberlin College and Colony from their founding to the beginning of the twentieth century. It still stood in 1933.

In July W. A. Heusner and Carl Dudley took over the Shuart Grader Company which became in time the Ohio Road Machinery Company. The Oberlin tax rate of 31.9 mills was the highest in the county. Reverend J. W. Bradshaw was called as pastor of First Church from Ann Arbor, Michigan.

General Jacob Dolson Cox, distinguished son of Oberlin, died April 5, at Magnola, Mass. He was buried in Cincinnati. For about a year General Cox, former governor of Ohio, and distinguished commander in the Civil War, had been making his home in Oberlin. He was a graduate of the college and was a member of the Board of Trustees for almost a quarter of a century.

News in the late summer of authentic character confirmed the loss of Oberlin missionaries in the Boxer uprising. The Memorial Arch at the west entrance of the college campus was dedicated in 1903 in honor of the Oberlin victims. All but four of those who died in the uprising were Oberlin students or members of families of Oberlin students. The bronze tablet on the arch bears the names of thirteen missionaries and of five children who were massacred. Professor F. B. Rice resigned as director of the Musical Union after thirty years of service. He was succeeded by Professor George W. Andrews.

In October President Barrows announced a change in the college regulation which had required attendance at morning prayers in boarding houses. From that date attendance at these services was not enforced.

The Board of Commerce on November 9 discussed municipal ownership of gas and electricity. C. T. Beckwith stated that Albert H. Johnson, original owner of these utilities, had made an investment of $53,000. Mr. Beckwith said he himself owned but one share of stock and served as manager without pay. He announced that he was authorized to sell both plants with all equipment to the village for $30,000.

Oberlin's population by the 1900 census was 4082. Elyria had a population of 8971.

1901

There were five hundred signatures to a petition presented to W. B. Bedortha by Oberlin people asking him to be a candidate for Common Pleas Judge. The Elyria bar supported A. R. Webber, who was nominated at Medina. Before voting began Mr. Bedortha addressed the convention and withdrew his name. John D. Rockefeller made a gift of $200,000 to the college conditioned on the raising of an endowment fund of a half million dollars. This condition was finally met. E. H. Holter, for twenty six years in the jewelry business here, sold his store to W. P. Carruthers.

Records showing water pumped in 1900 in Oberlin made a total of 36,560,000 gallons. In 1932 the total pumpage was in excess of 129,000,000 gallons. Merton Mason was elected chief of the fire department. In July an ordinance was passed for the paving of West College Street from Main to Prospect. Estimates of costs were nearly double the cost of the East College Street paving put in about two years before. Council at this time granted a franchise to the Cleveland-Elyria Western for the lay-

ing of tracks on West College Street. The spiritual and municipal guides of John Alexander Dowie's Zion City were patterning
their city sewer system after that of Oberlin. In October died
Professor Fenelon B. Rice, known as the "Father of the Oberlin
Conservatory." He came to Oberlin in 1869. President Fairchild resigned in November from the Board of Trustees of the
college. At a meeting in December the Oberlin Board of Commerce pledged the town to the raising of $5,000, toward the half
million endowment fund of the college. Citizens of the village,
including faculty members, finally pledged $8,000.

1902

Early this year the old Chemical Laboratory building, not
needed by the college since the erection of Severance Chemical
Laboratory, was torn down. This building, known as Cabinet
Hall, was built by the school district in 1851 for school purposes
and was bought by the college in 1874, when a new school building was erected on South Main Street. In February Charles R.
Comings, in 1933 head of the firm of A. G. Comings & Son,
and for many years associated in business with his father, returned
from three years of service with the regular army in the Philippines. In March the Republican caucus nominated Mayor Fauver by acclamation for a fourth term. He was elected. His opponent on the Democratic ticket was Luther Munson.

James Harris Fairchild, former president of the college, died
March 19, at the age of 84. He was for 68 years identified with
the college as student, teacher, trustee, and president. Mr. Fairchild was one of the three or four great men who shaped the
character of Oberlin College and who contributed to its growth.
His interest in the community was genuine and he made notable
contributions to the growth and betterment of the village as he
carried on his chosen work. President Barrows described Mr.
Fairchild as "leader, philosopher, saint, and friend." "He was,"
said Mr. Barrows, "the last of the great pioneers and founders
and will be remembered as the wise master-builder of this academic structure." Professor Henry Churchill King said: "Ober-

lin has had no richer character in all its history." A leading New England clergyman said of Mr. Fairchild's work in the presidency: "In all that period he made not a single false step, uttered no public word that was not based on sound and defensible logic, led the college through its radicalism to conservative and careful thought and an administration befitting the changing times."

Oberlin was shocked and grieved on June 3 of this year when President John Henry Barrows died after a brief illness of pneumonia. His body was borne from his home to Second Church, where services were held, and from the church to Westwood Cemetery, on the shoulders of students. Seventy-two students of the college rendered this last loving service. These were divided into relays of eight, as the coffin was borne through lines of grieving people. Mr. Barrows was elected president in 1898 and had made for himself a splendid record as a scholar and as an executive. His hold upon the community was as strong as it was with his associates in the college. More than 3,000 people passed by his body as it lay in state at the time of the funeral.

In July Warren J. Sage was appointed as a fifth letter carrier. He was still in service in 1933. In June Captain J. F. Randolph, manager of the Oberlin News, and William H. Pearce, editor, retired from active duty. Professor C. W. Morrison was elected director of the Conservatory to fill the vacancy created by the death of Fenelon B. Rice. He served until 1924, and his death occured in 1927. He was for years on the board of directors of the Peoples Banking Company. The first car over the new traction line to Norwalk was run June 29.

W. H. Pearce in a communication lists business men who were in business in 1877 in Oberlin and who were still active in 1902. This list included E. J. Goodrich, E. P. Johnson, L. T. Whitney, A. Straus, J. M. Gardner, T. H. Rowland, George S. Pay, T. J. Elliott, P. R. Tobin, W. B. Durand, L. L. Munson, W. T. Henderson, G. M. Glenn, Dr. J. F. Siddall, Attorney J. H. Lang, Judge John W. Steele. This quarter of a century had seen the change from frame to brick business blocks and the replacement of gas and gasoline lights with electricity.

Oberlin Colony

In July Charles Nelson Cole, in 1933 dean of Oberlin College, began his work here as an instructor in Latin. In the early fall Frank W. Tobin bought a half interest in the F. E. Burgess drug store, where he had been employed for seven years. Soon thereafter he took over the entire store. Deacon John S. Peck, father of Professor John Fisher Peck, who was many years an honored teacher in the Academy here, died at the age of 84. He was a student here in 1839.

At the meeting of the trustees of Oberlin College on November 19 Professor Henry Churchill King was elected president of the college. Mr. King was graduated from the college in the class of 1879, and from the Seminary three years later. He was tutor in the preparatory department from the time of his graduation until 1882. In 1884 he was made Associate Professor of Mathematics and in 1891 was made Professor of Philosophy. He had served as registrar in the early nineties and was dean of the college at the time of his election to the presidency. He served as president until his retirement in 1927. Mr. King's administration covered the period of the greatest financial growth and expansion of the college. His fine personality and the respect for his views held by Charles M. Hall accounted very largely for the bequest made by Mr. Hall in his will. Mr. King was always a tireless worker, holding a firm belief in the mission of Oberlin College and willing to give all he had for the promotion of the purposes of the college. Over this period of a quarter of a century he had given without stint, unselfishly and intelligently. He met with rare tact changing conditions which marked the World War period and the years following it. He retired with the respect and affection of the citizens of Oberlin who had taken satisfaction in the work which he had done. Mr. King was living in 1933 at his attractive home on East College Street.

In the fall of this year the Oberlin Gas and Electric Company was disturbed by a proposal of the Logan Natural Gas Company, whose pipe line was closely approaching Oberlin, to furnish gas to the village. At the same time the Oberlin Gas and Electric Company was selling artificial gas at $1.50 a thousand. In

The Story of a Century

December the Logan Company asked of Council a franchise for distributing natural gas here. President Beckwith, of the Oberlin Company, submitted a written statement that his company would ask for a franchise for distributing natural gas. He promised ample service and plenty of gas before the end of 1903. The ordinance was submitted fixing a price of thirty cents a thousand for the first four years, with slight increase for the six following years. These prices were subject to a discount of two and a half per cent. It was provided that the city should have 100,000 feet of gas free yearly. Mr. Beckwith expressed every confidence that his company would either develop a natural gas field or would be able to purchase from other producers. There was no charge of bad faith made at the time, but the record indicated a spirit of hopefulness which in the end proved expensive for Oberlin citizens. The franchise was granted to the Oberlin Gas and Electric Company and the application of the Logan Company was refused, although gas was at the doors of the village when the application was made and the price was about one-fifth of the price of manufactured gas which Oberlin had been buying from the Oberlin Gas and Electric Company. Mr. Beckwith's company secured no natural gas, and when a year or two later a committee from the Oberlin Board of Commerce waited on the Logan company and asked them to come to Oberlin with their fuel, the company responded that they were not interested. The final proposal of the Logan company was made to Council in August, 1903, when it offered natural gas service by October of that year if a franchise were granted. The price for the first year was twenty-five cents. In the years which have passed Oberlin residents have expended for gas service many more thousands of dollars than would have been necessary had the Council granted a franchise to the Logan company. In 1933 Oberlin was paying eighty-eight cents gross, the highest price in the State of Ohio, for its natural gas. A few years following this fiasco the mistake made by Council became an issue in the Republican primary campaign and brought about the first upset in an official Republican slate in the history of the village.

Oberlin Colony

1903

The year opened pleasantly with a New Year's reception given by President and Mrs. King at their home on East College. Five hundred residents of the community called between the hours of 2 P. M. and 10 P. M. Mr. and Mrs. King were assisted in receiving by Messrs. and Mesdames Alfred Fauver, John W. Steele, Miles J. Watson, A. H. Currier, Lyman B. Hall, and Edward I. Bosworth. A coal famine in January elicited the statement from the Oberlin Gas and Electric Company that the company might go out of business if conditions did not change.

The College Chapel was destroyed by fire on Sunday, January 25. This was the most spectacular fire in many ways in Oberlin history. The building, built in 1854-55, was remodeled in 1871. From 1860 to 1870 the Second Church congregation held services in the building and it had been used for years as a place for community gatherings. An addition was made to the building in 1884, following the erection of a new tower the year preceding. The fire was discovered by C. K. Whitney. The loss was $40,000.

The 'Oberlin Electric and Heating plant was given a franchise for steam heat. The incorporators were L. B. Fauver, L. E. Burgner, A. M. Loveland, J. D. Yocom, C. K. Whitney, and A. G. Comings. That the Oberlin Gas and Electric Company had conducted an astute campaign to protect its interests was shown at a Board of Commerce meeting in February at which time Judge Steele, M. J. Watson, and Dr. Bunce were among the very few who did not think natural gas inferior in all respects to manufactured gas.

Superintendent E. A. Miller proposed a four-year high school, which was chartered in December, this year. Mr. Miller tendered his resignation to become Dean of College Men for Oberlin College. Ward Nye was made superintendent in his stead. C. S. Hopkins, who came with his father, Fay Hopkins, to Oberlin in 1834, died February 19. At the March caucus Mayor Fauver was for the fifth time nominated for mayor. This action was taken by acclamation. A. A. Wright, F. F. Jewett, and W. B. Bedortha were elected to the Board of Trustees of Public Affairs, the new name for the water board. Colonel Ralph Plumb, 87, who had become a multimillionaire since leaving Oberlin, died at Streator, Illinois. He built the brick residence at the southwest corner of South Professor and Forest Streets in the Civil War days. He left Oberlin in 1865. Council passed an ordinance providing a maximum speed of eight miles an hour for automobiles within the corporation limits. A collision of Cleveland Southwestern and Columbus traction cars near Cottesbrook, July 19, resulted in the death of E. L. Garvin, Oberlin, and injuries to thirty others. Damage suits, running into many thousands of dollars, followed the wreck. The Oberlin fire department won a first prize at a convention at Amherst. John White, colored, who had worked for President Mahan, died in October. He came to Oberlin in 1838. In November C. T. Beckwith sold his post office block to the Oberlin Business College.

1904

Mayor Alfred Fauver died February 29. He was a soldier in the Civil War and was serving his fifth term as mayor. He had been a resident here since 1891. O. F. Carter, president of Council, succeeded Mr. Fauver as mayor and M. G. Dick was made president of Council. M. J. Watson was appointed to the vacancy created on the Council. Captain A. B. Parsons entered the grocery business here. John Ramsey, colored, was still living in May and claimed to be 121 years old. He came to Oberlin in 1840 and worked on the construction of First Church.

W. H. Pearce, for twenty-five years editor of the Oberlin News, died in April. The following month occurred the death of General Giles W. Shurtleff. He was the captain of Company C, 7th O. V. I., the first company answering the call for troops at the outbreak of the war. He was captured in the battle of Cross Lanes with other members of his company and served a year in Confederate prisons. After his release he was on the staff of General Wilcox and was later made Lieutenant-Colonel of the Fifth United States colored troops. He was twice wounded and was given the brevet of Brigadier General at the close of the war. He was treasurer of the college, 1887-94, and was made a member of the Board of Trustees when he resigned as treasurer. He engaged in real estate and loan business here after his resignation and was active in town affairs to the time of his death. He had served as mayor and as member of the Council and was a recognized leader in the village. He was described as a champion of law and righteousness and a born fighter of heroic mould.

In August the State Savings Bank opened for business with W. C. Clancy, cashier and H. L. Bassett, assistant cashier. Ten thousand people witnessed the firemen's parade in Oberlin, August 17, when the annual convention of the Lorain County Firemen's Association was held.

In the death of William Brown Bedortha on October 10, Oberlin lost one of its most valued citizens. Mr. Bedortha, who was born in 1854, spent his entire life in Oberlin. As a youth Mr. Bedortha served as an apprentice in the office of the Oberlin News, where he worked for five years. For four years he conducted a printing office of his own and for one year following was manager of the News. In 1877 Mr. Bedortha entered the office of Judge John W. Steele for study of the law and three years later was admitted to the bar. In twenty-four years of practice he earned the reputation not only of finished proficiency in an exacting profession, but, more than that, of high honor in the conduct of his business. Said one who knew him well: "His quiet questions and his timely good humor would drive many a dark cloud away. He always addressed himself to the best there was in a man and rarely failed to secure a response. It was natural for him to deal directly and openly under all circumstances. The great and final impression which he made upon those who had business with him was that he was a 'sympathetic, clear, sincere and open hearted man.'" In the course of a memorial address delivered by Professor A. S. Root, the speaker related the public service rendered by Mr. Bedortha and paid tribute to his outstanding qualities. He concluded by saying: "Fair and square in every business relation, the 'soul of honor,' we had hoped for many years to have the benefit of his counsel and the joy of his permanent presence with us. It will be many a year before we have ceased to mourn him."

That Mr. Bedortha was recognized as a leader of the Lorain County Bar was further emphasized in a memorial address delivered by Judge David J. Nye in which he said: "In a county of able and trusted lawyers he stood in the front rank. He did not practice law as a mere trade, but he took up the profession as a high and noble calling and pursued it for the good he could do to his clientage and to mankind. He gained the esteem of every member of the bar of Lorain County. They all knew his ability and integrity. When the present Common Pleas Judge became a candidate for another position, the entire Bar of Lorain County joined in a petition to have Mr. Bedortha become a candidate for the office."

Resolutions paying tribute to Mr. Bedortha were passed by the Lorain County Bar Association. Here in Oberlin he is remembered not only as an able lawyer, but as a citizen of splendid character who rendered outstanding service to his community.

1905

In January announcement was made of the gift of Andrew Carnegie of $125,000 for the building of Carnegie Library. At the funeral of C. T. Beckwith, February 8, Dr. Henry M. Tenney, of Second Church, called attention to the fact that Mr. Beckwith had been for sixty years a resident of Oberlin, and, prior to the mistake he made in the Chadwick affair, had had a record of sound judgment and helpfulness. Mr. Tenney made reference to Mr. Beckwith's service with the church and to his contribution to the community as president of the Board of Education. To this task he gave much in time and money.

In April occurred the death of Albert A. Wright. Mr. Wright was acting president of the college between the time of the resignation of President Ballantine and the election of President Barrows. He served in the Civil War and did valuable work in the geologic surveys of 'Ohio made in 1872 and 1882. He shared with Judge Steele the credit for fine work done in the establishing of the water works here in Oberlin. He had served on the Board of Water Works Trustees since its organization in 1887. In April Clarence R. Graham was made chief of the fire department to succeed Merton Mason, resigned. Mr. Graham, who was manager of the telephone exchange here at the time, was still serving as fire chief in 1933. C. E. Van Ausdale, assistant chief, served as chief while Mr. Graham was in war service in France.

Judge John W. Steele, a sketch of whose life is given in this volume, died Wednesday, April 26. On recommendation of Congressman A. R. Webber of Elyria the president appointed J. N. Stone as postmaster at Oberlin to fill the vacancy caused by the death of Judge Steele, following an election held a day or two previous at which 671 votes were cast. Women were permitted to vote at this election, which was entirely informal and not very effective, since Mr. Stone, who received the nomination, had but one vote, while L. P. Chapman had 373, A. E. Griffin 216, and Noah Huckins 52. In May A. B. Spear, cashier of the old Citizen's Bank, pleaded guilty to making false entries in the banking books and was sentenced to seven years in the penitentiary. William H. Chapin began his service with Oberlin College as an assistant in the Chemical Laboratory. Mr. Chapin was still with the college in 1933 as Professor of Chemistry. He rendered good public service as a member of the Board of Trustees of Public Affairs. He has been active in village matters in his residence here and has made notable contributions to village history through a series of articles which have appeared from time to time in the Oberlin newspapers and the Oberlin Alumni Magazine. The first stake for the new Oberlin-Lorain traction line was driven July 11. The road was never built. In July Grove Patterson edited the Oberlin Tribune while Carl Kinney took a vacation in the west. In 1933 Mr. Patterson, a member of the Board of Trustees of the college, was recognized as one of the leading journalists of America. He was in 1933 editor-in-chief of the Toledo Blade. The corporation ticket this year was O. F. Carter, mayor; C. H. Snyder, clerk; A. P. Behr, treasurer; C. E. St. John, F. F. Jewett, and F. W. Tobin, Board of Public Affairs; M. G. Dick, A. D. Booth, and H. J. Morris, council; Scott Van-Ausdale, marshal. In November C. W. Savage was made director of athletics of Oberlin College, a position which he still held with credit in 1933.

1906

The Peoples Banking Company was incorporated early in the year. The original board of directors was made up of L. E. Burgner, J. T. Henderson, George Preston, F. E. McKellogg, Dr. W. C. Bunce, E. E. Sperry, H. B. Thurston, Dr. Charles H. Browning, H. F. Smith, M. J. Watson, and C. W. Morrison. J. T. Henderson was elected president and H. F. Smith, vice president. They held the same offices in the bank in 1933. Mr. Morrison was second vice president, Mr. Burgner, secretary, and Horace Waite, cashier. The new bank took over the property of the Northern Ohio Bank which had been started in the early fall of 1905. C. W. Balson and L. W. Campbell bought the grocery of W. H. Cooley & Son. Cooley & Son then bought the shoe store of W. J. Stone. J. B. Hart died March 9. He was a member of the firm of Hart & Vincent. A new Methodist Church on North Main Street was dedicated March 25. It cost $26,000.

Ramsey and Wabash interests were contending in rival coal routes running north and south through Lorain County west of Oberlin to connect Lorain and other lake ports with the coal fields of Ohio and West Virginia. In April several hundred men were working on the two roads near Oberlin. Both companies were paying round prices for right-of-way. John Dudley, Oberlin farmer, received $7500 for a right across his farm west of town. The Congressional convention which nominated J. F. Laning of Norwalk endorsed the candidacy of Honorable A. G.

Oberlin Colony

Comings of Oberlin for Secretary of State. Mr. Comings was defeated in the state convention for the nomination.

John M. Siddall, son of Dr. J. F. Siddall, Oberlin dentist, was one of a group of eight nationally known editors and writers who purchased the American Magazine. Mr. Siddall, one of the ablest of the sons of Oberlin, made of the magazine in his work as editor an outstanding publication of its kind. His column "Sid Says" was widely quoted for its sound wisdom and good sense.

In June it was announced that the half million dollar endowment fund had been completed, insuring the Carnegie gift for a new library. In July Dr. S. E. Miller, of Kipton, was nominated for coroner on the Republican ticket. Following his election in the fall he removed to Lorain where he lived until 1912, when he came to Oberlin to reside. In 1933 Dr. Miller was still a resident here and was one of the recognized leaders in the medical profession in the county. Merton L. Mason, member of the fire department for twenty-three years and former chief, died in July. In August died John D. Carpenter, vice president of the Oberlin Bank and a resident here fifty years. He owned much real estate and was regarded as the wealthiest citizen of the community at the time of his death. In August E. J. Davis established the Sugar Bowl in the Park Hotel block. He was still in business in the same location in 1933. H. F. Smith sold his drug store in September to O. M. Harter. Mr. Smith had been in the drug business here as clerk and proprietor since March, 1887.

Initial discussion of a hospital for Oberlin was had at the September meeting of the Oberlin Board of Commerce. G. N. Carruthers died in September. He was the father of W. P. Carruthers, a well known Oberlin resident in 1933, and had lived here since 1888. He was a graduate of the college. In November a petition for a Beal Law election was filed with the mayor. The election was held the following month with an overwhelming victory for the dry cause.

1907

In January Arthur Saxton was elected Master of Oberlin Grange. He was for many years a well-known farmer living east of Oberlin. The Oberlin hospital association was incorporated in February. The incorporators were Dr. F. E. Leonard, Mrs Nancy Squire, S. M. Cole, Mrs. M. G. Street, Reverend J. W. Bradshaw, Dr. R. D. A. Gunn, Dr. George C. Jameson, Dr. A. B. Everitt, Dr. W. C. Bunce, O. F. Carter, Dr. M. T. Runyan, Mrs. B. F. Shuart, C. N. Cole, Frank J. Dick, and Dr. C. H. Browning. The association later elected as trustees O. F. Carter, F. J. Dick, Dr. C. E. St. John, J. D. Yocom, and C. W. Morrison. The residence of Mrs. Alice Williams, at 21 South Cedar Avenue, was leased and the hospital was opened August 20.

In February the community returned temporarily to the evangelistic days of President Finney when Reverend Mr. Lyon came here for a series of revival services held in a specially built tabernacle. More than seven hundred "came forward." In April construction began on the Carnegie Library and a contract was let for Finney Memorial Chapel. In May occurred the death at Kalispel, Washington, of Flavius E. Pease, oldest son of Deacon Peter Pindar Pease. In June Philip D. Sherman was appointed instructor in English in the college. In 1933 Mr. Sherman was Professor of English and had rendered good service to the community as a member of the Board of Education and as a citizen generally interested in the affairs of college and village. Contracts for the paving of West Lorain and North Professor Streets let in July completed a paving program which had extended over several years. James M. Worcester died August 29 at Pittsfield where he had lived since 1845. He was of a family prominent in the affairs of 'Oberlin and Pittsfield since pioneer days and was the first member initiated into Oberlin Lodge of Masons soon after its institution in 1867. Schools opened in September without the services of Miss Tacey Anderson, a teacher here for thirty-five years.

In the first Republican primary held in Oberlin, replacing the caucus, which had been in operation here from year to year since

Oberlin Colony

the days of the founders, O. F. Carter was defeated for mayor by Joseph Wolfe. Mr. Carter fell a victim to public dissatisfaction with the handling of the gas question by the Council. Two or three members of the Council were defeated at the same time. At the election Wolfe had 586 votes and Luther Munson, his Democratic opponent, 334. This was an unusually large vote for the opposition and indicated that the heat of the primary campaign had created some ill feeling among Republicans. It is tradition that the day following the election Mr. Munson, who had been confident of success, announced with cold deliberation that he had a record in a written list of the number of people in Oberlin whose pre-election promises were not worth a tinker's dam. The entire Republican ticket was elected, including H. T. Marsh, clerk and A. P. Behr, treasurer. In October Glenn Gray, the greatest athlete in the history of Oberlin College, figured strongly in the Oberlin football team's defeat of Case by a score of 22-0. The Oberlin team also included George Vradenburg and "Bud" Waters. The "tight money market" of the fall of this year, when scrip was used in many cities, was not felt in Oberlin.

THE SCHOLAR IN PUBLIC LIFE

CHAPTER XIV

JAMES MONROE, teacher and legislator, was a young man of twenty-one when in 1844 he entered the Junior class of Oberlin College. Teachers in the college were impressed in his first year's work by the poise, the mental ability, and the broad experience which marked Mr. Monroe even in his student days. That this is true is shown by a statement of President Fairchild: "During my sixty years of teaching at Oberlin I have known many bright scholars, but never have any surprised me as did this young student from Connecticut." Inheritance as well as native ability accounted for these characteristics.

Mr. Monroe was born of Quaker parentage at Plainfield, Connecticut, July 18, 1821. His father was for a time a lawyer. The son received his early education in the common schools, at Plainfield Academy, and later under private instruction of John Witter of Plainfield. At the age of fourteen Mr. Monroe began teaching in the public schools. Before he was twenty, and before he came to Oberlin to complete his formal education, he was a lecturer for the American Anti-Slavery Society. This platform work brought him contact with such leaders in the anti-slavery movement as Garrison, Phillips, Douglass, the Burleighs, Edmund Quincy, and others. Despite his youth, he had high standing among the strong men of that day who were advocating the freedom of the colored race. For two years he traveled in the interests of this reform and occasionally in his pleas from the platform felt the force of mob spirit which ran from verbal abuse to actual violence. Never combative in disposition, Mr. Monroe's methods were not those of Phillips or of Garrison. He followed his own bent in seeking to arouse sympathy for the down-trodden race and to persuade his hearers in this manner to enlist in their cause. It is said that the finished eloquence of Wendell Phillips, polished by a liberal education, persuaded young Monroe to leave the platform that he might complete his own education.

Oberlin Colony

In view of this early career of Mr. Monroe, it is not surprising that he desired to come to Oberlin. The college in those days was known as friendly toward the Negro through opportunities offered for his education, although the Institute and its adherents did not follow men like Garrison, who opposed membership in any of the political parties of the day. With a background such as this, with outstanding ability reënforced by a fine and impressive personality, Mr. Monroe in his student days was recognized as a leader. Largely through the influence of President Finney, he abandoned adherence to the Quaker Church and joined the First Church in Oberlin, retaining membership throughout his life. He finally became thoroughly convinced that the evil of slavery would be wiped out more quickly through the efforts of political parties and he early allied himself with Chase, Gerrit Smith, and others in the movements which finally led to the forming of the Republican party, of which organization he was for many years an outstanding member.

After his graduation with the degree of A.B. in 1846 Mr. Monroe became a tutor in the college. In 1849 he was graduated from the Theological Seminary. He won his Master's degree in 1850. From 1849 until 1862 he was Professor of Rhetoric and Belles-Lettres in the college. While pursuing his college studies and giving attention to his teaching duties, Mr. Monroe took an active and intelligent interest in public affairs. He was particularly watchful of the principles and events which brought about the organization of the Republican party, and he had no small part in this work. In 1855 he was a delegate from Lorain County to the convention which organized the new party in Ohio. In the opening campaign he was nominated for the State Legislature and was elected with ease. He served two terms of two years each in the Ohio House of Representatives and one term, from 1860 to 1862, in the Ohio Senate. While higher honors were later accorded him, it is probable that his most valuable contribution to the state and the nation was made in his legislative service in Ohio.

JAMES MONROE

Oberlin Colony

In his autobiography Professor G. Frederick Wright, who was a student at Oberlin in 1855 and for many years a member of the faculty, says: "Professor James Monroe, who had been as a young man in Connecticut a devoted and successful anti-slavery lecturer, was my teacher in Rhetoric and Belles-Lettres. Into this department he brought the rich ripeness of his early experience in presenting talks in the most convincing manner to the cultivated audiences he had been accustomed to face in New England. In voice and manner and in richness of thought he could not be excelled. Naturally he continued to be interested in the anti-slavery cause, and as the war approached he was elected to the State Legislature and became one of the most influential members in shaping the course of the state in those troublous times.

"President Finney however was much exercised in his mind over Professor Monroe's entering the political arena, and at one time preached a most powerful sermon to try to dissuade him from running for the Legislature. The scene was one of the most memorable of my experience in Oberlin. Professor Monroe sat in a conspicuous place in the church, and listened with rapt attention as the eloquent preacher endeavored to prove that a man of high moral principles who had entered the arena of moral reform could not run for office without lowering his standard and compromising his character. Such a man cannot get the votes of the people except he come down to their level. Professor Monroe, he contended, is too good a man to do this. He can't afford to do it. He should remain on the high pedestal of moral principle where he now is and strive to draw all men up to it. If he gets down to the level to which he will have to fall if he gets the votes of the people he will never rise again to his original high standard. 'Professor Monroe,' said the preacher, 'is too good a man to run for the Legislature of Ohio.'

"Just then Professor Peck, who sat near, rose in his place and lifted his hand in token that he wished to speak. President Finney turned his great eyes toward him and perceiving what was wanted said, 'Speak on, Brother Peck,' and sat down while Professor Peck finished the sermon in trying to show that we were not going to lose Professor Monroe from the ranks of high moral reform, but were going to have him in both capacities as reformer and legislator. When Professor Peck finished his well-chosen remarks, Finney, with tears in his eyes, prayed that we might all be led aright and dismissed the meeting.

"Professor Peck's previsions were correct. Monroe was elected and never betrayed his trust. Indeed some have surmised that Finney, in his sermon, was trying to secure Monroe's election by showing that he was so good a man that his constituency would honor themselves by voting for him, thus showing that their level was higher than was generally supposed."

When Mr. Monroe began his work at Columbus in 1856 Salmon P. Chase was one of the acknowledged leaders of the Republican party in Ohio and in the nation. Abraham Lincoln was slowly emerging from his inconspicuous position as a circuit-riding lawyer in Illinois and was recognized as a leader in the new organization who must be taken into account when plans were made. The elections of 1854 had demonstrated that the new Republican party organized in that year was threatening the hold of the South through the Democratic party on national affairs. The strife in Kansas and early in 1856 the Dred Scott Decision, with the unnecessarily stupid statements of Chief Justice Taney, made in announcing it, had combined to make plain the fact that the day of compromise had passed. No prophet was needed in 1856, certainly not in 1860, to foretell that palliative methods could not solve the issue of slavery. In the legislative battles which preceded actual strife and which tended to unite the North in support of the Union, Mr. Monroe had a conspicuous part. The character of this service to the state was set forth by General Jacob Dolson Cox, later Governor of Ohio and a colleague of Mr. Monroe, on the floor of the House. General Cox said: "In four years of service in the House, Mr. Monroe became noted for qualities which distinguished him in all his career. His absolute fidelity to conscience was first. He was in politics to advance a great reform by noble means, and his devotion was so evident and so sincere that no one could doubt it. He was in advance of many of his co-workers, and sometimes seemed to them too radical; but what he thought it his duty to do was done with a quiet courage which could not be dismayed. Yet he was as marked for his charity and suavity as for his conscientiousness. His appeals were all to high motives and noble principles. Personal censoriousness and dogmatic egotism were never seen in him. Those who did not go with him felt that their conflict was with the best impulses of their own souls and not with him. It was most interesting to see the regard approaching personal affection which some of his strongest opponents showed for him."

Needless to say, Mr. Monroe did not stand as a candidate for the legislature merely for the purpose of holding office. He had in mind four things which he expected to accomplish in event of his election. Three of these he brought about in the course of his service in the Lower House. The fourth was realized at a later date largely because of the sound arguments which he presented in its favor. The first three proposals were the passage of a liberty bill, killing what he regarded as the unfair and illiberal provisions of the Fugitive Slave Act, the establishment of a state reform school, and the protection of the common school system. The fourth plan, which did not materialize in the course of his service in the Lower House, was the passage of such preliminary legislation as was necessary to strike the word "white" from the Constitution, giving the right of franchise to the Negro. Before going to Columbus he talked freely with members of his party and with prominent men of the state and of the county as to the best means of accomplishing not alone these several things but anything for the promotion of the interests of the state and the people. Word of Mr. Monroe's ability had preceded him to Columbus and he was placed on the standing committees on common schools, the penitentiary, and the revision of bills. His position as chairman of the committee on common schools gave him power to do what he had in mind with reference to the protection of the law then on the statute books promoting the common school system. This had been passed by a Democratic legislature, but a man of Mr. Monroe's type very properly took the view that the interests of the state were served by the maintenance of good legislation from whatever political source.

A reading of Mr. Monroe's Thursday lecture entitled "My First Legislative Experience," published the year prior to his death, is a liberal education in wise and successful politics. Mr. Monroe points out that half the Republicans of the house were conservative and leaned a little toward the Democratic side in matters touching abolition. They lacked what Oberlin regarded as anti-slavery *principles*. These men looked askance at the proposal of a personal liberty bill and asked what it was like and whether or not it was abolitionism. They were concerned as to the attitude of their constituents and as to the possibility that such measure might divide the newly formed Republican party. Mr. Monroe states that he reasoned with these brethren, comforted them as well as he could, and bided his time about the introduction of the bill. At the same time he discussed the situation with Governor Chase, who had endorsed his plan of avoiding trouble by moving slowly. Mr. Chase promised his influence in support of the measure. About this time occurred a tragedy at Cincinnati, which involved the slaying by a colored mother of her young daughter to prevent the return of the child to slavery. Both had been captured under the Fugitive Slave Act and the incident stirred up feeling against that law throughout Ohio. Ex-President Hayes tells of a former pro-slavery neighbor in the city of Cincinnati who said after the event: "Mr. Hayes, hereafter I am with you. From this time forward, I will not only be a Black Republican, but I will be a *damned abolitionist*." Governor Chase called on Mr. Monroe following this incident and urged that action be had on his proposed bill to insure through state authority the enforcement of the writ of *habeas corpus* in the case of persons held under the Fugitive Slave Act. Mr. Monroe assured the Governor he was ready to proceed when the time seemed ripe, as it then was, and the two agreed that the measure should be introduced. The bill was accordingly drafted and passed both branches of the legislature. Its salient provision was that the writ should be directed to the sheriff of the county who should take the person detained out of the custody of the officer detaining him and bring him before the judge issuing the writ. This took the issue from federal courts into the courts of the state. That this measure passed was very largely due to the wise work of Mr. Monroe.

In his fathering of the bill for the care of juvenile delinquents in reformatories separate and apart from the penitentary Mr. Monroe conferred a great benefit on society. At the time of its passage many young criminals were at large or were pursuing careers of crime from homes unfitted for their correction. In many instances juvenile delinquents were confined in the jail with hardened criminals, and in the year when this bill was passed there were more than two score boys ranging from twelve to seventeen confined in the 'Ohio penitentiary. As the result of Mr. Monroe's measure the reformatory at Lancaster was established. Since that time the idea has been expanded through a girl's reformatory and a reformatory for women at Marysville. While promoting to successful issue these two constructive measures, Mr. Monroe rendered valuable service by preventing all efforts to emasculate the then excellent law in force for the expansion of the common school system. All these destructive proposals he was able to kill through his position as chairman of the committee on common schools. While he was conspicuous as the first man to make a speech in the Ohio Legislature in behalf of an amendment to strike the word "white" from the Ohio Constitution, he found that the time was not sufficiently far advanced to insure its passage. He admits he was moved by the appeal of members of his party who feared that a record vote on such a proposal would have a tendency to split the party and drive conservatives from its ranks. In relating the incident Mr. Monroe said that the arguments did not appeal to him as altogether satisfactory. He goes on to say in commenting on the incident: "In a free country there seems to be only this alternative: you may have a party sound to the last man upon the desired reform but so few in numbers that it is difficult to pick them out of the election returns, or, you may have a party strong enough to control the state or even the nation, but prone, as regards advanced thought, to hesitate, to compromise, to defer. On reflection, whether wisely or unwisely, I decided not to demand the final vote. When I reached home I was severely criticised, both for the amendment in itself as being narrow and illiberal, and also for the manner in which I had dropped it."

In his second lecture on "My First Legislative Experience," delivered in 1892, Mr. Monroe sets forth in detail his reasons for uniting with the Republican party at the time of its organization. After some discussion of the Convention of 1848, which preceded the organization of the Republican party by several years, he says:

"The disapproval with which many Liberty men regarded the party of 1848 was extended, though in somewhat modified form, to the Free Democracy of 1852 and the Republicans of 1856. Even at a later period, some of them made bitter attacks upon the administration of Abraham Lincoln. They regarded the new party as having been, from the beginning, one of compromise for the sake of power, rather than one of principles.

"I may say that when the Free-Soil party was formed in 1848, my sympathies were with the earnest abolitionists who refused to join it. I liked neither the candidate nor the platform. I thought those Liberty men were right who said that the Free-Soil party was not the one to which they had belonged. It did not meet my ideal of the party which the Democrats demanded. I knew there were thousands of honest anti-slavery men in it, but they had been misled. I did not vote for Van Buren and Adams. I kept aloof from the new party for some time. During this interval, with my friend Professor Hudson, I voted for such men as we believed to be reliable, without any thought of influencing their election. Each successive year the men who voted as we did became fewer and fewer. I might have continued voting in the line of succession to Gerrit Smith and William Goodell until this time, had it not come clear to me one day, as I was thinking it over, that, in a country where suffrage is universal, you cannot carry a great national reform without votes. Most of the anti-slavery voters had gone into the Republican party. Many of them found the standards of opinion lower than they desired, but they were constantly striving, and with a good degree of success, to elevate them. I finally decided that my place was with these men. If the new party were not moving as fast as I could wish, they were, perhaps, moving as fast as public opinion would sustain. If they were not trying to carry out all the truth which I deemed important, they were trying to carry out some of it, and what they were trying to do it seemed probable they would soon have strength enough to accomplish. I became willing that anti-slavery principles should be brought forward one at a time, if, by so doing, a party could be secured strong enough to give to each successive principle a triumph. I was content to accept, first, the doctrine of no more slave territory—next the abolition of slavery throughout all the national domain—next the partial abolition of slavery in the states—next its total abolition everywhere, and finally the Thirteenth, Fourteenth, and Fifteenth Amendments —'first the blade, then the ear and then the full corn in the ear.' Hungry men might wish that the full corn in the ear should be produced at once, but the constitution of nature is otherwise. It seemed a pity not to be able to do all the desired good things, but there was compensation for the delay in the increased numerical strength which the delay secured. I came to the conclusion that, in the present condition of the world, it would not be practicable to organize a party with voters enough to accomplish anything, whose average moral tone would not be below the just standard. Hence I voted for Hale and Julian in 1852 and thence forward acted with the Republican Party."

This careful setting forth by Mr. Monroe of his reasons for going along politically with the Republican party is interesting not alone from the standpoint of history, but is equally interesting as emphasizing the sound common sense with which in his public career he reënforced a finished education and a mental endowment much beyond the ordinary. The statement is reminiscent of a remark of Theodore Roosevelt that in seeking through public action the success of his own principles he always found it wise to work with whatever tools were at hand. The careful consideration by Mr. Monroe of the ends desired by opponents of slavery recalls Lincoln's thoughtful endorsement of the Republican party which came two years after it had first placed candidates in the field.

The service of Mr. Monroe as Senator from 1860 to 1862 was marked by the same high conception of public duty and by the sound approval of his constituents.

The part which Mr. Monroe had had in the forming of the Republican party in Ohio and the support which he had steadily given to its principles, together with his admitted fitness for the office, gained for him, in 1863, the position of United States Consul at Rio de Janeiro, Brazil. Here again his conduct was marked by tact, wisdom, and devotion to duty, for which he was warmly praised by Secretary of State William H. Seward. Soon after his return from Rio a friend of Mr. Monroe overheard a conversation between two strangers on a railroad train. Both were apparently business men of wide experience. One said to the other: "We had lately at Rio a consul, Mr. Monroe, who was a thorough gentleman and statesman, just and upright, and sparing neither labor nor pains to be of use to his country's residents abroad." For a time while at Rio Mr. Monroe served as *charge d' affaires* in the absence of the United States minister.

After seven years at Rio, Mr. Monroe returned to Oberlin, influenced, in part at least, by assurance of a strong movement among Republicans of the district for his election to Congress. He was nominated, elected, and served with distinction in the National House of Representatives for five successive terms, from 1871 to 1881. At the end of his fifth term he announced that he did not care to return to Congress. In 1883 the chair of Political Science and Modern History in Oberlin College was endowed by his friends, and he returned to teaching. Here he spent thirteen years of his long and active life, retiring in 1896. The following year he published his volume of lectures and addresses. On July 6, 1898, after an illness of a few days, Mr. Monroe passed from life at the advanced age of seventy-seven.

In 1847 Mr. Monroe married Elizabeth Maxwell of Mansfield, Ohio, who preceded him in death. In 1865 he married Miss Julia R. Finney, daughter of President Charles Grandison Finney, who died February 8, 1930. Mrs. C. N. Fitch of Staten Island, N. Y., is a daughter.

In his five terms of service in the Congress of the United States, covering the ten-year period from 1871 to 1881, Mr. Monroe was brought into contact with the leading men in public life in America in those days. He knew Blaine and was present when the "Plumed Knight" delivered his dramatic challenge to Proctor Knott and produced in the House the Mulligan letters. He knew also Frye, John A. Bingham, James A. Garfield, William McKinley, and Charles Sumner. He had listened to the eloquence of Tom Reed and Hale of Maine, Roscoe Conkling, George F. Hoar, Ohio's "Sunset" Cox, and scores of others who figured in the public eye in that decade. In one of his most interesting lectures, delivered to students of Oberlin College after his retirement from public life, Mr. Monroe discussed leading speakers in Congress in the period of his service in that body.

The concluding paragraph of this lecture contained a thought which in no small degree influenced the life of Mr. Monroe from the time when in early manhood he espoused the cause of the slave from the lecture platform until the close of his public career. In bringing to a conclusion his discussion of public men, Mr. Monroe said:

"The young people of my audience are now, perhaps, disposed to ask what is the practical relation of this discussion to their own attainments and future work? What does it mean for you? You will say that the men of whom I have spoken had special gifts, such extraordinary powers in certain directions as you cannot hope to emulate; and you inquire whether they had not some qualities in common—in common with each other, and with all useful public speakers—which you might hope to reach. I reply that they had such qualities—qualities which were the common soil out of which grew all of their gifts, and which must sustain the power of eloquence wherever it is possessed. Of two of these qualities I will speak.

"In the first place, I notice in all the distinguished men whose names I have introduced a certain *scholarly* quality. By this I do not mean that they had mastered the amount of Latin and Greek usually prescribed in a college curriculum; though, as a matter of fact, they had generally done this. I do not mean that they had acquired more or less of science or philosophy or modern languages; though, doubtless most of them had studied these branches of liberal culture. I do not mean that they were graduates from college, though it so happens that about three-fifths of them were. But what I do mean, more than any other one thing, when I say that these men, almost without exception, had a certain scholarly habit of mind, is that they were men who could not bear to think or speak in a confused or slovenly manner. Their thought must be clear and they must give it clear expression. They must know what they wished to say and say only that. They could take no satisfaction in obscure or clumsy purpose. When I listened to the best thoughts of some of the best of these men, it seemed to lie in their minds like a diamond in the bottom of a spring, so clear was it in itself, and so clearly revealed. This scholarly quality is the fruit of much close and systematic thinking, of much weighing of thought and expression, of much self-discipline, of many modified discoveries of self-deficiencies, of much collision with other minds, whether in books, in society, or at school—collision which imparts polish, and sometimes strikes fire. This scholarly quality is within the reach of you all.

"Another quality which I noticed in nearly all of these men was *earnestness* of character. They may not have been professors of religion, though I think most of them were. They were, at least, in earnest. They were no triflers. Life and its responsibilities and its rapidly approaching close were not to them a jest. There was unlimited work to be done, and but little time to do it. Ennui and indifference had no place in their souls. They found the world interesting. Its burdens, its progress, its memories, its destinies, its fears, its hopes—all claimed their sympathy. Their hearts swelled and sometimes their eyes filled when they discussed the welfare of a great empire which they and their hearers might do something to promote. There was some principle, some doctrine, some policy, some cause which they loved better than life, and they made you feel it. They belonged to a generation that had momentous and terrible issues to meet. Some of them had exposed their lives for their country upon the battlefield. Some of them had had a share in the breaking of the chains of the slave . . . Even those of them who had been on the wrong side of the great issues had been terribly in earnest. Earnestness was the common quality of these men, and it showed itself not only in action, but in living thought expressed in words that burned.

"This quality also may be yours. Earnestness is a quality of character, and character, even the highest, is, with God's help, of your own forming. The great issues are not all dead. New ones constantly arise. The groan of burdened humanity is still heard. Sin and oppression still make their desperate fight. The voice of God still calls . . . Never was there a time when an earnest heart, a clear thought and a word that fits it, could do better work in the world than they could do now."

In a quarter of a century devoted to public life Mr. Monroe made appeal to men in all classes of society. His constituents respected him for his loyalty to principles; his associates in the Legislature and in Congress admired him for his trained intelligence, his consideration, and the spirit which moved him to fight fearlessly for a cause without attacking an antagonist. His friends here in Oberlin Community and College loved him as a kindly, courteous neighbor, interested in the welfare of both village and college and anxious to aid in carrying forward any movement for their growth and betterment. This unselfish disposition was strongly manifested in the fruitless trip made by Mr.

The Story of a Century

Monroe at a time of grave danger to himself in an effort to bring back, at the heart-broken request of a poor black mother, the body of John Copeland, one of the Negro youths executed with John Brown after the raid at Harper's Ferry.

On the summer afternoon of the funeral of Mr. Monroe the American flag, which he had served in life with fervent zeal, was displayed at half mast on the campus. Business was suspended in the village where he had been an honored resident for more than half a century and fitting tribute was paid in First Church to the earthly memory of a good man.

JUDGE JOHN W. STEELE

CHAPTER XV

IN one hundred years of history Oberlin has had the good fortune to shelter or produce many men of ability and admitted distinction. In that century of the life of the village the public good has been advanced by unselfish citizens, both scholars and men of humbler walks of life. It has been the rule in the administration of public affairs that the elected or appointed servants of the village have rendered uniformly unselfish and reasonably intelligent service. If the roll were called of all citizens who have contributed in notable degree to the public welfare and to community progress, there might be some dispute as to who was second or third. It is probably true of no other community of corresponding size that there would be no confusion in the mind of anyone as to who came first. The vote of the humble citizens, whose interests he guarded, of the men of fixed place and ability who worked with him, and the voice of all those who followed his career would fix the choice on John W. Steele.

There is a disposition on the part of many who speak of individual greatness to set forth at length and in detail the offices and titles held by those who in their judgment tower above the common mass. Measured in such fashion it would be difficult to justify the place which John W. Steele holds in the memory and affection of the people of Oberlin more than a quarter of a century after his death. He was Judge Steele to most of those who knew him, and occasionally Colonel Steele. The first title was earned by good service in the Probate Court in the prime of his manhood. The second title was honorably won in the cause of his country in the Civil War. This does not clearly tell the story, since others have given honest and faithful service on the bench and many thousands of his comrades in blue were fearless and faithful on the field of battle. Colonel Steele was for twelve years postmaster of Oberlin, and here again he served with intelligence and fidelity. But Oberlin in her first century of history has had several postmasters with a clear conception of public duty, who cared for the office faithfully and well. While the titles of Colonel and Judge and of Postmaster all indicate selection for special duty in the field of active life and are thus a part of the career of Judge Steele, they do not explain the man. They are only incidental to an understanding of the work which he did, not alone for Oberlin, but for a much wider area in the course of his life. To say that his name was synonymous with good citizenship, with devotion to the public welfare, and with passionate love of justice is to paint a picture which leaves out of consideration his gift of friendship. While his comrades of the war days honored him as the ideal soldier, in his later years he was warmly loved by the little orphans of the Children's Home, who properly took no heed of titles or public honors, but showered their marks of innocent and unquestioning affection upon the man they knew.

A friend of Judge Steele said with quiet emphasis: "He was a great man; too great a man to have been confined through his life to a small village. He could have made notable contributions to state and national life." There are many who knew Judge Steele who will endorse this statement. A constant battle with ill-health from the time of his discharge from the army at the close of the war, almost without interruption to the day of his death, went far to fix his residence here and to confine his activities to Oberlin. That fate or providence made this choice necessary was fortunate for the people of Oberlin not only in his day, but for Oberlin people of the present.

Inheritance played a part in the well-rounded character of Judge Steele. He was a son of Dr. Alexander Steele, a pioneer resident of Oberlin and the first practicing physician in the community. He was born at Middleburg, Ohio, a suburb of Akron, December 21, 1835. Dr. and Mrs. Steele were on their way to Oberlin from New York to make their home when their son was born. Three months after his birth they established their residence here where Dr. Steele practiced his profession to the time of his death in 1872. The son attended the public schools in Oberlin in early life and was enrolled in the preparatory department

Oberlin Colony

and Oberlin College from 1851 to 1858. Tradition has it that he was suspended in the latter year for participation in some sort of initiation into a secret organization not identified with college work. There were no fraternities in the modern sense at that time and little is definitely known as to the circumstances. It is said that a coffin figured in the initiation and gave some foundation for the suspension. Following this incident young Steele went to Ann Arbor, Michigan, for the study of law. While there he made his home with an aunt. He was later admitted to the bar at Cleveland, Ohio.

The outbreak of the Civil War came soon after Judge Steele was graduated from the Law School at Ann Arbor, Michigan. It was about August 1, 1861, when Judge Steele and Captain Alonzo H. Pease agreed to make an effort to raise a company for the Forty-first Regiment of Ohio Volunteers, then in process of forming at Jefferson, Ashtabula County. Captain Pease, who was a son of Hiram A. Pease, Oberlin pioneer, had acquired a small knowledge of military affairs in the Ohio Militia in which he had served as captain of a company. The suggestion for the organization of the volunteer company came from Captain Pease, who felt sure that he and Steele together could raise the needed number of men in and around Oberlin. Judge Steele was eager for service and promptly accepted the offer. The work of enlistment began about the middle of August. The two secured enlistment rolls and without further authority began their work. Several from Oberlin and points nearby signed these rolls before Captain Pease and Judge Steele found that this method was at least informal and decided to suspend the work. Proper authority was granted to them September 4 and the effort to form the company was pushed in Lorain and adjoining counties. Meetings were held at Pittsfield, Huntington, Camden, and Wakeman. James Monroe and Henry E. Peck, of the faculty of Oberlin College, made talks at these meetings and gave aid in the work of recruiting.

Within ten days from the time of receiving authority to form the company Pease and Steele had an enlistment of fifty-two men. These reported to Oberlin on Monday, September 16, 1861. The people of the town gave them a fine reception. Dinner was served at the Palmer House. Patriotic addresses were made by citizens and on the afternoon of September 16 the company formed at the public square and marched to the depot, amid the cheers of citizens who gathered to see them leave.

The company reported to Camp Wood, Cleveland, where they joined the regiment then under command of Colonel William B. Hazen. Early in November, 1861, the regiment, badly armed with useless muskets furnished by the state, was taken to Camp Dennison, near Cincinnati, where it received further training and more adequate equipment. The Oberlin company was mustered into the United States service October 29, 1861, with Alonzo H. Pease, Captain; John W. Steele, First Lieutenant; and Albert McRoberts, Second Lieutenant. Recruits to the number of thirty had been added after the arrival of the company in camp.

Judge Steele says in a formal history of the company published in 1897: "Probably not far from seventy-five percent of the enlisted men were farmers, fifteen percent mechanics, and the remaining were of various other pursuits. They were mostly descendents of New England stock, who settled the Western Reserve. They were fairly well educated, industrious, honest, and thrifty. Most of them enlisted from a patriotic sense of duty. Many of them were connected with Protestant denominational churches and were zealous in their religious beliefs. Soon after their enlistment they organized weekly religious services and kept this organization up through their term of enlistment. As a characteristic of the company: Soon after entering Camp Wood the majority of Company H members drew up a written remonstrance against profanity among the officers of the regiment. This remonstrance was written in moderate language and rather in the tone of a petition than a complaint. A committee was appointed who presented the remonstrance to the Colonel. They were told that such action was subversive of military discipline and were not a little surprised at the spirit in which the petition was received; they, however, ventured the remark that profanity was not only in violation of the commandment, but also a violation of the United States regulations for the army.

"From a letter just received from Captain Horatio P. Kile, who commanded the company twenty months, I clip the following: 'The men of Company H were as a whole as grand, noble, and brave a lot of men as could be mustered into a company organized in a community; therefore, to its survivors, descendants, and friends is due a recognition of their worth and work.'"

Captain Pease, who was forty at enlistment, resigned his commission at Camp Wickliffe, Kentucky, January 9, 1862. Judge Steele was promoted to Captain February 3, 1862, and assigned to Company E of the Forty-first.

After a brief service with his regiment in the field Captain Steele's peculiar fitness for staff duty, because of his keen mind and legal training, was recognized, and he was appointed on the staff of General John M. Palmer, where he served as Judge Advocate and as an officer in the corps of engineers. After preliminary service in this capacity he was promoted to the rank of Major and assigned as an aide-de-camp on the staff of General D. S. Stanley, commander of the Fourth Army corps. His military service was marked by high intelligence and coolness in time of stress. He participated in numerous battles, including the major engagements of Shiloh, Stone River, Chickamauga, Franklin, and the Atlanta Campaign. It was while serving as aid-de-camp that Major Steele won the Congressional Medal of Honor. The war department records say: "During a night attack of the enemy at Spring Hill, Tennessee, on November 29, 1864, upon the wagon and ammunition train of Major Steele's Corps, he gathered up a force of stragglers and others, assumed command of it, though himself a staff officer, and attacked and dispersed the enemy's forces, thus saving the train." His final service was in Texas in opposition to Kirby Smith, after the backbone of the rebellion had been broken. He was mustered out of service March 27, 1866, with rank of Lieutenant-Colonel.

The Story of a Century

The Forty-first Ohio is listed as one of the three hundred fighting regiments in the Civil War. In addition to a number of minor engagements it had part in the Battles of Shiloh, Stone River, Chickamauga, Orchard Knob, Mission Ridge, Resaca, Picketts Mills, Kenesaw Mountain, Atlanta, Franklin, and Nashville.

That Colonel Steele's associates in the army put a proper value on his service and ability is shown by the fact that he served as Recording Secretary of the Society of the Army of the Cumberland from the date of its organization in 1870 to the time of his death. The annual reports of this organization contain many paragraphs of quotation from talks of members which show the high esteem and affection in which Colonel Steele was held by his army comrades.

Of many stories growing out of Colonel Steele's war service two may be told as shedding some light on his wit, his sense of justice, and his coolness in battle. It was of record that he had not had the friendliest of relations with a certain general officer in the army with whom he had been associated. After the close of the war court martial proceedings were instituted against this General. Colonel Steele carefully avoided the summons sent out for him to testify in the case, saying that it was generally known that he and the General were not friendly, and, that since he could say nothing good for the officer on his trial, he feared that anything he might say against him would be construed as willingness to take an opportunity to even up old scores. When in later years the General's widow remarried and became subject to certain public criticism growing out of her relations with her second husband, a man of national fame, Colonel Steele remarked dryly, with the famous twinkle in his eye, that he must decline to join the hue and cry against the lady, since frankly he had a tender spot in his heart for her because he was sure she had led her first husband "a hell of a life."

In one of the leading battles of the war when the conflict was at its height and men were falling right and left, Colonel Steele, who was then serving as a staff officer with the rank of Major and carrying the usual leather order book, was observed to fall. One of his comrades hurried to his side, and, picking him up, anxiously asked him: "Where are you hit, Major?" Major Steele replied, "In my euchre deck." The dispatch book with a bullet hole in it is still in the possession of members of Judge Steele's family, but the euchre deck has gone.

But all the misfortunes of war could not be met with jest, even by a man of Colonel Steele's strong character. In a later battle near the close of the war he was struck in the chest by a shell and one of his lungs was almost destroyed. It was while he was serving as Judge Advocate in Texas that tubercular activity started in his remaining lung and his Negro servant brought him to his home in Oberlin. His father's knowledge of medicine, coupled with his own good constitution, brought about his recovery to such a point that in 1866 he became a candidate for the nomination of Probate Judge of Lorain County to which position he was elected, beginning his service in December, 1867. In his first contest for political office Judge Steele manifested his strength with his constituents and his fellow citizens of Oberlin and the county by finishing as winner in a field of four contestants. Seven ballots were taken in the convention. On the first ballot Judge Steele had only seventeen votes as compared with thirty-eight for his highest competitor. On the final ballot he was nominated with a vote of sixty-eight to forty-one for his only remaining opponent.

The Court of Probate sixty years ago, as is the case today, was the court of record having closest relations to the people of the county. Judge Steele brought to this work a sympathetic disposition, a thorough knowledge of law, and a desire to be helpful to men and women. These attributes were reënforced and rounded out by an unusual measure of the saving grace of common sense, and all combined to make his service on the bench of definite value to the county. This result came about in no small degree because this was the sole end that Judge Steele sought. While he had no difficulty in securing a second nomination and election, his public conduct was never modified nor his judgment clouded by any desire to serve selfish aims. His second election in 1870 was followed by his resignation the following year on account of impaired health. He had been advised by his father that he would have to give up any career which would keep him indoors.

On his election as Probate Judge, Colonel Steele was united in marriage to Miss Ella Frances Clarke and in his family life, covering a period of almost forty years, he found his greatest happiness. Of three daughters and one son born of this marriage, two daughters survive. They are Mrs. Burt D. Whedon and Miss Eloise Steele, both of whom live in New York. For a time after their marriage Judge and Mrs. Steele made their home on North Main Street.

Following close upon his resignation as Probate Judge and in furtherance of the advice of his father that he seek to regain his health by work in the open, Colonel Steele joined his brother-in-law, Frederick Norton Finney, in the work of building the Canadian Southern Railroad. He moved with his family to Ontario where he made his headquarters while this work was in progress. Three years later he went to South America where he was employed in a survey of a railroad route down the Magdaline River. Senator Dorsey, well known in Oberlin and prominent in national politics then and later, was at the head of the project. Colonel Steele spent about eighteen months on this task without financial profit, since the firm conducting the work was forced into bankruptcy. This activity was followed by his appointment by the United States Government as an inspector of mail routes in the West. These were established largely in unbroken country and the mails were mainly transported on horseback. This service led to his appointment as an investigator in the Star Route scandals. In this period he was in close contact with various Indian uprisings, notably the White River Massacre. He returned with his family to Oberlin in 1882, occupying as his home what is now (1933) the Townsley residence on East College Street, but for several years the property of Professor Clarke, father of Mrs. Steele, by whom it was inherited at her father's death.

Oberlin Colony

Soon after his return to 'Oberlin, Judge Steele quietly began a campaign for supplying the village with an adequate water service and with modern protection from fire. As a result of suggestions made by him in a communication to the Oberlin News, a public meeting was called and endorsement was given of his general plan for this important improvement. He gave without stint of his time and his engineering knowledge to a thorough investigation of conditions. Several proposals were considered before the final adoption of the plan for securing a water supply from the east branch of the Vermilion River. The selection of this source of supply and the discovery of its complete fitness for a water service for Oberlin were both made by Judge Steele in company with another engineer. This final choice came at the end of a long and careful personal inspection by Judge Steele of all apparently promising sources. It was in 1887 that the major section of the work was completed. Judge Steele walked many miles over the territory in and around Oberlin in his earnest effort to determine the best procedure from the standpoint of public economy and efficiency. The water works system stands as a monument to his rare interest in Oberlin and its welfare. He was ably seconded in this work by his close friend, Attorney William B. Bedortha, and by Professor Albert A. Wright, and W. B. Gerrish, the city engineer, who contributed much of value to the project. Not content with this achievement Judge Steele followed it with a campaign for a modern plant for the disposal of sewage. This came in time largely as a result of his efforts. These two improvements contributed immeasurably to the healthful condition of the village, which has been maintained since that time.

'On his return from service in the army Colonel Steele gave evidence of those qualities of public leadership which marked his career. In his service as Probate Judge he had extended his acquaintance and made many warm friends. In his work for modern improvements in Oberlin he added to his list of friends and strengthened greatly his hold upon the public confidence and the public affection. The bond was all the stronger because of the fact that in this work, as in the discharge of his judicial duties, Judge Steele was looking only to the public welfare. He found too much joy in friendship to stultify the relationship with any selfish appeal. His selection for postmaster at Oberlin in 1889 was a result of his admitted leadership in his party and in his community. He was always a stout Republican, basing his party adherence on belief in the party's principles and in intelligent understanding of its purposes. His employment as postmaster, in a day when the duties of the office were lighter than they are now, gave him time for outside activities which not only benefited his health but added to the pleasure and the satisfaction of his friends. Service of five years as postmaster from April 23, 1889, to January 9, 1894, was interrupted by the appointment of Flavius A. Hart, a Democrat, who served from January, 1894, to January, 1898. Judge Steele was again appointed to office on this latter date and served until his death. His appointment and re-appointment to this office meant recognition both of party service and of unquestioned fitness for the place. For almost a quarter of a century Judge Steele was the recognized leader in the community and a recognized leader of his party in the county and state. On at least one occasion he was called to Washington for a conference with President McKinley.

On the occasion of Judge Steele's retirement at the end of his first term as postmaster in January, 1894, the Oberlin News has this to say of his public service:

> Colonel John W. Steele has filled the position of postmaster of Oberlin for more than four years, and during his administration—in his first year—for the first time in the history of the village, its postoffice was deemed worthy of the privileges of the free delivery system and its organization was laid upon him. It has since continued to be a free delivery office, with an increase of one in the list of carriers. The business of the office has maintained a steady growth, and to provide for this enlargement and for the better accommodation of the public, he has made such additions to his clerical force and added such improvements in the office appointments as will serve this purpose—so that his successor will step into the traces finding everything well appointed and well equipped for smooth progress from the outset of his official career. The administration

of the affairs of the office during Colonel Steele's incumbency has been efficient and, in an eminent degree, satisfactory to the large number of people who patronize it, and in the passing of the duty of the place to another, the citizens of Oberlin and vicinity will lose a faithful and accommodating servant, and the post office department a trustworthy and able official.

Colonel Steele has not only performed faithfully and well the routine duties of his charge as postmaster of our village, but he has rendered this community signal service in many other directions. To him, in very large measure, is due the existence of the excellent water works system of the village. Through his efforts and personal appeals, the voters of the village were brought to see the great need of public provision for an adequate supply of water for all purposes, and the feasibility of the plans he proposed for procuring it. After it had been decided to bond the town to make this improvement, his good judgment, his large acquaintance with and devoted attention to the many details of the whole project, including the preparation and marketing of the bonds, and particularly his intelligent, painstaking care in deciding upon the source of the water supply, were of very great value to the community. These services were given without price, as was also his service on the Board of Trustees after the system had been established and put into successful operation.

In the construction of our public school system, now nearly complete, his aid was nearly as complete and valuable as that given in the water works and as in the former case was also without cost to the community.

This much we have said of Colonel Steele's interest in the welfare of the town and the part which he has taken in promoting it, not in disparagement of the service of other citizens in these and other public improvements, but because the opportunity seemed to be present when the News might, with perfect propriety, speak of the worth and service of a citizen who, having done much, is little given to exploiting his own deeds.

In a tribute to Judge Steele on the occasion of his funeral Azariah S. Root says of his public career: "It must be said of Judge Steele that he was in the true sense of the word a politician. He loved the game with all his heart; his service in war, railroad construction, as Probate Judge, and as postmaster had given him an opportunity to size up and understand human nature and the motives by which human nature is influenced, so that he was a past master of the art of influencing and controlling his fellow citizens, and yet in all these twenty years no one has ever dreamed of connecting with the name of Judge Steele the suggestion of anything except the most honorable conduct. He was not a politician for graft, or for selfish advancement, but because he loved the game, and because he was by instinct and by trait a natural leader of men. Those who know more intimately the game of politics than do most of us, are, I think, the ones who will bear the most sympathetic testimony to the truth of this statement. In all our local affairs the chief concern of the Judge was to find a good man and persuade him to become a candidate, and having persuaded him to run, he did all he could to nominate and elect him and to make his administration a success."

These words of Mr. Root come close to making a perfect definition of a good citizen. However, to this fine tribute may be added the statement that an interest in humanity, a helpful feeling, an outstanding unselfishness, gave to Judge Steele a following more or less unique in the history of the county and the state. Frequent trips by horse and buggy over Lorain County made by Judge Steele from time to time had as their basis a genuine interest in the well-being of the people he went to see. It was not a conscious building of a political following. It was the sincere cultivation of the feeling of friendship, and the political following came as a result. Rambles in the woods with close friends or with young men in whom the Judge saw promise of useful living bore fruit in added prestige for Judge Steele, but no one would contend that these rambles and these frequent visits had such an end in mind. They were often the occasion for a friendly word of advice, always given with the good taste which marks the fine gentleman. It is related that while Colonel Steele could not lay claim to a broad knowledge of woodcraft, plants, and trees, he had for this branch of nature, as he had for varying problems of life, an inquiring mind. Frequently in such walks through the woods he would ask of his companion as to a certain plant. When his friend could not identify it, it was Judge Steele's habit to take a few leaves and, at his leisure, find out about it. A few days later he would surprise his friend with a statement describing the plant in detail. This habit of careful inquiry seems to have covered his life, contributing to a well-rounded practical education.

Oberlin Colony

One of the factors making for the greatness of Judge Steele and for his ability to render conspicuous public service was his earnestness in any task which he undertook, his ability not only to find the facts but to arrange them, and his steady interest in life which had its basis in a keen power of understanding and analysis. This side of his well-rounded character is shown in an incident which occurred in March, 1894, at the Wellington Fair.

There was staged by the fair management an unusual program labeled "An open lesson in heredity." Committees consisting of three prominent physicians, representing Cleveland, and Judge Steele and Professors G. Frederick Wright and F. F. Jewett of Oberlin College, representing Oberlin, were invited to be present and to engage in this unique contest. The test was to ascertain how much the family resemblances between parents and children would enable an observer to judge of their relations. Four well-known families of Wellington, each consisting of father, mother, and three children, were sitting promiscuously upon the stage, and each one plainly numbered. Then each member of the two committees, without consultation, undertook to group the families correctly by numbers. The families were then presented to the audience as arranged by the committee and then finally arranged correctly. Each judge was allowed fifteen minutes for the inspection of the members of families, with the privilege of having each walk a few steps and count ten. According to the printed rules, each committeeman was credited three points for each classification of husband and wife; ten points for each assignment for son or daughter to both parents correctly; one point for each assignment of son or daughter to one parent only. It required thirty-six points for a perfect arrangement. The following was the score: Dr. H. F. Biggar, 6; Dr. T. P. Wilson, 2; Dr. W. B. Hinsdale, 9; total for the Cleveland team, 17. Professor G. F. Wright, 2; Professor F. F. Jewett, 2; Colonel J. W. Steele, 26; total for the Oberlin team, 30.

When the proposal was first made that the county build a home for the care of orphaned children Judge Steele doubted the wisdom of such action, basing his objections on the fear that parents might be led to avoid their responsibilities to their children in the knowledge that the county would care for them. When he became convinced of the merit of the suggestion—and, while firm in his views, his mind was open to conviction—Judge Steele lent his great strength to the movement and very largely through his influence the home was built at the edge of Oberlin. He served for several years as a trustee. It was his habit after the completion of the home to visit it each morning before going to his office work. Friends tell of the joy of the children on these occasions and of their depth of affection for Judge Steele. His final visit to the home was made a short time before his death. He had much to do with the landscaping at the institution and took proper pride in its beautiful appearance.

A few weeks prior to his death Colonel Steele called upon Professor W. G. Caskey, living in the house adjoining the Steele home on the east. Mr. Caskey was working in his yard at the time. Judge Steele said to him quietly that he knew he had but a short time to live and would like to talk with him awhile. With his customary courtesy and thoughtfulness, he suggested to Mr. Caskey that if he had a chair he could accompany Mr. Caskey about his lawn and they could talk as Mr. Caskey continued his work. The plan was followed. Judge Steele talked quietly of conditions in Oberlin and urged Mr. Caskey that if the time came when he could render service in the village he would do so. This promise Mr. Caskey kept in later years and was for several terms a valuable member of the Village Council. Judge Steele further said that J. N. Stone, who then, as now, was active in Republican politics, was the logical man to succeed him as postmaster. It is significant of the influence of Colonel Steele that only a few weeks after his death Mr. Stone was appointed to the position, despite the fact that several other candidates were in the field. At the end of the discussion Colonel Steele invited Mr. Caskey to go across the lawn to his own home next door. Judge Steele called to a young man who was working about the place, explaining casually to Mr. Caskey that he had given the man work because he seemed to have been side-tracked in his effort to become a minister and was out of employment. By direction of Judge Steele the young fellow brought a small elm tree to an indicated spot and, when placed, the Judge and Mr. Caskey planted it. The two then returned to the Caskey home and the Judge accompanied Mr. Caskey to the front door of the house. Standing there, where the tree was in plain sight, Judge Steele said to Mr. Caskey: "Now I think you understand. In years to come, when I am gone and forgotten, you can stand here and see this tree and keep in mind your promise to me." The tree still stands and the promise was kept.

At a mass meeting of Oberlin citizens held in the college chapel Saturday evening, April 4, 1891, Judge Steele was one of the chief speakers on the selected topic "How to make Oberlin a model home." He had reduced his remarks to writing and it is in keeping with his character that there was no attempt at oratory and no appeal to anything but common sense. After showing the small but steady increase in population and the growth in tax values for the preceding ten years, Judge Steele said:

> We have had a steady, healthy growth in both population and wealth, and have fair assurance that this growth will continue if we do our duty as citizens. We are a community of 4300 people with a marked peculiarity. I think of no village of its size made up as we are; a village in which so many are engaged in what are called the higher pursuits—professors, teachers, clergymen, and students—from waxing professors to waning theologians. A larger proportion than most villages. It is unjust to say that we are nearer to the other extreme than most villages. We are an incongruous lot of people.
>
> This $2,000,000 worth of houses, lots, chattels, and cash and these 4,000 people arranged and living in reasonable order make up Oberlin, as it is, a village in which we may justly take a modest degree of pride. How can we make it a model village? What is the town and what are its necessities?
>
> To the first question I answer Oberlin is almost wholly a college town. Its best interests are in the success and prosperity of the college. How many of us know or, if we know, appreciate the fact that nearly half a million dollars from this society is annually distributed among our people. This properly applied to the improvement of the college and town is of vital interest. Each succeeding year the class of students comes from homes better fitted with the conveniences and even the luxuries of life, and the luxuries of one year are only the necessities of

the succeeding years. We've got to keep moving. No psychology or theology will make a person who is accustomed to a marble lavatory, satisfied with a wash bowl on a stump. Self-inflicted torture is out of date, and the hair shirt of the monk is not as comfortable, attractive, feasible, or sensible as the silk gown of the prelate. The world moves and we have got to move with it. In fact we ought to move a little ahead of it.

Discussing the need for a new sewer system, which came a few years later largely as the result of his efforts, Judge Steele said, in answer to the contention of some of the citizens that the village could not afford this modern improvement, that one serious outbreak of typhoid fever would cost more in dollars and cents than would a sewer system. Continuing his discussion of needed public improvements Colonel Steele said:

We should have established grades for our streets, so that a citizen may lay sidewalks and place curbing with a reasonable degree of certainty that his walk won't be more than a foot out of line with his neighbor's walk. If a system of sewers is to be adopted, we should have the plans and specifications, showing the size, elevation, and grade of each line of sewers, so that as fast as the construction of sewers becomes necessary or desirable each new division made may be set in as part of a whole system. As nearly as I can find out we have expended $3700 on public sewers, with no assurance that we can make a foot of it fit in with any general system that may hereafter be adopted. Our cart is before the horse in the matter of sewers. I am not advocating sewers; I don't know that they are the best way of caring for this emergency. That is what we ought to know and we can only know it through careful and painstaking investigation.

Now where is the town so well supplied as this, with men capable of making this investigation? Where is the town with so many men so well fitted by education or experience for investigating public needs and suggesting the proper methods of making them, and where is the town in which it is so hard to get competent men to undertake the work?

During the past week I have solicited many persons, who in my poor judgment were especially fitted for public service, to accept a position for only one term, and found only one who accepted and who withdrew afterwards and named another. Each one was overloaded with the duties on his shoulders. Each pleaded that he had more than he could do, and each pleaded this with good cause.

Here we are: the little tot comes home with his books to get his lessons for the next day. Mr. Superintendent, his lessons ought not to be longer than he can manage at school. The student has ten pages of Greek where he ought to have five. My dear professor, you would not have to burn so much midnight oil to keep out of the way of your classes if you would give them lighter punishment in the way of lessons.

The merchant ought to close his store at six, give his clerks a chance to rest and a chance to love, cherish, and obey, according to the original contract. This is done in all cities and in most of our adjoining towns and causes no inconvenience to customers when once accustomed to rules.

In other words, we can make Oberlin a model village when we recognize our public duties as good citizens ought, when we recognize the fact that it is a duty to do our share of unpleasant but necessary work, *when we so arrange our private affairs as not to close the door against our public duties.*

I learn that last Sabbath a sermon was preached from each of our pulpits on the duty of citizens to turn out to the caucuses to see that good men were nominated to fill good offices. Yet when I went around beseeching good men to accept these offices, I found that they all thought that the sermons were pointed at some other good man.

It was a lasting mark of the greatness of the man that while Judge Steele manifested no interest in formal religion by church attendance or church membership, he held the unqualified respect of men who attached first importance to these things. In a day when in Oberlin the question of the liquor traffic was a live one, with almost the entire community ranged on the dry side, Judge Steele could earnestly support a candidate for Congress who had been labeled as a friend and possible agent of the liquor interests. He did this because of his honest conviction of the ability and sound character of the candidate, and, while the man in question was defeated for the nomination, it is a significant fact that the Oberlin territory was controlled by Judge Steele and lent its support to his candidate.

In an address at Colonel Steele's funeral President Henry Churchill King, after characterising Judge Steele as one of the most interesting and genuine characters of Oberlin, says: "Temperamentally disinclined to the conventional and merely traditional, it was a part of the native and inbred honesty of the man that he could not live a simply imitated life. We are coming to understand now what was not so clear in the days of his young manhood that we cannot require the same kind of response from widely different temperaments. The situation was not simple but bewilderingly complex for some in those days. Doubtless many elements entered into the resulting decisions, much doubtless—that with his marked modesty—he himself would not wholly approve; but as I have come into closer touch with Judge Steele in these steadily mellowing later years and rejoiced in his friendship, I have not been able to doubt, that in those earlier years, with his temperament, he found certain common roads practically closed to him, certain experiences practically impossible. And he could not merely pretend or borrow or imitate . . . Not finding the key to them in himself, he naturally reacted for the time against them, and he himself seemed to be shut up to the way of practical service. And that way he has trod, we can all bear witness, as few have trodden it."

The difficulties of which President King speaks were not such as Judge Steele would discuss with any friend, however close. He had a dignified reticence which all respected. He had a standard of ethics which few were disposed to question. It is tradition in Oberlin that when any problem of a public nature came up the first inquiry was, "What does Judge Steele think about it?" His community activities were supplemented by a wholesome interest in the welfare of his friends and neighbors. Scores today tell of this interest and of the wisdom of his counsel. It must not be thought that Judge Steele was in any respect a busybody. He had a fine dignity, a superb sense of the fitness of the occasion, and never offered friendship or advice where it was not freely welcomed. One of the leading business men of present-day Oberlin tells of a whispered reference made by Colonel Steele, as he lay on his bed of death, to an incident of years before which had a ludicrous aspect, but which was marked by the thoughtful aid of Colonel Steele who had rescued the young man from a position of threatened danger. This was one of many instances of Judge Steele's helpfulness and consideration.

In appearance Colonel Steele resembled Mark Twain, a fact which had been frequently called to his attention. He had a noble head, and eyes which reflected not alone his understanding, but his keen wit and love of fun. In temperament he was quiet, seldom, if ever, manifesting anger. As one friend put it, he could be well out of humor and show the fact that he was displeased, but he would still be courteous. He was not given to argument, but was unmatched in quiet persuasion. In politics he was a master of finesse in the best sense of the word. He never made use of a weapon which would soil his hands.

When, after the failure of the old Citizens Bank, following the operations of Cassie Chadwick, Andrew Carnegie gave a fund of $15,000 for the reïnbursement of students in the college who lost money by the failure, and of indigent persons whose losses could not be otherwise replaced, it became the duty of President King, of Oberlin College, to make selection of a person to administer this trust, he appointed Judge Steele. Mr. King said in commenting on the selection made: "I turned instinctively to Judge Steele as the ideal person for this work." This last task of a public character performed by Judge Steele had at his hands careful, intelligent, and conscientious attention. He was at that time in failing health and was forced in his activities to combat the inroads of the disease which within a few months caused his death.

It remained for President King, who had selected Judge Steele for this task, which proved the last which he was able to perform for the people of Oberlin, to set forth clearly in his tribute at Judge Steele's funeral the character of the man whose life had meant so much for Oberlin. In closing his address Mr. King said: "He was characteristically, in his beliefs, a man of deeds not of words—hiding his inner life; but his close friends learned to see that a sometimes brusque manner was the shield of a marked sensitiveness and a real tenderness that yet could not be wholly hidden. And those did not know him who had not seen in him that delicate courtesy that seems often to belong to the true soldier—a courtesy that was more than a courtliness, full of genuine human feeling, and free from all affectations and every trace of condescension. He was a rare friend and a rare public servant."

The Story of a Century

The death of Judge Steele on April 26, 1905, followed an illness of several weeks of organic heart trouble. Professor Albert A. Wright, associated with Judge Steele in the campaign for a modern water plant for Oberlin, had died on April 2 of this year and Attorney William B. Bedortha, close friend and associate of Judge Steele in law and politics, had passed away the preceding fall. First Church was filled with friends of Judge Steele on the occasion of his funeral on Saturday, April 29. Participants in the final service were Dr. Bradshaw, pastor of the church, Professor A. S. Root, President King, and Honorable E. G. Johnson.

When the story of Judge Steele's achievements has been told there is still something left, more or less defying analysis even on the part of those who knew him well. His work for the village earned for him respect and gratitude. Back of what he did was a unique character which in life won for him love and affection and which, a generation after his death, insures his place as Oberlin's first citizen. Those who knew Colonel Steele in his prime, when nothing of a public character was promoted without asking his advice, recall a figure of dignity, a countenance registering understanding and friendship and broad tolerance. Always neatly dressed, Judge Steele favored white shirt and collar and a black bow tie. When weather conditions were favorable and other business did not claim attention the Judge would hitch his bay horse to his buggy, pick up a congenial companion, and start on one of his hundreds of trips through this section of the country. These trips frequently had no particular objective, but they always had a purpose. It might be that Colonel Steele had something in the way of advice to offer to the man who accompanied him. It might be that he wished to call upon some party adherent who showed signs of straying from the fold. At times the horse would be hitched to the side of the road while the Judge and his companion rambled through the woods and fields. Many of these trips were devoted to a search for the proper water supply for 'Oberlin. Many were devoted to a tactful, quiet effort of the Judge to learn of the plans of some young man starting in his business life. Needless to say his fine manner inspired complete confidence and this confidence was rewarded with counsel and suggestions beyond value in money, for Judge Steele's interest, first and last, was in humanity. In his many and varied contributions to public service he was impelled by a sense of duty. In his contact with men the moving force was an unselfish desire to give help. Even the humblest citizens of the community sensed this feeling. It was a rare day when someone did not appeal to Judge Steele for the settlement of a dispute of some character. These submitted questions ranged all the way from the proper pronunciation of a word to the adjustment of what seemed a final break between life-long friends. When Judge Steele had rendered his opinion—and it was never rendered without careful thought— the dispute was at an end. This complete confidence, not only in his judgment but in his integrity, had its basis in a thorough understanding of the qualities which made the man.

It must not be thought that Colonel Steele was perfect in all things. It is possible that had this been true his life and character would not be the inspiration which it is to men of less endowment. He was strong in his likes and stern and unyielding in his hatred for hypocricy and double-dealing. While not habitually a user of profane language he could, on occasion, voice his views with words not made for the drawing room. But the occasion was never a trivial one and the expressions were in general used to condemn unfairness or injustice. Ill health, growing out of his army service, earned for Judge Steele a reputation in certain quarters for indolence. That this charge lacked a basis in truth is evidenced by Colonel Steele's day-by-day record in the preliminary survey and construction of the water works and the sewer system in Oberlin, as well as by his interest in other public projects. He had a type of mind which resented the tread-mill of an unvaried occupation. He liked diversion in his work and diversion in his friendships. It is of record that while his few close friends were men of the finest type, he gave association to one or two whose record was a little below this standard. It was not their weaknesses which attracted Judge Steele, but virtues concealed from those who had not looked beneath the surface.

The Story of a Century

Judge Steele lived in Oberlin at a time when those who largely controlled public opinion here regarded use of tobacco as more or less sinful. Those who did use it did so in the main under cover. Judge Steele enjoyed a cigar and used tobacco openly, without bravado, and quite likely without any thought that there was anything unusual in his quiet belief in his right to govern his own conduct, so long as such conduct did not infringe upon the rights of others. It was foreign to his nature to be other than he seemed to be, both in trivial matters such as this and in the larger matters which go to make up life. This fine spirit of unquestioned independence and manliness won for him the respect of many who could not always endorse his views.

Luther Munson, a picturesque figure in the history of Oberlin, attracted the interest of Colonel Steele, and the two frequently discussed public affairs. Munson was a Democrat and Steele was a Republican, but even in those days of partisan bias this did not affect their free understanding. Munson had a good mind, a keen wit, and was a great reader. It was known to some that Munson, at his little store, occasionally dispensed hard cider. One evening when Steele and Munson were talking together, a young man in whom Steele had shown great interest entered the store and drank a glass of what was known in those days as "hard liquor." When the young man had emptied his glass and set it down, the Judge turned to him and said: "How often do you drink this?" The young man replied that he did not know. The Judge said to him quietly that once a year was plenty often enough. This advice was salutary for the young man, and it did not offend Mr. Munson.

This homely incident is one of a countless number setting forth the kindly character of Colonel Steele. He knew instinctively to whom he could give advice with the certainty that it would be followed. His kindness of heart was controlled by a marvelous tact. These two virtues, supplemented by a gift of leadership and a deep sense of public duty, accounted for the reputation which he built in life and still account for the memory of his greatness.

THE WOMAN FAILS TO PAY

CHAPTER XVI

THE most depressing day in the financial history of Oberlin was Monday, November 28, 1904. This date marked the closing of the Citizens National Bank of Oberlin and the collapse of the Cassie Chadwick financial bubble. People of the village were stunned on the morning of this date when they read a notice posted on the bank door that the bank was closed until further notice and that its affairs were in the hands of bank examiners.

More than a quarter of a century after the Chadwick drama there was still uncertainty as to all the facts. It finally developed that President C. T. Beckwith, of the Citizens National Bank, had for a period covering almost a year prior to the bank's closing, loaned at various times large sums of money to Mrs. Cassie L. Chadwick of Cleveland. These loans were made by Mr. Beckwith without the knowledge of the board of directors, but with the collusion of Cashier Arthur Spear. Mr. Beckwith, who made loans from bank funds to the Chadwick woman, aggregating $240,000, also loaned to her about $100,000 of his own money. While he failed to consult the board of directors on the loans, the record seems to indicate that he sought rather the growth of the bank than personal profit. It was charged that presents of value were made to Cashier Spear by Mrs. Chadwick from time to time.

Knowledge of the wholesale operations of the Chadwick woman first came in a suit brought by Herbert D. Newton of Brookline, Massachusetts, to recover $190,000 which he had loaned to her. Connection of the Citizens National Bank with Chadwick loans was first known in Cleveland. Reports drifted to Oberlin on Friday and Saturday preceding the closing of the bank and there was a mild run on the institution Saturday afternoon and Saturday night, but there was at this time no general knowledge of the condition on the part of the bank's patrons. It developed that in the summer preceding the failure of the Bank Attorney W. B. Bedortha received information which made him suspicious and

The Story of a Century

he got from President Beckwith an admission of the fact that these loans had been made. Mr. Bedortha, one of the strong men of Oberlin in those days, carried the secret in his breast almost to the time of his death in October preceding the crash. Meantime he was working earnestly in an effort to cure the situation. When he found this impossible he took into his confidence Judge John W. Steele, also a director, who gave of his best efforts to find a remedy. The directors generally were not cognizant of conditions until the Sunday prior to the bank's formal closing.

President Beckwith had back of him years of conservative banking. Examination of the bank showed that all the loans save those made to Mrs. Chadwick were sound and adequately secured. Mr. Beckwith held as security for the loans he had made a note for half a million dollars bearing the name of Andrew Carnegie, then head of the steel trust. This he was confident was genuine, and when Carnegie announced that he had signed no such note, the veteran president began to break physically and died a few weeks after the bank's closing. He and Spear were indicted on several counts for violation of the federal banking laws. Spear was sentenced to prison and died of tuberculosis soon after his discharge after serving his sentence. The bank was liquidated by the federal government and ultimately the depositors were paid a little more than 67 cents on the dollar. Losses sustained by Oberlin College students were made good by Mr. Carnegie, as were also losses sustained by aged people without means of support. This generosity cost Mr. Carnegie about $15,000.

It is possible that but for the operations of the Chadwick woman Oberlin might not now have the handsome Carnegie Library. After the statement had been issued by Mr. Carnegie that he would make good student losses and certain other losses entailed by the unwarranted use of his name by Mrs. Chadwick, President Henry C. King of Oberlin College, on the occasion of a visit to New York, called upon Mr. Carnegie to thank him for his action. In the course of the conversation Mr. Carnegie asked President King as to library facilities in Oberlin College. The president responded that they were not what the college would like to have in the conduct of its school work. Mr. Carnegie then said to Mr. King that he would endow a library for the college. This he did and the present handsome Carnegie Library was completed in 1908 at a cost of $165,000.

While the amount of borrowing done by Cassie Chadwick at the Citizens National Bank was probably not the high water mark of her operations, Oberlin became the center of the picture by reason of apparent proof enabling the government best to make a case here in Ohio. Mrs. Chadwick was arrested in a New York hotel and was brought back to Cleveland for trial. At this time was divulged the unusual history of a woman born in poverty who in less than a year's time, with no security save her cold nerve, was able to borrow from banks, not only here in Ohio but at other points, sums estimated to exceed $1,500,000.

Cassie Chadwick, who blazed a new trail in modern high finance in the days preceding match kings and utilities barons, was born at Eastwood, Ontario, Canada, in 1857. Her name was Elizabeth Bigley. Her father was employed as a section hand. While yet in her teens Elizabeth forged a note, but was released on the ground that she was not mentally responsible. In 1890 she was convicted at Toledo on a forgery charge and sentenced to prison. She was paroled after three years by William McKinley, then Governor of Ohio. In 1897 she married Dr. LeRoy S. Chadwick, a reputable physician of some wealth, residing in a large mansion on Euclid Avenue, Cleveland. In the years prior to her marriage Mrs. Chadwick had lived under several aliases, including Madame Lydia de Vere, and Madame La Rose. She posed as a clairvoyant and was for some time mistress of some sort of semi-social, semi-public house, in the conduct of which she was supposed to have met her husband. Her marriage to Dr. Chadwick and her residence in a magnificent home in Cleveland brought her definite standing. People talk today of her shopping splurges. Tradition has it that she bought at one time eight grand pianos and sent them to eight close friends with her compliments.

It was in the spring of 1902 that Mrs. Chadwick's fertile brain devised the plan which spread financial wreckage in a number of banking centers, contributed to the death of several men of established reputation, and brought her more than a million dollars, no dollar of which she had when she entered the Ohio penitentiary. At this time she engaged the services of Virgil P. Kline, then the leading lawyer of Ohio and attorney for the Standard Oil Company. She told Kline that she wanted him to accompany her to New York for a call on Andrew Carnegie. She had claimed to be the niece of Frederick Mason, a member of the Carnegie financial organization. Her story to Kline was that Mr. Carnegie, as trustee, held a fortune of $11,000,000 left her by Mason. She asked that Kline go with her to make settlement with Mr. Carnegie, who, she said, desired to be relieved of this responsibility. At their arrival in New York they took a carriage to the Carnegie home. At the suggestion of Mrs. Chadwick, Mr. Kline remained in the carriage, as the woman said that Mr. Carnegie might be prejudiced by the presence of a stranger. Mrs. Chadwick went to the colossal Carnegie home, gained admission, and was in the house fully half an hour. When she returned to the carriage she showed to Kline a package which she said contained railroad bonds and displayed at the same time notes for $2,000,000, apparently signed by Mr. Carnegie. Taking Mr. Kline further into her confidence, Mrs. Chadwick told the attorney, in strict secrecy, that she was not the niece of Mason, but that she was a natural daughter of Mr. Carnegie and that this great wealth was given her that the "Steel King" might do justice to her. She was right in her apparent belief that such a great secret would not be forever kept and that the report would be spread over Cleveland, where it would do her the most good.

It was soon after this historic trip to New York that Mrs. Chadwick appeared at the Wade Park Bank in Cleveland, of which Ira Reynolds was secretary, and Frank Rockefeller, brother of John D. Rockefeller, was president. Mrs. Chadwick presented Mr. Reynolds a package, which she said contained a deed of trust for more than $10,000,000 and notes for $5,000,000, all signed by Andrew Carnegie. She advised Mr. Reynolds that she desired to place this property in a safe deposit box and she gave to the cashier what she said was a detailed list of the package, which Mr. Reynolds did not open. It is probably of significance that Mr. Kline, who was deceived by the woman on the New York trip, was recognized as the attorney-in-chief for the Standard Oil Company. It may be assumed that the bank, headed by Frank Rockefeller, was closely related to Standard Oil interests. A day following her visit to the bank Mrs. Chadwick telephoned to Mr. Reynolds in great agitation that she had lost her copy of the memorandum listing her notes and securities held in the safe deposit vaults of his bank for safe keeping. She asked if she might have a copy of the listing at once. Reynolds very obligingly complied with the request. He made a copy of the listing which Mrs. Chadwick had submitted and signed his name to the list.

While in those days when the Chadwick exposé was the general topic of conversation in America, there was much talk as to Mrs. Chadwick's hypnotic influence with bankers, there is probably more likelihood that an exhibition of the papers signed by Reynolds, showing securities valued at more than $10,000,000, made the way easier for the woman in her application for loans than did the fixing of her hypnotic eye on the prospective victim. It is fair to assume that the bankers of those days would have investigated with more thoroughness had Mrs. Chadwick applied for large loans armed only with notes said to have been signed by Mr. Carnegie. When these notes were supported by the apparently authentic listing of her securities, her way was fairly easy. While it was a shock to many who saw their dream of fortune wrecked, it was not altogether a surprise when examination of the package of securities disclosed the fact that its bulk was made up of pieces of brown wrapping paper. In the early spring of 1905 Mrs. Chadwick was convicted of conspiracy to violate the United States banking laws in her operations here in Oberlin and was sentenced to ten years in the Ohio Penitentiary. She died in October of 1907.

So strong was the belief of many who remembered Mrs. Chadwick in the days of her affluence that she always told the truth, there was much sympathy at the time of her trial. Even after her death it was currently reported that she had bribed her way out of prison and was still living in the style to which in the year or two before her conviction she had accustomed herself. Many would not give credence that she had had a shady career and a former prison sentence before she rode briefly but gorgeously on the top wave of financial ease.

At her trial, where she was represented by distinguished counsel, Mrs. Chadwick refused to make a verbal defense on her own behalf but contented herself with the statement that all of her outstanding notes would be paid. She further denied that she had ever claimed that she was a natural daughter of Andrew Carnegie. She failed, however, to supply any reason for possession of the alleged deed of trust. In an interview at the time Mr. Carnegie expressed some slight resentment that any one reading the deed of trust, which was written in very poor English, should hold the belief that it had been granted and signed by him. It will be remembered that Mr. Carnegie took as much pride in his literary ability in his later years as he did in his success as a builder and organizer.

After the failure of the Citizens National Bank and the arrest of Mrs. Chadwick it became known that the Cleveland woman had visited Oberlin first in a devious effort to secure a loan through the Oberlin Bank Company. Attorney A. Z. Tillotson, veteran member of the Lorain County bar and still practicing in Oberlin in 1933, related at the time of the bank failure here the story of a visit made to his office by Mrs. Chadwick early in April, 1903, It is thought that this is also the date of the first call made by Mrs. Chadwick on President Beckwith of the Citizens National Bank. Mrs. Chadwick told Mr. Tillotson that he had been recommended to her as an honest lawyer and as a member of the Baptist Church. She called attention to the fact that she also held membership in a Baptist Church at Cleveland. All this was precedent to asking Mr. Tillotson's good offices in securing for her a loan for $25,000. Mrs. Chadwick said that she must raise this amount of money without the knowledge of her husband and that she did not care to part with any of her securities. She showed Mr. Tillotson a note signed in the name of Charles A. Stewart. She told him this was the signature of the former treasurer of the old Euclid Avenue Trust Company. She also displayed a receipt for $30,000 signed by Virgil P. Kline. This she said was a receipt for an attorney fee. Mr. Tillotson brought the conversation to a close with the statement that such a loan could with difficulty be secured in a town of Oberlin's size, especially in view of the fact that no recognized security was offered by Mrs. Chadwick. The woman replied that that was what she had come to find out, and, apparently not offended by Mr. Tillotson's attitude, paid him a fee of $10 and left his office.

It was known at the time that the Chadwick bubble burst that the Citizens Bank was not the only institution in northern Ohio from which the woman had borrowed. At least one bank in Elyria lost in the crash and several banks in Cleveland are said to have accommodated Mrs. Chadwick with large sums. An Elyria bank, in an effort to make good some of its losses, sold the pictures in Mrs. Chadwick's Cleveland home. They were bought by an enterprising man, who kept them on exhibition, charging 50 cents admission. A constant stream of people went through the Chadwick home, gazing with amazement, if not delight, on the plaster cast of the negro boy holding a card tray, the cut glass with the sealskin upholstery, a huge oil painting of pigs drinking from a trough, and the countless pieces of lingerie crowding all the closets. A discouraged reporter referred to the display as a collection of utter "junk," but that did not stop the sightseers, who enjoyed looking at the $7,000 organ which Mrs. Chadwick had bought in the days of her prosperity.

THE CENTURY CLOSES

THE NEW OBERLIN

CHAPTER XVII

THE OBERLIN, both college and colony, in the years from 1833 to the outbreak of the Civil War was the Oberlin primarily of Charles Grandison Finney. In a little less degree it was the Oberlin of President Mahan and the Reverend John Morgan. Modified to some extent by after-war conditions, both town and college continued to be the 'Oberlin of Finney until after the election to the presidency of James Harris Fairchild in 1866. The warm evangelism of the earlier days was for the next quarter of a century tempered not only by the broad tolerance of Mr. Fairchild but as well by steadily growing contact with the outside world, which was bound to modify in some degree the traditions of the community and the college. When Henry Churchill King was inaugurated president in 1903, following the completion of a drive for an endowment fund for $500,000 and following the death in 1902 of President John Henry Barrows, college and town were both emerging in increasing measure from the isolation which had made Oberlin unique in the field of education. Restricted finances had contributed in no small part to this isolation, and the fairly straitened circumstances of both community and college had bound the two in a close union for almost three-quarters of a century. For about twenty years after its founding the college was precariously supported by gifts and term bills. The first endowment for the institution was obtained in 1852 and at the close of the Civil War in 1865 the total endowment was only a little over $91,000. This had grown to $680,000 in 1895 and was about $1,500,000 in 1908, when town and college observed their seventy-fifth anniversary.

Developments, both inside the school and in the world beyond, in the quarter of a century beginning in 1908, contributed to the making of modern Oberlin. The discovery in 1886 by Charles M. Hall of the electrolytic process in the manufacture of aluminum was to change Oberlin College from a school struggling with financial problems to one of the richest educational institutions in America. The great wealth which came to Mr. Hall and which resulted in his gifts to the college of more than $12,000,000 was made possible by tremendous economic changes in the nation. The long period of inflation and easy money, during and following the World War, changed the outlook of Oberlin people as it did that of people in all lands. "Father" Shipherd may have exercised sound judgment in his effort to build around his college and colony a wall which would keep both from contact with the sinful world, but traction lines, automobiles, and the mushroom growth of wealth put a final period to his dream.

The modern building program of the college, which greatly affected conditions in the village, had its beginning in 1907 with the construction of Finney Memorial Chapel and Carnegie Library. In the twenty-five years prior to 1908 the building program of the college included Sturges Hall, Warner Hall, Spear Laboratory, Peters Hall, Lord Cottage, Severance Laboratory, and Warner Gymnasium. This entire program of a quarter of a century represented less in expenditure than the cost of the two buildings dedicated in 1908. From 1908 until the end of 1932 the building program of the college represented an expenditure of about $2,400,000.

The community which emerged from the World War was of necessity not the Oberlin of pre-war days. In both college and town was apparent a changed attitude. President King, who gave to the college in twenty-five years of service as president the best of a life devoted to duty, found on his return from war service in France and the Near East that both school and students had been transformed in the fiery furnace of hatred growing out of war. The location here of the Student Army Training Corps affected college discipline. This in some degree accounted in 1919 for the lifting by the general faculty of the ban on smoking, which had been in effect, although the rule was not always observed, for a period of eighty-six years. This change was only one of many indications of a new day in both college and community.

The Story of a Century

Touching the material interests of the community, it is safe to say that modern transportation, which had its growth mainly in the twenty-five years previous to 1933, worked the most pronounced change in conditions in the village. When traction service began at about the opening of the twentieth century Oberlin merchants were first faced with the problem of out-of-town buying. This problem did not become acute until the passing of about two decades, when the Ford car came into general use, in the period of prosperity following the World War. The introduction of chain stores at about this same time added to the troubles of the small-town merchant. The day of isolation was over. People went to other towns to buy, not so much on the ground of economy but in order to travel and to visit these other towns.

The steadily increasing financial growth of the college in this twenty-five year period inevitably resulted, perhaps unconsciously, in a modification of the relations existing between the college and the community. When President Fairchild led his own cow to and from his pasture land, the support of the college by the community was essential to the progress of both. When near the close of the one-hundred-year period the college had total assets of more than $20,000,000, the condition was not the same. There was cordial coöperation in many things between town and college, but there was of necessity no feeling of dependence on the part of the college toward the community. They had unconsciously drifted apart, doubtless without fault on either side. These changed conditions were reflected in 1912 when residents of the community sought to have endowment of the college invested in stocks and bonds placed on the tax list. They were also reflected in the establishment of a college market in 1920 for the serving of dormitories and boarding houses. This action made serious inroads in the income of Oberlin business men. It is not to be understood that the action of business men seeking larger tax returns for the village or the action of the college in establishing its market was based in any degree on other than what was thought, by the business men in the one instance and by the college in the other, to be economic justice and sound business ethics. That the interest of the community in the college and its welfare had not disappeared under changed conditions was manifested in the college financial campaign of 1923 when it was sought to raise an endowment and building fund of $4,500,000. Oberlin Village pledged more than its quota of $140,000 in a campaign in which total pledges were in excess of $3,000,000. In similar manner the college was coöperating with the village in 1933 in the effort to establish a municipal light and power plant here. This hearty coöperation was especially pleasing to Oberlin residents, who were well aware of the fact that without such participation on the part of the college it would not be possible successfully to operate such a plant.

Within this final period Oberlin shared with the nation a definite change in what is commonly known as spiritual outlook. Oberlin churches were supported and maintained much as in the past. Church attendance, however, was not such as characterized either the days of Finney or the days of Fairchild, despite the fact that able pastors occupied the pulpits. There were a number of reasons for this. Motion pictures had begun to gain in popularity in the war period and before the close of the final quarter century of Oberlin's history, with the invention of "talkies," their hold on the public became still stronger. The radio in these later years made a like appeal. Many sat at home on Sundays and listened to sermons preached in Chicago or Detroit or New York. It is possible that the mode of transmission created as great interest as the weight of thought. It was in these days something other than the day of Finney and Mahan, the theologian and the minister. These two great men would not have appealed to the Oberlin citizens of the post-World-War age. There remained a belief in churches, but not a general faith in a Calvinistic God, a Presbyterian God or an early Methodist or early Congregational God. Faith in goodness remained, but adherence to formal doctrine was lessened. There was basis for the claim that this was an age of materialism. It was beyond doubt an age of inquiry and an age of challenge to established beliefs and customs. Youth who had risked their lives in the trenches did not take kindly to the strict guidance of their elders who remained behind the lines. Mark Sullivan in *Our Times* lists some of the releases from fears and says frankly: "In this period man's mind was sharpened though not necessarily deepened. Man was released from many arbitrary imperatives, from authoritative 'thou shalts' and also 'thou shalt nots.' A command, whether its source was religion, government, or public opinion, unless it appealed to the reason of the individual, was often ignored and could always be questioned without sacrifice of society's esteem." Mr. Dooley, speaking for those who resented these post-war changes, said that for himself "Th' Apostles' Creed niver was as con-vincin' to me afther I larned to r-read it as it was whin I cudden't read it, but believed it."

The new Oberlin and the new world of this period were again reflected in the fact that near its close the annual budget of the First Church was about two and one-half times the original cost of the church when it was built, although the membership was not as large as it was in 1860, when Second Church was formed by a group of members from First Church. This support was extended to this and to other churches, which operated on similarly increased budgets, by memberships having more dollars available and by dollars of much less purchasing power than in the early days of the community. Personal budgets and personal expenditures had kept pace with those of public character. Near the close of the period the building of a new high school at a total cost of $250,000 emphasized the fact that the community as a whole was willing to go along with altered conditions. The South Main Street school, abandoned because state inspectors held it did not comply as a structure with state laws and because Oberlin residents claimed it was injuring the health of pupils, was still in use in 1933 for school purposes in Oberlin College. In line with this change was the adoption near the close of the period of the city manager form of government, with the employing of a manager at about $4,000 a year replacing a mayor who, up until a few years of this time, had been paid $300 a

Oberlin Colony

year. In both these instances and in the case of the extension of street paving the argument was made by a majority of the community that more efficient service warranted the additional expense. A town hall built in 1919 at a cost of about $40,000, the improvement of storm sewer service in the village, and the rebuilding of the conduit line from Kipton to the water works were the last major expenditures for the period by the village. Within this same period assembly rooms were added to the Pleasant and Prospect school buildings.

It will be understood that the changes noted were not a result of a carefully planned spending orgy by either college or community. They were a part of the era of expansion which exploded in 1929 and scattered portions of which were being salvaged in 1933. There was no conscious departure from early ideals on the part of the college administration in these final twenty-five years. No abler man than President King has been at the head of the college since its founding. His ability was supplemented by sound faith and earnest belief in the traditions of the college. He carried forward the work of the school to the high credit both of himself and of the college. In public expenditures and in public changes the community through its chosen officials kept step with other communities in Ohio and in the nation. Proposals which would have shocked the fathers of early days as manifestations of financial madness were regarded in this period as necessities in the program of expansion. In the game of "keeping up with Lizzie" Oberlin played her part.

1908

John G. Olmstead was coach of the Oberlin basketball five. He served for several years as editor of the Alumni Magazine and was a citizen of Oberlin in 1933. Dr. J. E. Barnard, still in the practice of dentistry in 1933, this year bought the office and practice of Dr. H. G. Husted. Dr. Husted later returned to the practice of his profession here in Oberlin. By a vote of 98 to 16 citizens approved a bond issue for the making of sewer beds and the treatment of sewage according to principles approved by the State Board of Health. The bond issue was for $16,000. The First Church was remodeled at a cost of $25,000, almost twice the original cost of the building. W. W. Thompson retired from the hardware firm of Watson & Thompson. Mr. Watson was still conducting the business in his own name in 1933. The development of Reamer Place and of Edgemeer Place was begun.

Howard L. Rawdon was elected superintendent of the Oberlin Public Schools. In 1933 Mr. Rawdon was rounding out twenty-five years of service in this capacity. He had also served two years as high school principal. Much of the credit for the improvement of Oberlin schools and for their high standing with other educational units is due to Mr. Rawdon. A feature of the Seventy-fifth Anniversary of Oberlin College was the dedication of Finney Memorial Chapel, the gift of Frederick Norton Finney, honoring the memory of his father, President Charles Grandison Finney. The chapel stands on the site of the home built for President Finney when he came here in 1835. On this same occasion Carnegie Library was dedicated. It was the gift of Andrew Carnegie, steel king. Miss Tacey Anderson, who had taught in the public schools since 1875, resigned at the end of the school year. Miss Anderson's teaching was all done at the high school on South Main Street, built in 1874. Miss Alice M. Foote, a teacher in the public schools 1887-1905, 1906-08, ended her service this year except as to a final year taught by her 1930-31.

In June W. B. Gerrish resigned as city engineer following a dispute with Council as to salary. He was succeeded by W. F. Schickler. Mr. Gerrish had rendered good service to the town in almost a quarter of a century of employment. He worked with Judge Steele and Professor Wright in the establishing of the water works and of the sewer system here. Mrs. Edith Mason (Christy) was elected president of the Ohio Department of the Woman's Relief Corps. In 1926 Mrs. Christy was honored with election as president of the national organization.

Oberlin Colony

Professor Maynard M. Metcalf built a handsome home on Forest Street, which was later sold to the Oberlin Kindergarten Training School and still later was acquired by Oberlin College. The Metcalf name has been identified with Oberlin since the early days. Maynard Metcalf was Professor of Zoölogy here from 1906 to 1914. Irving W. Metcalf was a member of the Board of Trustees 1900 to 1925. He was still living here in 1933. Keyes D. Metcalf was graduated here and is now with the New York Public Library. Thomas Nelson Metcalf, athletic coach and Associate Professor of Physical Education here for several years, is now head of the Department of Physical Education at Chicago University. Wilmot V. Metcalf, a graduate of the college in 1883, was a resident here in 1933. General Wilder S. Metcalf was graduated from the college in 1878. Miss Antoinette Metcalf was reference librarian here 1904 to 1910. A catalogue of Oberlin College issued in 1926 shows thirty-eight of the name of Metcalf who have graduated from the school.

The Oberlin Volunteer Fire Department won two first prizes in August at a County Convention held at Lorain. The Autumn Club was the name given this year to an annual luncheon held for elderly people of the village. The first was held in 1900. Henry Braithwaite returned to his position as engineer at the water works after an absence of three years. He began there in 1886. Doren E. Lyon, who had held the place for three years, became eventually an employee of Oberlin College and in 1933 was still serving as superintendent of buildings and grounds.

1909

Frank J. Dick bought the grocery which had been conducted for twenty years by his father, M. G. Dick. The son had been with his father for the twenty years of the latter's ownership. Ezra L. Burge, who died at the age of 74, had served as marshal, street commissioner, and health officer of the village. He was a veteran of the Civil War. Dr. Henry M. Tenney, after twenty years of service, resigned as pastor of Second Church, effective in September, 1910. On his retirement Dr. Tenney was made pastor emeritus. He died in 1932. Thomas R. Mayhew, who died in February, had conducted a meat market and livery barn here for many years. He was 85 years old. He was buried in a coffin made to his order and kept in his barn for twenty years prior to his death. Early this year agitation had begun for a new high school building, which did not materialize until after the World War. In February Professor A. S. Root presented a plan for a building which would cost $50,000. T. J. Elliott resigned as superintendent of the Sunday School of the First Methodist Church, a position which he had held for thirty-six years. H. C. Wangerien began his services on the Council through appointment by the mayor. He was elected for several terms in succession. Oberlin College began work on the Men's Building. W. B. Durand, veteran insurance agent, died at the age of 69. He was for twenty-five years clerk of the township, was a director of the Oberlin Bank, and had been superintendent of the Sunday School of the First Baptist Church for thirty-nine years. He came to Oberlin in 1865. B. O. Durand is a son. It is interesting to note that Mr. Durand, T. J. Elliott, E. P. Johnson, and E. J. Goodrich, all were superintendents of Sunday Schools in the churches of the village for periods ranging from thirty-five to forty years.

The Oberlin fire department added two first prizes and one second at contests held at Elyria and Lorain. At the age of 86 Thomas Edwards performed carpenter work in improvements made at the home of his son, W. G. Edwards, on East College Street. Mrs. Thomas Edwards had one of the prize war gardens of the village in the World War period, planting and caring for it at the age of 94. W. G. Edwards and J. L. Edwards, still living here in 1933, are sons of Mr. and Mrs. Thomas Edwards. John E. Wirkler succeeded Professor John Fisher Peck as manager of the Oberlin College Glee Club. Mr. Wirkler was still performing the task with outstanding success in 1933. Both Mr. Peck and Mr. Wirkler contributed to the community in many ways outside the work of the Glee Club. W. D. Hobbs and Ira W. West were in charge of the first annual picnic of the Halcyon Club held at Ruggles Grove in August.

The death of Mayor Wolfe, in September, after a long illness, brought about the nomination of O. F. Carter for mayor at the primaries. Mr. Carter had been defeated by Mr. Wolfe two years previous. He was opposed at the election by Samuel Moore, who had recently come to Oberlin as a resident. Some of the bitterness growing out of the Wolfe-Carter campaign was carried over into this scrimmage. Mr. Carter at the election had 450 votes and Mr. Moore 324. Moore's vote was far beyond the normal Democratic vote in the village. At the primaries in September was nominated with Mr. Carter an unusually good Council, several members of which were continued from year to year. It was composed of H. C. Wangerien, W. G. Caskey, H. F. Smith, C. P. Doolittle, C. H. Snyder, and T. A. Bows. At the celebration of the seventy-fifth anniversary of First Church in September note was made of the service of E. J. Goodrich as superintendent of the Sunday School for forty years and of the service in the same capacity of James M. Fitch for twenty-five years.

Peace reigned for one evening in the banking business in Oberlin in this year when on October 5 Oberlin bankers were guests at a get-to-gether party at the home of Mr. and Mrs. L. E. Burgner. Dr. J. F. Siddall, a dentist here fifty years, was drowned in the cistern at his home. Roy Tillotson and Dan Dudley were members of a high school football team defeated by Oberlin Academy 3-0. R. W. Godfrey invented a starter for an automobile which would do away with cranking. Mr. Godfrey, who was a machinist here for many years, also invented an automatic device for the placing on and taking off of phonograph records. He never realized on either idea. Frank H. Foster was elected master and Eugene Dick, secretary of Oberlin Lodge 380, F. & A. M.

1910

Henry J. Morris died February 5. He was in the meat business here for years and was a member of a family prominent in Oberlin affairs for more than half a century. He gave good service on the Council and was a director of the State Savings Bank. He was generous in public gifts. Mayor Earl R. Morris is a son and George W. Morris and L. J. Morris, in business here for a number of years, are brothers.

Mayor O. F. Carter died in April. He had conducted a hardware business here, had served on the Board of Education, the Village Council, and as mayor. He served two terms as County Treasurer. C. P. Doolittle succeeded him as mayor. The state registrar of automobiles reported that this year there were 27,600 cars in Ohio. In 1932 there were 2,000,000 of all types.

In July died Mrs. A. A. F. Johnston, one of the most useful of the citizens of Oberlin. At the funeral services Reverend Henry M. Tenney said: "She was a great administrator as well as one of the world's great teachers. The indebtedness of Oberlin College to her is beyond the power of words to express, and our Oberlin Community, how greatly it is indebted to her! She has always loved it, and has had its welfare and the interests of all its people upon her heart."

Mrs. Johnston was the organizer, and president until her death, of the Village Improvement Society. Her purpose was to make Oberlin a beautiful residence village and through her efforts many unsightly spots were removed and homes and yards made attractive. One of her ambitions was to establish a parkway through the village bordering Plum creek, and before her death she had acquired certain sections which are now the property of the Society.

The federal census gave Oberlin a population of 4365. In 1900 the population was 4082. Reverend Jason Noble Pierce accepted the pastorate of Second Church. Timothy Dwight Ingersoll died at the age of 93. He came to Oberlin with his father in 1833, and delivered packages from his father's store, the

first store operated here. He was a great-grandson of Jonathan
Edwards. The Good Eats Club held a meeting in the large
barn of Ira West and disposed of a venison dinner made possible
by a deer shot on a western trip by Mark Whitney, then in
business here.

1911

Oberlin citizens were supporting a movement for a tuberculosis hospital. Plans made by the county commissioners in 1910
provided for a building accommodating fifty patients at an estimated cost of $16,000. The County Tuberculosis Hospital, now
in use and completed in 1932, cost about $425,000. It was built
to accommodate seventy-five patients. In April E. A. Stevens
bought the Preston dry goods store and moved from his location on South Main to the Preston store on North Main. Mr.
Preston had been in business here ten years. After a long illness
Dr. John W. Bradshaw resigned as pastor of First Church, a
charge which he had held with notable success for ten years. He
was succeeded by Reverend W. H. Spence of Rutland, Vermont.
Dr. Bradshaw died at Batavia, Illinois, in 1912. Reverend W.
H. Scott, rector of Christ Episcopal Church for eleven years,
went to Cincinnati to a new charge. At the primaries in Septem-
ber J. D. Yocom was nominated for mayor over J. L. Edwards.
Others on the ticket elected in November with Mr. Yocom were
H. T. Marsh, clerk; A. P. Behr, treasurer; R. T. Paden, mar-
shal; G. W. Morris, H. C. Wangerien, W. G. Caskey, O. E.
Peabody, C. P. Edwards, council; F. W. Tobin, W. D. Hobbs,
F. F. Jewett, board of public affairs; A. S. Root and E. E.
Sperry, board of education.

The Pittsfield Gas Company, organized by Fred L. Hall,
then in the real estate business here, and Mr. Green of Cleveland, drilled in a 2,000,000 foot well on the George Morris
farm southeast of 'Oberlin. In October a franchise was given the
company to furnish gas at thirty cents a thousand. In October
Mrs. Howard Huckins was elected president of the Ohio Feder-
ation of Women's Clubs. Mrs. Huckins was one of the founders
of the Woman's Club here. Beginning with the early years of

the twentieth century Oberlin women have shared to an unusual degree in club work in the village and through state organizations. Allen J. Monroe, mail carrier in Oberlin since 1889 and prior to that date employed at the store of A. G. Comings & Son, died this year. He enlisted in the army in the Civil War before he had reached the age of 16. H. B. Dobyns, who this year bought the F. E. Decker grocery store, later went to California and there gained a fortune in oil. Phil H. Ohly bought the Corner drug store, which he was still operating in 1933.

1912

J. N. Stone was made president of the Oberlin Board of Commerce. Mr. Stone was in 1933 secretary of the Oberlin Business Men's Club and he has held office with business organizations in the community for more than a quarter of a century. H. H. Barnard, in the grocery business here for twenty-five years, died suddenly in the office of his son, Dr. J. E. Barnard. Mr. Barnard was a veteran of the Civil War. The Board of Health provides for the licensing of milk dealers and for inspection. Marx Straus, who died in Elyria at the age of 83, opened a dry goods store in Oberlin in 1852. He later added clothing and this department was bought in 1860 by his cousin, August Straus. Marx Straus sold his store here in 1880 to A. J. Frederick.

Comrades of Henry Lincoln Post, Grand Army of the Republic, met in April with the Oberlin Board of Commerce and advised the Board that their numbers had become too few and their years too many for them to continue in charge of the decorating of the graves of soldier dead on Memorial Day. This request for help came fifty-two years after the firing on the flag at Fort Sumter. In compliance with the request of the Post members the duty of arranging for Memorial Day services was placed in the hands of certain civic organizations of the village, with the Oberlin Christian Union in immediate charge. Several years following the World War this duty was formally turned over to the members of Karl Wilson Locke Post, American Legion.

Oberlin Colony

The death of E. J. Goodrich occurred June 24. Mr. Goodrich, who was born in Connecticut in 1831, opened a book store in Oberlin in 1856 in a frame building at the southeast corner of Main and College Streets, where the Goodrich block, now known as the Oberlin Savings Bank Company block, still stands. For years his store was known as the largest of its kind in the country in a town of the size of Oberlin. Mr. Goodrich was a member of First Church for over half a century and retired in 1908 from the office of superintendent of the Sunday School which he held for forty years. He was a trustee of Oberlin College from 1878 to the time of his death. In his active years in business here he was held in high regard by the community and from year to year proved his good citizenship by unselfish work for the good of both village and college. When Stanley Morris resigned as principal of the high school J. C. Seeman was appointed to fill the vacancy, serving until his death in 1922.

In July complaint was made that the Oberlin Gas & Electric Company was using natural gas from the Pittsfield field to fire its boilers to make artificial gas which was sold to Oberlin citizens at $1.00 a thousand. The first cost of the natural gas was thought to be 15 cents a thousand to the Oberlin Gas & Electric Company. The company's rebuttal was that it was trying out the Pittsfield field to make sure there was sufficient natural gas to serve Oberlin. John H. Scott, colored, a figure in the Wellington Rescue and a resident of Oberlin since 1856, where he was in the harness-making business, died at 85. In August Anson Cheney and J. Burle Blue bought the Goodrich book store. This change was followed in August by the sale of the E. P. Johnson store, one of the oldest in Oberlin, to Yocom Brothers. Mr. Johnson had been in business here forty-seven years. Yocom Brothers, still doing business in 1933 as the Yocom Brothers Company, had then been here six years. Active members of the firm then were the late E. K. Yocom, banker and business man and a leader in the First M. E. Church, and J. D. Yocom, for three terms mayor of Oberlin and, like his brother, active in church and civic affairs. The conduct of the business of the Yocom Brothers Company in 1933 was in the hands of Ernest Yocom and Herbert Yocom, sons of E. K. Yocom.

The second of a number of hospital fairs given to raise funds for the community hospital was held in a tent on the campus October 4 and 5 and resulted in the clearing of $1500. Funds raised in this manner went far toward the support of the hospital and finally made up an endowment fund of $10,000, known as the Dr. Charles H. Browning Fund. Among the scores of citizens who had part in this good work were Mr. and Mrs. H. F. Smith, Mr. and Mrs. W. D. Hobbs, Mr. and Mrs. Louis E. Burgner, Dr. and Mrs. C. H. Browning, Dr. and Mrs. F. E. Leonard, and Mr. and Mrs. A. G. Comings. H. T. Marsh resigned as village clerk and was succeeded by Willis A. Hart, who had been employed as efficiency clerk. Mr. Marsh, who was a son of J. B. T. Marsh, former college treasurer, was for a time manager of the News Printing Company and after his retirement as clerk conducted a printing office of his own. Charles Bassett, who died in September at the home of his son, H. L. Bassett, at the age of 93, was one of the early settlers in Russia Township. Mr. Bassett was a descendant of Miles Standish. His father, William Bassett, came to Ohio in 1834 and bought a farm in Russia Township, which is still owned by H. L. Bassett, former vice-president of the Oberlin Banking Company and for a number of years cashier of the State Savings Bank Company.

Coincident with the turning of natural gas into the mains of the Ohio Electric Power Company from the Pittsfield gas field, announcement was made of the appointment of Paul Loewe to succeed Albert E. Hay, a picturesque figure, as manager of the company here. The Pittsfield company at this time claimed a production of 11,000,000 feet a day. Despite this apparently adequate supply, which early in 1913 was estimated at 20,000,000 feet a day, the wells proved shallow and it was finally necessary to purchase gas first from the Logan Gas Company, when the price was increased to 50 cents, and later from the Ohio Fuel Supply Company, when the price went to a gross of 88 cents.

Oberlin Colony

1913

Irving L. Marsh took over the management of the Park Hotel, which he held for several years, finally going east to enter business. He died in 1932. County Auditor C. A. Horn holds that endowments funds of Oberlin College invested in stocks and bonds are not subject to tax. A demand for the taxing of such college property was made by several leading citizens of Oberlin. The matter was taken into court and was finally determined by a decision of the Supreme Court of Ohio in favor of the colleges of the state. A. H. West buys the harness store of P. R. Tobin, who came to 'Oberlin in 1862 and who had been in business on South Main Street more than fifty years.

In March occurred the most disastrous flood in the history of Ohio. While Oberlin had but a small share in the way of property loss, citizens were shocked by early reports, later proved untrue, that 13,000 people had been drowned at Dayton and Springfield. The final toll of death in the state was about 400. Records kept by Professor F. F. Jewett showed a total rainfall in Oberlin between 10 A. M. Sunday, March 23, and noon on Tuesday, March 25, of 6.69 inches. Water stood four feet deep at the intersection of South Professor and Vine Streets. It was necessary to suspend work in both the public schools and the college for two or three days. H. C. Wangerien was elected president of the Oberlin Bank Company to succeed E. P. Johnson. Oberlin lost three valued citizens in the deaths of Mrs. Lucinda Comstock, mother of the late Seth G. Comstock and Mrs. O. C. Gibson; Jacob Burgner, father of Louis E. Burgner and former superintendent of schools at Fremont; and M. G. Dick, for twenty-one years in business here and for twelve a member of the Village Council.

Mrs. Mabel Fauver Gibson, in 1932 a teacher in the high school here, and Mrs. Clara Lehmann were elected members of the Board of Education. The Board in 1933 had in its membership Mrs. Mabel McKee and Mrs. W. L. Tenney.

1914

W. D. Hobbs completed his new block on East College Street and opened a restaurant. He had then been in business here for about twenty-two years. Mr. and Mrs. P. G. Worcester, who came to Oberlin to live in 1894, celebrated their silver wedding anniversary April 29. Frank L. Wilson opened his mill and cabinet works in the S. M. Cole plant, a location which he occupied in 1933. In March H. G. Waite resigned as cashier of the Peoples Banking Company and was succeeded by I. L. Porter. Mr. Porter continued to hold this position in 1933 and the intervening years had seen, on his part, rare and unusual service to the community in many and varied forms. Reverend Jason Noble Pierce resigned as pastor of Second Church to accept a pastorate in the East. He was succeeded by Reverend Charles H. Williams. In May M. A. Houghton was appointed postmaster of Oberlin by President Wilson. He finished first in a field of six applicants. In June occurred the death of Dr. William C. Bunce, a physician here for thirty-five years. His father, also William C. Bunce, was a pioneer physician in Oberlin. Captain Alva B. Parsons died after fourteen years as a member of the firm of Wright & Parsons. Oberlin citizens were boasting of the village having built eight and one half miles of brick pavement in the twelve years preceding July of this year. In 1933 the village had fourteen miles of brick pavement, an unusual record for a town of its size. In July Irving M. Channon bought the Goodrich book store from Cheney & Blue. The Oberlin tax duplicate showed realty values of $4,486,180 and personalty values of $1,249,365. W. M. White opened the White House dry goods store on West College Street.

While Oberlin was transacting business as usual the World War clouds were gathering in Europe in the late summer to break in storm in early August. Americans at this time had no thought that this nation would play an active part in the tragedy. Mrs. Anna Elizabeth Butler, mother of Mrs. W. H. Cooley and widow of John Butler, died here, aged 92. In October the Lo-

Oberlin Colony

rain, Ashland and Southern Railroad announced the opening of regular passenger train service between Lorain and Custaloga. The first passenger train out of Lorain was wrecked about two miles north of Oberlin. J. N. Stone was elected state Senator, an office which he held for two terms, giving excellent service to the state and the district.

The death of Charles M. Hall on December 27 resulted eventually in additions to the endowment funds of Oberlin College totaling more than $12,000,000. Soon after the death of Mr. Hall it was announced that gifts to Oberlin College would amount to about $3,000,000, but, since these gifts were largely in stock of the Aluminum Company of America, they grew in value and the final total upon settlement of the estate in 1926 was $10,192,000. The income paid to the college by the trustees of the Hall Estate, prior to final settlement, was $1,654,747. Mr. Hall had made numerous gifts to the college prior to his death. Charles M. Hall, who was a son of Reverend and Mrs. Heman B. Hall, was graduated from the college in 1885. The year following, working under the handicap of a laboratory erected in the home of his parents on East College Street, he invented the electrolytic process for the manufacture of aluminum. He had been a student of Professor Frank F. Jewett in Oberlin College and it was at the suggestion of Mr. Jewett that young Hall began his investigation. At the time of his invention aluminum was selling for $12 a pound. His process made it a common metal of commerce which brought the price to a point where it might be used in manufacturing. The gift made to Oberlin College was due in no small measure to Mr. Hall's great respect and affection for President Henry Churchill King, with whom he had been in contact for many years as a member of the Board of Trustees of the college.

E. E. Sperry, senior member of the firm of Sperry & Pfaff and prominent in Republican politics of the county in his more than twenty-five years of residence in Oberlin, was elected postmaster of the Ohio Senate. Mr. Sperry has been for a number of years deputy clerk of the County Board of Elections.

1915

Negotiations were begun this year by the college for the purchase of the town hall, The First Methodist Episcopal Church, The First Baptist Church, and other properties between East College and East Lorain Streets on the north side of Main Street, to the end that the site might be cleared for the erection of a memorial honoring the mother of Charles M. Hall. Mr. Hall, in his will, left $500,000 for this specific purpose. Early in 1933 it was uncertain when this work would be started. The fund in the meantime was reported to have increased to $1,000,000.

A. L. Jones, marble dealer, died in March at San Antonio, Texas, where he had gone for his health. He succeeded his father in business here. W. T. Henderson, veteran barber, died in April at the age of 79. He came to Oberlin in 1857 and opened a barber shop which he conducted until 1914. Mrs. C. W. Kinney was made president of the Prospect Parent-Teacher Association, formed this year. The Pleasant Street Association had been operating for a year or two. E. P. Johnson, veteran merchant, died early this year. His father, I. M. Johnson, was a pioneer in business here and the son succeeded him. Mr. Johnson helped organize the Oberlin Bank Company and the Oberlin Telephone Company and was for thirty-seven years superintendent of the Sunday School of the Second Church. Soon after the death of Mr. Johnson, Levi T. Whitney retired from active business after having been engaged as clerk and proprietor in commercial pursuits here for fifty-seven years. His interest in the clothing firm of L. T. Whitney & Son was sold to Jasper V. Hill and the new firm became Whitney & Hill. Mr. Whitney came to Oberlin in 1858 from Pittsfield. He first worked as a clerk for S. D. Hinman and later for I. M. Johnson & Company. The firm of Johnson, Whitney & Cole was formed in 1870 and a year later the firm of Whitney & Company succeeded. Mr. Hill began work for Mr. Whitney at the age of 13 and in 1933 was sole proprietor of the store, having purchased the interest of C. K. Whitney in 1923. Miss Celia Burr, teacher in the public schools, resigned. Miss Burr taught 1876-83 and at the end of the latter year left Oberlin for a period of a few years. She resumed her teaching here in 1895 and continued the work for twenty years. Miss Burr was living on West Lorain Street in 1933. In July Henry Pfaff and Earl Morris entered the clothing business under the firm name of Pfaff & Morris. Work was begun this summer on a new reservoir for the water plant with a capacity of 10,000,000 gallons. In November the trustees of the college voted to abandon Oberlin Academy, a preparatory school which had been in operation for many years.

1916

Reverend William H. Spence resigned as pastor of First Church. He was succeeded by Reverend Nicholas Van der Pyl. The college announces a gift of $100,000 for the construction of Allen Hospital. In February discussion began of the proposal to unite the First and Second Congregational Church. The Second Church was formed by members of the First Church in 1860. H. E. Arnold, proprietor of the Oberlin Laundry here for the past twenty-five years, was appointed as a trustee of the Lorain County Children's Home. George M. Glenn died early in the year at the age of 87. He had conducted a barber shop half a century. Gibson Brothers began building a new bakery on West Lorain Street, with a daily capacity of 10,000 loaves. When James R. Severance died, after twenty-two years as treasurer of Oberlin College, he was succeeded by H. B. Thurston, who held that position in 1933. After operating a steam heating plant for twelve years at a loss, the Oberlin Gas & Electric Company discontinued the service. In October was dedicated the new Rust Methodist Episcopal Church. Captain J. F. Randolph, who died in November, had been a resident here for twenty-five years. He was a director of the State Savings Bank Company. A part of the consideration for the sale by the village to Oberlin College of the Town Hall for $20,000 was an agreement by the college that the village should have free quarters for offices in a proposed Civic Building.

1917

E. K. Yocom was elected president of the State Savings Bank to succeed M. M. Squire, resigned. When it became apparent early in the year that war might come between the United States and Germany President King, members of the college faculty, and students united in a message of encouragement and support to President Wilson. There was a shortage of gas in February, with thermometers standing nineteen below zero. H. C. Wangerien, George M. Jones, and H. B. Thurston were a joint committee to investigate the advisability of installing a municipal light and power plant in Oberlin. In April a mass meeting at chapel endorses Wilson's call-to-arms. President King was one of the speakers. Mrs. Emeline Farnsworth Wright, who died in April, was 95 and had lived here more than fifty-five years. The family home still stands at the north-east corner of Cedar and West Lorain Streets. In the midst of war's alarms the Apollo Theatre was showing Mary Pickford, labeled as "America's Sweetheart," and Bessie Barriscale, in the movies of the day. Mrs. Nancy Wolcott Squire, who died at 83 and who was the widow of Samuel Squire, was a real daughter of the Revolution, her own father having seen service. She had lived in Oberlin since 1872. In May the new First Baptist Church on East Lorain Street was dedicated. Ralph Miller, son of Dr. and Mrs. S. E. Miller, was appointed a cadet to West Point. Ira West, who had been showing motion pictures at the Rex Theatre for two years, bought the Apollo Theatre, which had been operated for three years by George F. Broadwell.

The moving picture industry in Oberlin had its start early in 1907 when a show was opened by Gibson Brothers in a room on the second floor in their building on West College Street. At about this same time Frank L. Wilson opened a moving picture show in the Martin block on East College Street. At about this period a third show was in operation for a time in the Wynn building on South Main Street. George F. Broadwell bought the Wilson show and for a time operated both the Apollo, in the

Oberlin Colony

Hobbs building on East College, and the Rex on South Main Street. These two shows were later acquired by Ira West, who finally closed the Rex, but continued to operate the Apollo, which he sold to Oscar Smith. After Mr. Smith's death Mrs. Smith conducted the business for a time and eventually sold it to Jerome Steel, who was in 1933 operating one of the best equipped show rooms in northern Ohio. The name Apollo was retained, but the building itself had been remodeled by its owner, W. D. Hobbs, especially for motion picture purposes. The theatres operated at the outset in Oberlin gave a limited form of entertainment. At that time the flicker incident to motion pictures had not been conquered. Prices, under pressure of keen competition, were sometimes as low as 5 cents at matinee performances. The "talkies" were first shown at the Apollo May 11, 1929.

The Oberlin Grain & Milling Company bought the Ward & Whitney Mill. W. H. Walker was still secretary and manager of the concern in 1933. Professor John Fisher Peck was general chairman in charge of a Red Cross Drive which raised $5,300. The special Red Cross Committee included Mrs. Louis E. Burgner, Mrs. W. G. Caskey, Mrs. R. A. Budington, and Mrs. J. E. Barnard. Jesse Lang died in July, aged 92. He was in college here in 1844 and had been a citizen of the village since 1870. The Republican ticket elected in November included W. H. Phillips, mayor; W. A. Hart, clerk; C. R. Graham, treasurer; and H. C. Wangerien, W. G. Caskey, G. W. Morris, O. E. Peabody, H. F. Smith, and A. W. McIntosh, council.

Late in the fall war conditions had brought on a fuel shortage which was most acute in 'Oberlin and throughout northern Ohio. Shipments of coal to the northwest by the lake ports had been delayed because of the demand for fuel in factories making war munitions. In October Judge W. B. Thompson, of the Court of Common Pleas of Lorain County, named a fuel administration, with a representative in Oberlin. At this crucial time, when coal was scarce and hard to get, the gas shortage in Oberlin became more acute. Many resorted to the use of wood for fuel. The college and the public schools suffered for lack of coal and the schools were closed down for a few days. There was some chance that church services might be discontinued. While much inconvenience resulted from conditions, there was no actual suffering. A little later Oberlin with the rest of the nation practiced heatless Monday under the advice of Fuel Administrator Garfield. Wilbur Pay and E. C. Leonard, two well-known Oberlin boys, were flying over the front in France. Leonard was wounded in a duel with a German plane. The First M. E. Church burned December 6. The building had been bought by Oberlin College. George C. Prince, who died near the close of the year, had lived here since 1884 and had been engaged in real estate and banking.

1918

The war was brought closer home to people of Oberlin when they were given cards through which they bought sugar in limited amounts from time to time. Wheatless days were established by Food Administrator Herbert Hoover. War trucks made it a point to reach Oberlin by night where they were liberally fed by the good women of the community and were assigned to quarters in Warner Gymnasium. Early in the year a war committee for the village was named by the mayor composed of Dean Edward I. Bosworth, George M. Jones, H. C. Wangerien, I. L. Porter, E. K. Yocom, M. A. Houghton, Charles A. Hammond, and Mrs. W. J. Horner.

Public schools were forced to suspend for two weeks in February because of unusually severe weather and a shortage of coal. A low mark of 22 below zero was reached. In February the Oberlin Gas & Electric Company began the purchase of energy from the plant at Lorain, shutting down their producing plant here. A. S. Glenn, one of the original carriers appointed here when free mail delivery was established in 1889, died in March. He had resigned in January, 1917, because of failing health. J. F. Alderfer, of the faculty of Oberlin College, died in service in France. Oberlin made the excellent record of exceeding her quota in four Liberty Loan drives and in the Victory Loan floated by the Government. A war committee composed of H. C. Wangerien, E. K. Yocom, President Henry Churchill King, and Dean Edward I. Bosworth fixed a quota of $48,000 a year for war purposes, exclusive of Liberty Loan activities, but including Red Cross contributions. When a drive was put on for this amount it was exceeded by several hundred dollars. Willis A. Hart, for six years clerk of Oberlin Village, died at Clifton Springs, New York, after a long illness. Eugene G. Dick was named as his successor. President King was given a farewell reception by Oberlin citizens on his leaving for France for Y. M. C. A. war service.

Oberlin College made another important contribution toward the prosecution of the war by installing here a Student Army Training Corps of 425. Captain Francis M. Root, son of Professor A. S. Root, was in command. The training was continued until after the close of the war. The members of the corps were mustered out December 21. Oberlin shared in an influenza epidemic in October which claimed many lives in America. There were but two deaths here with a record of more than one hundred cases. In the fall came news of the death on the western front of Lieutenant Thomas Quayle and of the drowning on the Ticonderoga of Private Wilfred Cobb, two well-known Oberlin boys. While Oberlin participated in the false Armistice Day, growing out of ill-founded newspaper reports, this fact did not lessen enthusiasm on Monday, November 11. The previous impromptu celebration was on Thursday of the week before. The official signing of the Armistice was announced in Oberlin when, under the direction of Fire Chief C. E. Van Ausdale, the whistle at the water works was sounded at 4:30 in the morning. Soon the streets were crowded and at six o'clock a parade of 2,000 people formed in charge of Professor Philip D. Sherman as marshal. Activities, both in the public schools and in the college, were abandoned for the day and at 10 A. M. a formal observance was held in Finney Memorial Chapel, attended by the largest crowd which ever filled the edifice. Addresses were made by Dean Edward Increase Bosworth, Professor William J. Hutchins, Reverend Charles H. Williams, and the mayor of the village. Prayer was offered by Professor George Frederick Wright. An organ program by Professor George W. Andrews and singing under the direction of John E. Wirkler of the Oberlin College Glee Club added to the impressiveness of the occasion. This ceremony marked the end of the war as it touched Oberlin life, save as receptions were tendered to 'Oberlin boys as they came back from service.

1919

Memorial services were held in the churches here for ex-President Theodore Roosevelt, whose death occurred January 6. Oberlin, as the original home of the Anti-Saloon League, was vitally interested in the fact that in January a sufficient number of states had ratified the Eighteenth Amendment to make it effective in the nation. By proclamation of the Secretary of State the law was declared in force and effect as of January 16, 1920. A greenhouse on North Cedar Avenue, built in 1871 by Andrew Congdon, was abandoned and portions of the structure were incorporated in additions made to the H. A. Cook greenhouse on South Main Street. Among Oberlin men returning from World War service were "Shorty" Pay, Edmund C. Leonard, Fred Hall, Jr., Everett Papworth, and Floyd Harley. Dr. H. W. Pyle, who had practiced his profession here twenty years, died in February. Fred Edmonds was appointed marshal on the death of Scott Van Ausdale. Voters approved a bond issue of $225,000 for a new high school building. A second vote was had, however, before the new building was put up. Oberlin over-subscribed the Victory Loan, as it had made a record of over-subscriptions in the Liberty Loans in war time. Louis E. Burgner was area chairman in all of these various drives.

In April Council passed a resolution for a special election in May on the question of a bond issue for $50,000 for erecting a municipal light and power plant. This was the initial gun in a dispute with the Ohio Electric Power Company over rates. A bond issue was approved by a vote of 307 to 23, but no bonds were issued, since litigation questioned the legality of all of the steps taken by Council. The ordinances were repealed and new ones passed for an election held in September, which again recorded the desire of Oberlin citizens for municipal ownership by a vote of 310 to 6. At this election a total issue of $58,000 was authorized. After almost three years of dispute Council made a compromise agreement with the company in the matter of rates.

J. R. Haylor this year bought the Channon book store. A contract for a new town hall was let in May and the building was completed at the end of the year at a cost of $40,000. In July Reverend Charles H. Williams resigned as pastor of Second Church and was succeeded by Reverend Jason Noble Pierce. Hundreds were present at a reception in September for President Henry Churchill King on his return from war service. The reception was held on Finney Chapel terrace. Welcome home, on behalf of the community, was extended to Mr. King by the mayor. In October Council, under pressure from gas users, who feared the supply would be cut off by the Ohio Electric Power Company, agreed to a maximum rate of 88 cents a thousand gross. Talcott tree, which stood in front of Talcott Hall for more than 70 years and which in that time shared honor with the Historic Elm, was cut down in the summer because its decayed condition made it dangerous for pedestrians. The tree was the college bulletin board in early Civil War days and in prior years. That the year closed with a fair measure of prosperity is indicated by ready sales of turkeys at 45 cents a pound, dressed.

1920

Dr. W. A. McIntosh was the first health commissioner under the Hughes Act creating a health district in the county, which had in 1933 been operated from year to year on an annual budget of about $20,000. Before this measure became effective Oberlin's health appropriation was about $300 a year. Under the operation of this law health charges in the village annually were close to $1800. When A. M. Loveland resigned as cashier of the Oberlin Bank Company, after 25 years of service with the bank, he was succeeded by H. F. Ashley, later cashier of the Oberlin Savings Bank Company and in 1933 an Ohio bank examiner. Mr. Loveland's resignation followed a breakdown in his health due to unusual duties in the World War period.

The congregations of both the First and Second Congregational Churches by vote approved a union of the two churches after about sixty years of separate operation. Dr. Henry M. Tenney, who was made pastor emeritus of the new United Church, preached a final sermon to his congregation at Second Church June 20. Reverend Nicholas Van der Pyl was chosen pastor of the new United Church, the name of which was later changed to the First Church in Oberlin.

This year marked a buyers' strike, following record high prices. In May sugar was selling in Oberlin stores at from 20 cents to 26 cents a pound, while the price in Lorain was 33 cents. In June occurred the death of the Reverend Chauncey N. Pond, who came to Oberlin in 1858. He was a veteran minister. Dr. W. F. Thatcher, a leading physician here since 1908, was killed by a traction car near Castalia. The population of the village by the federal census of 1920 was 4236.

1921

Carl Pfaff became junior member of the grocery firm of Sperry & Pfaff. At a special election in April voters approved by a vote of 599 to 100 a bond issue of $250,000 for a high school building. This second vote was the final action under which bonds were issued. Attorney C. A. Hammond, for several years city solicitor, died in April. Republican primary nominations in August were: Mayor, H. F. Smith; trustees of public affairs, W. H. Chapin, William Darling, D. E. Lyon; members of council, A. W. McIntosh, J. N. Stone, W. D. Hobbs, Harold King, Lynds Jones, C. R. Comings. The Oberlin Volunteer Fire Department won a first prize in a hook and ladder race at

Medina. Noah Huckins, who died in September, had been in business in Oberlin since 1889. In October occurred the death of Deacon George S. Pay, who came to Oberlin in 1865. In 1914 he sold his meat market, which he had operated almost continuously in his residence here, to Otis E. May, who still conducted it in 1933. Mr. Pay was a councilman for several years and had served as constable, marshal, and chief of the fire department. He was active in the First Church. Oberlin residents rejoiced in October in the defeat of Ohio State by the Oberlin College football team, coached by T. Nelson Metcalf. Oberlin high school boys playing on the team included Al Wheeler, McFarland, Bowen, and Tenney.

The final hospital fair made a net of $2150 toward hospital support. This completed the Charles H. Browning memorial fund of $10,000, and no further fairs were held. T. J. Rice, as stockholder, sustained substantial loss in a fire at the aviation field of the Lowell Aviation Company near Oberlin.

1922

By a compromise settlement made with the Ohio Electric Power Company a contract was made for 6 1-2 years for the furnishing of light and power to the village. Near the close of the year occurred the deaths of Professor Frederick Anderegg and Dr. Fred E. Leonard, members of the college faculty who were valued citizens of the community. August Straus, dean of Oberlin business men, died in April.

1923

T. O. Murphy, who had come to Oberlin to install a heating plant in the new high school building, established a plumbing and heating business. He later formed a partnership with Edward J. Sable and the firm was operating in 1933 as the T. O. Murphy Company. In April a union was completed of the Oberlin Bank Company and the State Savings Bank. The new organization was the Oberlin Savings Bank Company. Miss

OBERLIN HIGH SCHOOL

Oberlin Colony

Nellie Cheesman, who died this summer, had been in business on North Main Street for 15 years. She was a representative of one of the older families of the village.

The effect of the automobile on traction line service was shown in an application filed in August with the Ohio Utilities Commission by the Cleveland Southwestern Railway Company asking permission to abandon their service between 'Oberlin and Norwalk. George W. Gibson, whose death occurred this fall, had lived in Oberlin since 1881. He was constable for the township for 32 years and was chief of the fire company which won the United States championship and the world's championship in competition in volunteer firemen's races. In September use was first made of the new high school building erected this year. Reverend Frank Wade Smith, pastor of the First Methodist Church, left Oberlin for a charge at Delaware. He was succeeded by Reverend Charles B. Ketcham.

At the November election the city manager plan was approved by the voters of Oberlin in a vote of 540 to 423. The proposal had the active support of the League of Women Voters and the apathetic opposition of most of the business men. The proposal was first made by Honorable A. G. Comings. The plan was ably supported by Professor Karl F. Geiser, who was elected to the first Council under the new system.

A reflection of economic conditions is shown in the fact that turkeys for Christmas sold well at 55 cents a pound dressed. The total of Oberlin's tax value at this time was $6,888,935. At the close of the year announcement was made that the community had slightly exceeded its quota in the drive of Oberlin College for additional endowment of $4,500,000. Oberlin pledges amounted to $143,737.06. The quota of the village was $140,000.

1924

Professor L. F. Miskovsky, who died in January, had been principal of the Slavic Department in Oberlin College from 1894 to 1921, when the department was discontinued. He had definite standing as a respected citizen of the community. Oberlin honored the memory of President Woodrow Wilson on the day of his funeral, February 6. W. F. Schickler resigned as city engineer and as superintendent of the water works, positions which he had held for 15 years. J. B. Vincent, who died in the early summer, had been assessor for the village for a quarter of a century.

Oberlin Community raised $5,000 for the relief of sufferers in the Lorain tornado which, on June 28, resulted in a property loss of $25,000,000 and in the death of 62 persons. Oberlin sustained small losses in a rain storm which occurred here at the same time and which had the character of a cloud burst. Small boys swam in the water on the campus at the close of the storm. Among those who lost their lives at Lorain was Reverend F. E. Jeffery of Oberlin. Frank E. Peck, E. N. Walker, and W. G. Edwards were honored at a celebration by Oberlin Lodge of Masons in October of their more than 50 years of membership in the Masonic Fraternity. Among the guests was Honorable David J. Nye of Elyria who had been a member of the order for more than 60 years. The reign of high prices continued and retail quotations in December were: eggs 70 cents, cheese 60 cents, wheat $1.55.

1925

H. V. Zahm was named superintendent of the water works, a position which he held in 1933. Charles B. Wright, of Ravenna, bought the B & W Variety store, which had been established by Ernest Bastel and John W. Williams. Ira West sold the Apollo Theatre to Oscar Smith of Seville. Mrs. Roxa Ackelson died at the age of 89. H. G. Klermund in April acquired entire control of the Ford Agency here when he purchased the interest of Maurice Schubert. Mr. Klermund came to Oberlin in 1917 as an employee of Schmauch Brothers. Stock in the Oberlin Machinery Company, a corporation formed in an effort to market drills and chucks, was sold to the extent of $10,000. The effort was fruitless. The following year a receiver was named for the company.

Oberlin Colony

On May 16 a tornado at Pittsfield just south of Oberlin caused a loss of $100,000. Chief among the losers were Willoughby Harris, Ira West, and Alonzo Norton. Oberlin and Wellington business men worked for several days in helping property owners to clear up the debris. Relief work was instituted at the suggestion of Reverend William Smith, pastor of Pittsfield Community Church and in 1933 a resident of Oberlin. Oberlin people raised $1500 for aid. O. C. McKee and Ira Porter headed the committee.

In June E. C. Westervelt bought the old high school building on South Main Street which he later gave to Oberlin College. M. M. Squire, former Oberlin business man and president of the State Savings Bank, who left Oberlin in 1920, died in July at Claremont, California. Mr. and Mrs. George A. Mosher, who had been in charge of the Lorain County Children's Home for a quarter of a century, retired this year. Allen Hospital was opened this fall.

In December Don Herrick, of Albion, Michigan, was made Oberlin's first city manager. Ira L. Porter, who had been elected to Council, declined to serve after announcement had been made that there were no provisions for the enforcement of law under the sections of the Ohio statutes governing Oberlin's new form of government. W. H. Chapin and T. H. Rowland were members of the water board which retired when the city manager form of government became effective at the end of this year.

1926

Publication was made of the fact that at the close of the final year under the federal form of government Oberlin had a general bonded debt of $69,000, a sum which was exceeded by $1600 by sinking fund holdings and cash balances. This was an unusual record. The Haylor book store was burned January 13 with a loss to Mr. Haylor and J. V. Hill, clothing merchant, of close to $40,000. R. W. Allen retired from business when his interest in the furniture store of Allen & Sedgeman was bought by George T. Sedgeman. In March the Oberlin High School basket-

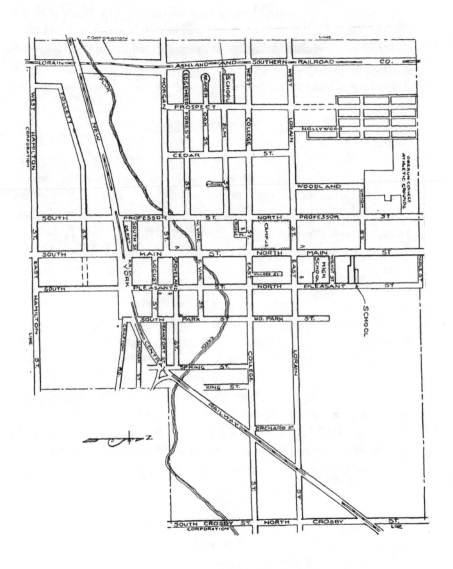

MAP OF OBERLIN 1933

ball team won the state class B championship. The team included Gaines, Barnes, Powers, Weiss, Thomas, Hamlin, Yocom, Dufty, and Gibson. John Atkinson was the coach. In April Frank Knapp, of Bellevue, bought a controlling interest in the Oberlin Telephone Company. Soon after this F. H. Gardenier retired as manager.

Professor F. F. Jewett died in June at Honolulu. Mr. Jewett is given much credit for the success of Charles M. Hall in a commercial development of aluminum. Mr. Jewett was Mr. Hall's instructor in college and suggested to the latter that he give consideration to such an investigation. Levi T. Whitney, veteran merchant, died in July at the age of 90. Attorney C. R. Summers was nominated for representative on the Republican ticket and served two terms. In September M. D. Wyckoff, who came to Oberlin in 1919, built a modern dry cleaning plant to which he has made additions from time to time. It is one of the most complete plants of its kind in Ohio.

Professor Harold L. King died in October. He was a son of President and Mrs. King and had given excellent service as a member of Council. He had been on the faculty of the college since 1916. Finney Chapel was filled at a memorial service for Mr. King at which addresses were delivered by Dr. W. F. Bohn and Dean Edward I. Bosworth. A unique work came to an end in the death of George C. Wood, who for 20 years had trained boys in athletics and clean living. Several hundred boys had been under his care in the 20 years of his activity.

1927

The Second Church building was sold to Oberlin College and was in use in 1933 for college purposes. Otis E. Peabody died in February. He had served on the Council and was in business here for twenty-five years. This year saw the clearing of the Oberlin campus in compliance with the provisions of the will of Charles M. Hall. French Hall and Society Hall were first wrecked, after which Spear Library was torn down. Professor C. W. Morrison died in May. He had retired as director of the Conservatory in 1924. Erection of a new First M. E. Church, on North Professor Street, was begun this summer. The cornerstone was laid July 7. The entire cost was about $90,000.

President King retired at commencement in June and was succeeded by Dr. Ernest H. Wilkins, of Chicago University, who was still serving as president of the college in 1933. C. R. Summers was elected Grand Master of the Odd Fellows of Ohio. Dr. Edward Increase Bosworth died in July. He had been in Oberlin as a teacher since 1883. He is generally recognized as one of the great men of Oberlin College and he held a unique place in the affections of the people of Oberlin. The death of Dr. Bosworth in July was followed by that of Azariah S. Root in 'October. Mr. Root had been with the college as librarian for forty years. His community activity was outstanding. He had been president of the Board of Education, president and secretary of the Board of Commerce, and at the head of the Village Improvement Society.

A cane was presented to Luther L. Munson on his 81st birthday in October by Oberlin business men. This cane was at Mr. Munson's death, by his request, given to A. G. Comings, who held it as the oldest business man in point of years at that time. Oberlin Lodge of Masons tendered a reception to T. H. Rowland on the occasion of his fiftieth anniversary as a member of the order. Reverend Nicholas Van der Pyl resigned as pastor of First Church.

1928

In February Julian S. Fowler was appointed librarian of Oberlin College. In this same month City Manager Herrick resigned and was succeeded by L. A. Sears, who was still serving in 1933. In an address before Oberlin business men County Auditor Welty pointed out that in 1900 Oberlin Village spent for all purposes $20,478.36. In that same year the Oberlin Board of Education spent $13,298.03. Ten years later these figures had grown to $40,541.91 for the village and $23,660.21 for the schools. In 1927 the village expenditure was $44,062.82 and

Oberlin Colony

that for the schools $90,052.93. In March Jerome Steel bought the Apollo and Rex Theatres. Mr. Steel, some years later, closed the Rex, but was still operating the Apollo in 1933. In June William F. Robinson, a respected colored resident and former slave, died at the age of 96. He had lived here 73 years and died in the home which he had built for himself in 1855. This same summer occurred the death of Mrs. Ruth Gager, 90, and Mrs. S. B. Farnsworth, 90, the latter the mother of Mrs. E. M. Ransom.

The white-way lighting system for the business section was completed in July. In August the highest retail meat prices in years were disturbing buyers. Steak was selling at 37 cents and 42 cents and spring chickens at 42 cents a pound. The new Sedgeman furniture store in the Bailey block on East College Street was formally opened October 27. George L. Close died in October as the result of injuries sustained in an automobile accident. He saw service in the World War and had been with the Oberlin Business College for about 15 years. Reverend James A. Richards, of Winnetka, Illinois, accepted the pastorate of First Church. Former Mayor C. P. Doolittle died in September. He was for some time superintendent of buildings and grounds for Oberlin College.

FACING A NEW CENTURY

CHAPTER XVIII

It was a smug and self-satisfied Oberlin which observed Christmas in 1928. As the year rounded to its close orthodox and unorthodox alike felt certain that the final proof of election to grace was to be found in the lasting prosperity of state and nation and of community and individual. Santa Claus in that year was unusually jolly and unusually generous. A great national campaign had been won on the uplifting slogan "A chicken in every pot." There were a few Jeremiahs to prophesy evil, but they were so greatly outnumbered that their popularity suffered. No one in 1928 dared sell America short. The country's plethoric prosperity was the envy of the less fortunate nations of the world and the pride and joy of those who shared it. God was, in those days, looking after his chosen people with a temporal growth such as was never known before in the history of the world. Oberlin shared in this and rejoiced in its great and deserved good fortune.

In 1929 a change came. Early in the year there were those who said aloud that there must be an end to the skyrocketing of stocks. Office boys, horse jockies, boot blacks, house-maids, and millionaires, who had all made paper fortunes by this upward climb, were loud in their denunciations of those who had in this year insisted that what went up must come down. The voices of the prophets were for a time drowned, but by October, 1929, the great truth registered that the value of industrial stocks for investment purposes is determined largely by their dividend-paying qualities. This truth seemed to strike home as a bolt from a cloudless sky. When paper values disappeared, experts argued for a time that this fact did not affect actual values and that the nation was but entering upon a period of needed and health-giving deflation. Whatever may be the accuracy of the qualifying adjectives, this period of deflation was still in operation in the spring of 1933. The years between the fall of 1929 and the spring of 1933 marked the most far-reaching and disastrous period of depression in the history of America. Oberlin, needless to say, shared in the disturbing collapse of the gas-distended balloon of quick riches. The depression was not felt to its full limit in Oberlin until early in 1933. The two years preceding were increasingly quiet in a business way and retail merchants suffered with growing intensity. The campaign in 1932, which resulted in the election of Governor Franklin D. Roosevelt to the presidency, was fought on the dual issues of the return of normal industrial conditions and the repeal of the Eighteenth Amendment. When President Roosevelt, the day following his inaugural, closed all the banks in the country for a period of several days for possible readjustment, it was felt that America had finally struck bottom in the decline of physical values and in the spread of unemployment. There were some signs later in the spring of a tendency toward slow recovery. The endorsement in 1932 of wet platforms and the selection of a wet Congress, which pushed through a bill for beer of 3.2 percent alcoholic content, forecast the ultimate repeal of the Eighteenth Amendment, which first had its birth in a small gathering here in Oberlin forty years before. Council in May, 1933, licensed the sale of beer here.

It would possibly have been as difficult for the founders of the colony and the college to have understood conditions in 1933 as it would have been for them to have gained an understanding of the limitless hope which marked 1928. Oberlin was rounding out its first century of existence in a spirit marked by gravity and sobriety, but marked no less by courage. If the people in the village in the century closed had lost much of the direct simplicity and self-denial of the pioneer, they had kept much of the stern courage which was characteristic of the founders. There was no disposition to quit under the repeated blows of adversity. There was apparent, on the other hand, a hearty determination to meet without hysteria or supine cowardice the disasters which fate or folly had brought upon the land. This much at least of the pioneer inheritance had survived, and it may well be that this spirit of manhood was the best the founders had to leave to those who should come after them in the race of life.

The Story of a Century

While in these years of distress statesmen were busied with the problem of crashing values and growing unemployment, Oberlin was occupied with its share of these great questions and with the things of less concern which mark the normal progress of small-town life. Early in 1929 announcement was made of the Rockefeller gift to the School of Theology for the construction of the Theological Quadrangle. This work was done the following year at a cost of $600,000.

Early in 1930 Mrs. Julia F. Monroe, daughter of President Finney, died at her winter home at Deland, Florida. In March a union was effected of the Oberlin Tribune and the Oberlin News. In the fall the flag of Henry Lincoln Post, Grand Army of the Republic, was formally presented to Karl Wilson Locke Post, American Legion. Henry Lincoln Post was represented on this occasion by Commander W. B. McClafflin and George H. Houghton, who were then the sole survivors of the organization. Mrs. William Morris, who died in October at the age of 92, had lived in Oberlin since 1854. Initial steps were taken at this time for the abandonment of the lines of the Cleveland Southwestern Traction Company. Service was discontinued in 1931.

It was announced in January, 1931, that the annual budget of the village for all purposes was $136,936.17. It is significant of changed conditions and possibly interpretative of some public ills that the total budget of village and school in Oberlin in 1900 was $33,776 as compared to a total of $258,000 for the conduct of schools and village in 1932. Announcement was made of permission granted to college women to smoke in their rooms. Luther L. Munson died early in 1931, aged 86. Professor Lynds Jones, who had retired from teaching after a successful career as a scientist, was made president of the Oberlin Board of Education. Before this time he had served most acceptably as a member of the Council. The death of H. A. Morgan, father of Harry Morgan and of Miss Grace Morgan, occurred in September. He had been a resident here fifty years.

Noah Hall, the initial college building put up for the housing of men, was erected in the spring of 1932, on Woodland Ave-

Oberlin Colony

nue. In April of this year occurred the death of Clarence J. Wright, of the firm of Wright & Parsons. Mr. Wright had been engaged in the grocery business as clerk or proprietor since 1893. He was active in First Church and represented the highest possible type of character. Wright Memorial Park, built in memory of Mr. Wright by citizens of Oberlin acting under the direction of the Oberlin Business Men's Club, was dedicated in the fall of 1932. The summer of this year witnessed the deaths of four other valued Oberlin citizens: John Hope, for twenty years in business, George Quinn, contractor and builder, A. J. Waite, freight agent for the New York Central for twenty years, and Dr. George W. Andrews, of the faculty of Oberlin College, who died in Honolulu. Dr. Andrews was internationally known as an organist and composer. He was for many years director of the 'Oberlin Musical Union. In the late fall a contract was let for the erection of a new post office on South Main Street at a cost of $85,000. This work, it was expected, would be completed before the end of 1933.

Among the veteran business men of the community as the century closed were J. T. Henderson, president of the Oberlin School of Commerce, formerly the Oberlin Business College, and H. A. Cook. Mr. Henderson began his residence here in 1883. His business career here began the year following. In addition to his duties at the School of Commerce Mr. Henderson has been president of the Peoples Banking Company since its organization. Mr. Cook, the oldest business man in town in point of continuous service, opened a buggy factory on South Main Street in 1880. In 1891 he established a bicycle store which he was still operating in 1933.

At the election in November, 1932, 'Oberlin voters went on record for the construction of a municipal light and power plant by a vote of 2018 to 180. An injunction suit brought by the Ohio Electric Power Company in the spring of 1933 threw the issue into the Courts.

Honorable A. G. Comings, an influential citizen of Oberlin for almost half a century, died in December, 1932, aged 76.

The Story of a Century

With face to the future, confident of what it would offer in the way of industrial recovery and sustaining hope in the battle of life, Oberlin College and Community were preparing in 1933 for the celebration of their centenary. The community observed on April 19 of this year the One Hundredth Anniversary of the coming of its founder, Peter Pindar Pease. Professor Lynds Jones was master of ceremonies and the address of the day was delivered by Professor Robert E. Brown. This observance was preliminary to the main ceremonies to be held at commencement time in June. Plans were made for a community day and for a historic pageant showing the progress of Oberlin College and Community since their founding. The community day address was then assigned to Grove Patterson, widely known journalist. The chief address for Oberlin College was assigned to Robert A. Millikan, eminent scientist. It was expected early in the year that, despite unfavorable economic conditions, 4,000 graduates of the school and former residents of Oberlin would be present for these ceremonies.

APPENDIX

A. THE OBERLIN FOUNDERS

John J. Shipherd was born in West Granville, New York, March 28, 1802. In preparation for college he attended school at Pawlet, Vermont. While at home on vacation he swallowed poison by mistake, thinking it medicine for a slight indisposition. His eyes were impaired to such an extent that he was obliged to give up the college course and his general health was permanently affected. He was married in 1824 to Miss Esther Raymond of Balstom, New York, and established a marble business   at Vergennes, Vermont. Under definite physical handicap he studied for the ministry under Reverend Josiah Hopkins of New Haven, Connecticut. He served for a year as a pastor at Shelburne, Vermont. For two years he was engaged in Sunday School work, making his headquarters at Middlebury, Vermont. It was while at Middlebury that he conceived the idea of establishing a school and colony in the "Valley of the Mississippi." He took an appointment from the American Missionary Society and turned westward without having a definite objective. When he arrived at Cleveland he met Reverend D. W. Lathrop, who had resigned as pastor of the church at Elyria and who recommended Mr. Shipherd for the place. Shipherd began his work in Elyria in 1830 and remained there until coming to Oberlin. In 1844, feeling apparently that his work at Oberlin had been completed, Mr. Shipherd went to Olivet, Michigan, to found a school similar to that here. He was then broken in health and lived only a few months after the establishing of his new colony. He is buried at Olivet. Mrs. Shipherd, who shared her husband's work, died at the home of her son in Cleveland in 1879 at the age of 82.

Philo P. Stewart was born at Sherman, Connecticut, in July, 1798. Ten years later, at the time of his father's death, he was sent to Pittsford, Vermont, to make his home with his grandfather. At the age of 14 he was apprenticed to an uncle in the saddle and harness business at Pawlet, Vermont. It was here he met Mr. Shipherd while both were students at Pawlet Academy. At the age of 23 Mr. Stewart was appointed by the American Board of Missions to a station among the Choctaw Indians in the state of Mississippi. He made the trip of 2,000 miles on horseback and arrived at his destination with $60 left of the $70 presented to him by the Board when he started. In 1827, after a period of rest in Vermont where he had gone because of failing health, Mr. Stewart returned to Mississippi accompanied by four recruits. Among these was Miss Eliza Capin, to whom Mr. Stewart was married in 1828. It was at the end of two years of further service on the part of Mr. and Mrs. Stewart that the state of Mrs. Stewart's health forced their resignation and they returned to New England. In the early spring of 1832, leaving Mrs. Stewart in the East, Stewart joined Mr. Shipherd in Elyria and the two made their plans for the founding of the colony and the college.

Mr. and Mrs. Stewart had charge of the boarding hall in Oberlin College from 1833 to 1836. The views of Mr. Stewart as to frugality and plain diet were such that his conduct of the boarding hall did not meet with hearty approval of students, even in those days of self-denial. Because of this, Mr. Stewart resigned in 1836 and with Mrs. Stewart returned to the East. While a guest in the Shipherd home at Elyria Mr. Stewart, who had a definite talent for mechanics, devised a stove for Mrs. Shipherd. After his retirement from his work here Mr. Stewart perfected this stove, which was widely sold and which brought him in time great wealth. He died in 1868 at the age of 70. His wife survived him a number of years.

B. THE WESTERN RESERVE

When Ohio was admitted into the Union of States in 1803—thirty years before the settlement of Oberlin—one of the terms of admission was that the fee simple to all of the lands within its limits, except those previously granted or sold, should vest in the United States. Prior to the admission of the state, ten or more divisions of land within its boundaries had been sold. One of the first of these sections was the Connecticut Western Reserve, known also at that time as New Connecticut. This section, covering an area of about 3,800,000 acres, lies in the northern portion of the state, with Lake Erie on the north, Pennsylvania on the east, Sandusky and Seneca Counties on the west, with the parallel of the forty-first degree of north latitude its southern boundary. Its extent from east to west is about one hundred and twenty miles, with a width of about fifty miles. These dimensions include the county of Huron, known as the Fire Lands, and comprising a body of about half a million acres. This particular section was a gift from the State of Connecticut to certain sufferers by fire in the War of the Revolution. What was

Oberlin Colony

known as New Connecticut in the early part of the nineteenth century was made up of the counties of Ashtabula, Trumbull, Portage, Geauga, Cuyahoga, Lorain, Medina, Huron, Lake, Erie, Summit, with the exception of two townships, parts of Mahoning and Ashland counties, and the island lying north of Sandusky.

In 1662 King Charles II of Great Britain made a grant to the then Colony of Connecticut of the charter rights to all lands included within certain specified boundaries. Geographical knowledge, both as regards monarchs and their subjects, was limited in those days. In making his gift the English king specified that the grant to Connecticut should include all lands contained between the forty-first and forty-second parallels of north latitude, extending from Providence Plantation on the east to the Pacific ocean on the west, with the exceptions of New York and Pennsylvania. This and other royal grants resulted in interfering claims on the part of colonies and states after the forming of the union. The Federal government in 1800 relinquished all claims upon the Connecticut Western Reserve and guaranteed the fee simple to the State of Connecticut. By the terms of the compromise the United States reserved the right of jurisdiction. This settlement made possible the forming of the State of Ohio and its admission into the Union.

Colonization of the Northwest Territory, which included of course the Connecticut Western Reserve, was hastened by the passage of the ordinance of 1787. The year previous the delegate in Congress from the state of Connecticut relinquished to the United States jurisdiction in the lands included in the Western Reserve. Nine years later, in 1795, Connecticut sold all of New Connecticut to Oliver Phelps and thirty-five others for a consideration of $1,200,000. The purchasers then formed the Connecticut Land Company. Some doubt as to conflicting claims to this land on the part of other states and further doubt as to the provisions of the ordinance of 1787 as to civil government in the Connecticut Western Reserve brought about a compromise which settled the entire issue. By the terms of this compromise Congress authorized the President, in April, 1800, to deliver to the government of Connecticut letters patent whereby the United States released all right and title to the soil of the Western Reserve and confirmed the title in those who had bought from Connecticut. At the same time Connecticut renounced and released to the United States complete civil jurisdiction over this territory. From this territory thus provided with means of government the county of Lorain was established December 26, 1822, eleven years before the settlement of Oberlin.

At the time of the forming of the county there was friendly rivalry among the people of Black River, Sheffield, and Elyria Townships for the location of the county seat. A proposal by Heman Ely, founder of Elyria, to give to the county land for a court house and jail and a donation of $2,000 doubtless convinced the commissioners on location that Elyria was the ideal spot for a county seat. They made this decision early in 1822 and the following year the court house was completed and the machinery of county government was put in motion.

The first township in the county was Columbia, organized in 1809. The last ones formed were Camden and Rochester, both in 1835. Russia Township was organized in 1825. In the land drawing at Hartford, Connecticut, in 1807, a quarter of a century before the settlement of Oberlin, the territory now known as Pittsfield Township was awarded to Ebenezer Devotion, William Perkins, and eight others. A Mr. Barker and two sons were the first white inhabitants. The father cleared a small tract and built a log cabin in 1813, but with his sons abandoned his home for military service. The township was surveyed into lots in 1819 and Milton Whitney was one of the largest owners at that time. The first permanent settlers in Pittsfield were Thomas and Jeffery Waite, sons of Thomas Waite, then a resident of Russia Township.

To the north and west of Russia Township, Brownhelm Township was organized in 1818. It was named for Colonel Henry Brown of Stockbridge, Massachusetts, who in 1816 came to the Western Reserve in company with Peter Pindar Pease, Charles Whittlesey, William Alverson, and William Lincoln. These men, with Seth Morse and Rensselaer Cooley, aided Brown in the building of his home. Morse and Cooley returned to the East that winter, but the others remained on the ground to do the work of clearing and preparing for the coming of other pioneers. Early residents of Brownhelm Township were Levi Shepard, Sylvester Barnum, Steven James, Solomon Whittlesey, Alva Curtis, Benjamin Bacon, and Ebenezer Scott who came in 1817, and, among others who came in 1818, Grandison Fairchild, Anson Cooper, Elisha Peck, George Bacon, Alfred Avery, and Enos Cooley. The first brick house in the county was built by Grandison Fairchild, father of President James H. Fairchild, in 1819. It was still occupied as a residence in 1933.

The first owners of the land which is now Russia Township were Titus Street and Isaac Mills. Before settlement actually began Mills sold his interest to Samuel Hughes and it was from Street and Hughes that a gift of land was secured by Shipherd and Stewart at the time of the founding of Oberlin. In 1818 Thomas Waite, a native of New York who had been living in Amherst, moved into Russia Township, clearing a section of land in the northwest corner. Two years later Daniel Rathburne and Walter and Jonathan Buck settled in the township. Other early residents were John McCauley, Lyman Wakely, Samuel T. Wightman, Jesse Smith, John Maynes, the Disbros, Daniel Axtel, Abraham Wellman, Israel Cash, Richard Rice, James R. Abbott, Henry and John Thurston, and Elias Peabody. In the summer of 1825 the first township election was held in a log school house. George Disbro, Israel Cash, and Walter Buck were elected trustees, Richard Rice, clerk, and Daniel Axtel, justice of the peace.

In the early years of the nineteenth century little had been done looking to the complete settlement of the territory now known as Lorain County. It was not until 1823 that work was begun on the court house at Elyria. At that time there was a settlement at Brownhelm, there were pioneer farmers in a northern section of Russia Township and in Pittsfield on the south, and a few other scattered settlements in other portions of the county. There was no development of the territory in and around what is now Oberlin before the coming of Deacon Pease in 1833. This condition was due to the fact that the soil in the Oberlin district was not as good as in other parts of the county and to the further fact that much of the territory was made up of swamp lands. A primitive road, which was nothing more than a clearing through the wilderness running into Oberlin from the north, made it plain to the casual traveler that the soil was mainly clay. It has been estimated by geologists that this clay extends to a depth of seventy-five feet. Time has proved, however, that when rightly treated the land will raise small grains and is peculiarly fitted for grazing.

C. THE PIONEER'S COURAGE

It is not possible for those living today to visualize the task which confronted the pioneer settler in the county one hundred years or more ago. Most of the first residents came either from Connecticut or Massachusetts. When they made the trip by land, as many did in the earlier days in covered wagons drawn by horses or by oxen, the time of the journey varied from four to seven weeks. When sailing vessels became common on Lake Erie the trip was cut to about two weeks. President Fairchild, in his *History of Brownhelm,* says that it was not unusual for young men to walk from Massachusetts to Ohio, carrying a few needed articles in a white canvas knapsack. While such a journey would in itself discourage the modern traveler, accustomed to brick or concrete roads and fast flying cars, the fact remains that the real difficulties of the early settler began with his arrival on the ground. There were forests to be cleared and homes to be built. The wresting of a modest living from the soil was then a thing of daily application to the task. Dwellings were built of logs, roughly plastered, with a single door. Oiled paper served for window lights where glass could not be secured. When prosperity arrived floors were made. Sometimes there were stairs leading to the attic room, but in most cases a ladder sufficed. A hole in the ground under the first floor served as a cellar. Private bedrooms were provided by curtains of sheets or quilts. These often disappeared as the needs of a growing family pressed, and the bed was left shelterless. In rare cases a family attained the dignity of a sleeping room separated from the living room by a board partition.[1]

While these details are selected from the history of the community of Brownhelm, established in 1817, it may be assumed that they are true in great measure of the homes of early settlers in Oberlin, only sixteen years later. There was without doubt deep satisfaction in the making even of a primitive home in the wilderness. This was a work of love and had its definite compensations. It is doubtful if the pioneer found immediate return and like satisfaction for his determined efforts in clearing the forests. This was a task which tested the faith and the courage of the strongest. The trees of those days were not the trees of these. One magnificent specimen of the time is said to have measured fifteen feet in diameter above the swell of the roots. The cutting down of such giants and the removal of stumps was

---

1 President Fairchild, *History of Brownhelm.*

no task for a man with a weak back or a weak heart. In his work the pioneer had only his axe, a yoke of oxen and a log chain. There were no engines at hand. The process of clearing was of necessity slow and it has well been said that a feeble race would have retired from the encounter. But there was sweet with the bitter, for the forests provided unlimited material for fencing and for fuel. No outlay of capital was required for the building of a home, unless the owner desired the luxury of window glass. The trees thus removed for clearing and for building included many thousands of fine specimens of whitewood, oak, ash, hickory, black walnut, and chestnut. These have been replaced by growing communities, and, in theory at least, the change has been for the advancement of humanity.

Living conditions were in keeping with the primitive character of homes. In the decade prior to the settlement of Oberlin there was little in the way of trading. The pioneer farmer hewed from the forests or raised for the use of himself and his family the products needed to sustain life. There were no railroads and no canals. The problem of food was more readily solved than that of clothing. Every woman was a spinner, but weavers were scarce. Sheep were few and when wool could be found the process of manufacture was slow. President Fairchild says in his *History of Brownhelm* that it was not a rare thing to see a boy in school with his summer pants drawn over the remnant of his last winter's wear. Home dressed deerskin occasionally furnished suits. Leather was scarce. Cattle were too valuable to be sacrificed for such comforts as shoes, tallow candles, and beef. Mr. Fairchild says: "The snow often came before the shoes and then the shoes themselves would be a curiosity—made as they were indiscriminately from the skins of the hog, the dog, the deer, and the wolf. I remember to have worn all these myself."

Food in the old days was, in simplicity, in keeping with clothing. There were no bakery wagons and the housewife made her bread in her home. Jointed corn or pounded wheat entered into the process. Pork was the staple article in meat diet with an abundance of venison and other wild game, of which in time the pioneer grew weary. The cultivation of the peach began in early pioneer days and it is on record that diseases and insects which in present day attack fruit trees were then in Northern Ohio unknown. It was not unusual for families to be without sugar for months at a time. Honey and pumpkin molasses served as substitutes. The food was placed in a common dish in the middle of the table. A knife and fork at each seat sufficed, or even one of them would do for the children. A drinking cup at each end of the table was ample. If bread and milk was the bill of fare, a single bowl and spoon could do duty for the entire family, going down from the oldest to the youngest.[2]

There could be little reading at night in these homes in the forests. Only the more fortunate families could have the luxury of a single tallow candle. This was lighted when visitors came. For general lighting a wood fire served. When the housewife had sewing or a member of the family desired to read, a saucer filled with hog's fat with a wick of twisted rag furnished the light. For an evening prayer meeting two dipped candles were provided.

When the pioneer fathers had cleared a portion of their land for farming purposes they were forced to till the soil by methods entirely primitive compared with those of today. Oxen were best suited for work among logs and stumps. Sometimes a single ox was made to do duty in plowing corn. The plowshare, made of wrought iron and pointed with steel, was brought from the East. When this point broke it was necessary, in the days of the first settlements, to send to Massachusetts for a new one. A little later these were replaced by a furnace in operation at Elyria. Mechanics devoting their time exclusively to a trade were slow to arrive in Lorain County. The pioneers were giving their entire attention to the clearing of their land and could not in general afford to support people in other lines of trade. Shoemakers, brick masons, and carpenters were often farmers as well.

Within the early years of the nineteenth century and for several years after the date of the settling of Oberlin, wild animals were plentiful in Lorain County. Wolves were more abundant than was pleasing to the farmer who had to protect his stock. In 1827 the county commissioners offered a bounty for wolf scalps and about that time wolf hunters were common in the settled portion of the county. Bears were not so numerous, but were frequently seen. Deer were more plentiful than cattle and farmers were often able to secure the family meat for a period of several days by shooting deer from their own back yard. In this connection President Finney says, dealing with his coming to Oberlin in 1835: "All around was an immense and unbroken forest, and the deer were so plentiful that they seemed to look out from the woods upon us, to see what we were about.

---

2 President Fairchild, *History of Brownhelm.*

Oberlin Colony

To escape from the pressure that was upon my mind, I would frequently take my rifle and go into the woods, and would seldom go forty rods from the clearing without seeing a deer. Brother George Clark, who boarded at Mr. Shipherd's, shot a deer, almost from the door of the house, that came out of the woods to see what we were about in 'Oberlin. Where this building now stands, was then a forest."

Since Oberlin's first settler, Peter Pindar Pease, had been a chief figure in the building up of Brownhelm, where he lived from 1816 to his departure in 1833, it is certain that he and such of his associates who came to Oberlin in the early days from other settlements in Lorain County knew in the main what they would again have to face in the way of stern effort in clearing the ground and making the way for the building here of a new settlement. It is an earnest of their courage and strength that they should undertake for a second time a work of this character.

D. OLD FAMILIES IN OBERLIN

There were few living in Oberlin in 1933 who were direct descendants of pioneer residents. The oldest family in Oberlin one hundred years after the founding of the colony and college was that of W. B. Gerrish, whose father, Nathaniel Gerrish, came here in 1834. Nathaniel Gerrish bought, in 1837, from Peter Pindar Pease, the lot on which the W. B. Gerrish home now stands. The original home erected by the father was destroyed by fire in 1875. J. V. Hill, Oberlin merchant, is a grandson of Lyman Hill, who came to Oberlin in 1837. The children of Mr. and Mrs. John W. Hill represent the fifth generation. J. V. Hill has in his possession a wallet which belonged to his grandfather and a work bench which the latter used in his operations as contractor and carpenter. The Misses Alice and Elizabeth Little, of East College Street, are granddaughters of Professor Henry Cowles, who came to Oberlin in 1835. Frank Beckwith, assistant postmaster of Oberlin, is a grandson of Woolston Beckwith, one of the pioneer merchants of the village. Mrs. Arthur Packard, of Woodland Avenue, is a granddaughter of Simeon Bushnell, who had part in the Wellington Rescue. Professor Florence M. Fitch of the faculty of Oberlin College is a granddaughter of James M. Fitch, who came to Oberlin in the thirties and for years conducted a book store and publishing house here. The father of Miss Celia Burr, of West Lorain Street, for a number of years a teacher in the public schools here, came to

Oberlin as a student in the early days of the colony. He was absent in his work as a preacher for a number of years, but finally returned here to live. Miss Fannie Wright, of Forest Street, is a daughter of Deacon W. W. Wright, influential citizen of the community in its early days. William Hovey, father of Frank Hovey, of North Pleasant Street, was in business in Oberlin before the Civil War. He came to Oberlin in 1851. H. L. Bassett, of West College Street, is a descendent of one of the pioneer families of Russia Township. His ancestors were farmers living outside the village limits. Phineas Royce, grandfather of Mrs. A. G. Comings, was one of the early business men of the village. He came to Oberlin in 1840 from Clinton, N. Y. Samuel Royce, father of Mrs. Comings, came to Oberlin to live in 1850. Andrew Clinton Comings, father of the late Andrew G. Comings, came from Vermont in 1867. Miss Ella M. Platt, of West College Street, is a granddaughter of Alanson Beach Platt, who came to Oberlin in the thirties and who operated a farm north of town. He and his wife, Elizabeth Beach Platt, reared and educated a family of eleven children. H. M. Platt was a son. Leonard Paige, a native of Vermont, had a farm north of Oberlin near the Platt residence in the early thirties. He and his wife were parents of seventeen children. Paige had purchased lumber for a new house at the time of the building of First Church and when solicited for contributions he abandoned his purpose of building and donated the lumber to the church, ending his days in his pioneer log cabin. Mrs. A. R. Kimpton is a granddaughter of Mr. Paige. Mrs. Earl D. Jones is a granddaughter of Dr. William C. Bunce, a pioneer physician. A son bore the same name and followed the same profession. Mr. and Mrs. B. F. Tenney are living at 178 North Professor Street in the house built in 1852 by Deacon Edward W. Andrews, who was the father of Mr. Tenney's mother, Mrs. Frances Adelia Andrews Tenney, wife of Luman H. Tenney. Deacon Andrews came from New York to Cleveland at the age of 16 when that city had a population of only 800. Miss Edith Clarke, 67 South Professor Street, is a daughter of Mayor J. B. Clarke. Her grandfather, Philip K. Thompson, who served several terms in the Ohio Legislature, came to Oberlin to live in the early '50's. Mrs. Theodore Keep was a daughter. The family home stood at the northeast corner of Main and Lorain Streets.

E. DID DEACON PEASE KNOW HIS DICE?

Were there two sides to the character of Deacon Peter Pindar Pease, first citizen of Oberlin? Was his unquestioned piety crossed with a strain that made it possible for him to "chuck" dice with even so great a man as Edgar Allen Poe? That Mr. Pease did gamble with Poe and that he collected from the poet the fruits of the game of chance is asserted in an article in the *Outlook* for September, 1920.

The story in question is told by Theodore Pease Stearns, a grand-nephew of Peter Pindar Pease, who states that he had it from the late Judge Harlow Pease, of Watertown, Wisconsin, a nephew of Peter Pindar Pease. Mr. Stearns, a former student of Oberlin College, gives the following version of the relations of the Oberlin pioneer and the great poet:

"When Poe was attending the University of Virginia, at Charlottesville, it fell to the lot of my great-uncle, Peter Pindar Pease, to make his acquaintance. Pease afterwards met the poet again in Boston, at a time when his biographer seems to have lost track of Poe, and later met him again in New York.

"It seems a pity that this companionship with this gifted genius should have fallen to the lot of as unsympathetic a person as my late kinsman. Indeed, the old gentleman never attached any importance to his association with Poe and it was only by persistent inquiry that my own uncle, Judge Harlow Pease, drew it from his uncle Peter. The facts were presented just as the judge passed them on to me.

"But Pease was a staunch prohibitionist and he believed Poe to be dissolute. He was a deacon of his church at Oberlin, Ohio (a determined pillar), and he regarded Poe as an outcast. Furthermore old Deacon Pease was deeply interested in the Underground Railroad before the war and he believed Poe to be a southerner. Finally the old gentleman cared nothing for any poetry outside his hymn book and therefore the entire scheme of Edgar Allen Poe's history and genius was without value to him.

"As a boy Pease was apprenticed to a saddle maker, Herman Tucker by name, and shortly before the early 30's he arrived at Charlottesville, Virginia, where Tucker opened a shop and my great-uncle became his assistant. Trade was pretty brisk and soon the little shop developed into a sort of curio store filled with second-hand articles, including a library which had fallen under the auctioneer's hammer in order to satisfy a plaintiff's debt and so came into the possession of Tucker. Among these books was a rare edition of Hogarth's prints, and this work the young assistant resolved to purchase on the installment plan from his employer.

"Two small payments had been made when Poe, then attending the college, happened at the shop one day, noticed the book, and decided to buy it. Upon Tucker's telling Poe that his clerk was attempting to purchase the work out of his meager earnings, the poet ask to be made known to my great-uncle and thus their acquaintance began. Poe immediately invited Uncle Peter up to his room, asking him to bring the Hogarth along with him that they might look it over, and the invitation was accepted.

"Next evening the call was made and after some parleying Poe suggested that they gamble for the book, agreeing to pay Peter the full price which Tucker asked in case he lost. If Peter lost he was to continue paying off the debt to Tucker and Poe was to keep the Hogarth. My great-uncle had been brought up to fear the devil and all his works with Calvinistic severity, but he resolved to take the chance of getting the book for nothing, so the dice were thrown. Poe lost and promptly paid over the money. Whatever became of the book I do not know. It is certainly not in the Pease library and uncle Pindar probably sold it. This incident occurred in May, 1826, as nearly as the old deacon remembered it.

"In July of the same year young Pease separated from his employer and returned to New England, settling in Boston, where he was again to meet Poe. It was while unloading a dray of hides on the water-front one blustering March afternoon that my great-uncle recognized in a pale, rather stoop-shouldered clerk, his former acquaintance who had diced with him in Virginia the year before."

Mr. Stearns relates a conversation between the two men and then states that Peter Pindar Pease did not see the poet again until 1831, when they met in New York where Poe had gone, he said, to secure the publication of a book of his poems by Harpers. On this occasion the two men simply exchanged brief greetings.

Mr. Stearns says that Judge Harlow Pease, in relating this story, cautioned him that he might not print any of it until after the relator's death.[1]

---

[1] The story Mr. Stearns tells is interesting, but of extremely doubtful authenticity. Records show that Deacon Pease was rearing his family in Brownhelm when these dramatic incidents are supposed to have occurred. The good man would have had little interest in Hogarth's prints and less inclination to gamble for works of art of this character. He was father of a child born in Brownhelm in 1825 and a second child was born to him in 1827. The known record of his life contains nothing to indicate that he would leave his wife without care and protection at such a time.

F. HIRAM ABIF PEASE

Hiram Abif Pease, brother of Oberlin's first settler, spent the greater part of his life in Oberlin. He died in 1889 at the advanced age of 92. He was two years younger than Peter Pindar Pease, having been born at Stockbridge, Massachusetts, in 1797. He spent the earlier years of his life at Brownhelm. For years he was employed as a wagon maker and was known as a good mechanic. He was among the early settlers of Brownhelm and it was his second son Alonzo Pease, for a time a captain in the Union army in the Civil War and later an artist of talent, who drove the oxen for Peter Pindar Pease when the latter came with his family to Oberlin. Several portraits of men prominent in the college in the early days were painted by Alonzo Pease and are now the property of the college. They include portraits of President Mahan, Dr. John Morgan, and Mr. and Mrs. Hiram A. Pease.

Hiram A. Pease, particularly in his later years, was different in temperament from his brother Peter. In his early life in Oberlin Hiram Pease followed the accepted high standard of religious solemnity. He was a member of the first class in the college and was a teacher in the Sunday School of First Church. In later years Mr. Pease developed a possibly latent sense of healthy humor. While still in a state of excellent health and apparently enjoying life, he took a large granite boulder to his shop and during his spare time polished one side that it might be used as a monument over his grave. He made express request of his family that after his death the following epitaph in verse be placed on the face of the stone on which he had spent so much time:

> Under this sod and under these trees,
> Lies the body of Hiram A. Pease.
> He is not here, only his pod:
> He's shelled out his soul, and gone back to God.

A descendant of Pease says that his request was not complied with because there was not sufficient room on the polished side of the stone. Mr. Pease is recorded as having said on numerous occasions that he wanted people to laugh when they came to his grave.

Mr. Pease was for years a deacon in First Church. He was active in the work of the Underground Railroad and was a stout friend of the colored people, both before and after their liberation. This friendship was manifested in the arrangements which he made for his funeral. By his request a colored undertaker prepared his body for burial and colored men were his pallbearers. President Fairchild preached his funeral sermon and paid tribute to Mr. Pease as a good friend and an earnest pioneer who had had a share in the making of 'Oberlin.

Mr. Pease was in many respects one of the most interesting of the strong men who were concerned with the founding of Oberlin village. In his early life he was active in church and Sunday School work and as a Sunday School teacher at Brownhelm had among his pupils President James H. Fairchild. Either the spirit of adventure or an abiding faith in "Father" Shipherd led Pease to go with the small colony of forty or more who went from Oberlin to Olivet, Michigan, to found a similar school and community there under the direction of Mr. Shipherd. Mr. Pease did not stay long at Olivet and returned to Oberlin where he thereafter lived. He at one time took an interest in spiritualism but finally, in the later years of his life, abandoned religious belief of any character, stating that he did not know about the future.

G. SOME STORIES OF FINNEY

Tradition carries down to the present many stories relating to President Finney. A student of backward disposition had purposely avoided contact with Mr. Finney outside of his classroom, that he might not be embarrassed by saluting him. Despite this care, he met the great man on the campus one day. Mr. Finney stopped and, fixing the youth with his magnetic eyes, asked him, "What's your name?" When a stammering response was made, Mr. Finney said: "Do you love God?" When the young man replied that he did, the president smiled benevolently and said: "Then we shall be good friends." Ever after that time, for more than a quarter of a century, Mr. Finney spoke to the relator of the story whenever he met him.

It is known that President Finney did not favor the forming of the Second Church by taking away a part of the congregation of the First Church, of which he was pastor. The movement had such strength, however, that the separation came about, but it is significant that the organization of the new church was effected while President Finney was abroad in England. On the return of Mr. Finney, Professor John M. Ellis called on him and in the course of the conversation made an effort to explain to Mr. Finney the reasons for the action taken. Mr. Ellis assured Mr. Finney that the separation did not grow out of any unfriendly feeling or dissatisfaction with the First Church or its affairs. Mr. Ellis further said that the church had become so large and the building so crowded that those of the congregation who organized the Second Church thought it best that a portion withdraw and give others, who so much needed to hear Mr. Finney, an opportunity to enjoy his preaching. The man who told the story years afterwards said: "With that inimitable Finney look that used to carry such tremendous force and logic with it, President Finney replied, 'John, you folks that have gone off to form this Second Church need my preaching more than anybody else.'"

A student here in 1837 related after the beginning of the twentieth century a story of President Finney's success in praying for rain. There was a severe drought in the summer of 1837. Crops were failing and pastures were burning up for lack of rain. Plum Creek was dry. The teller of the story says that cattle went up and down the street lowing for water. Black River was almost dry. In the midst of this distress Mr. Finney suggested a day of fasting and prayer. The entire community responded with a hope that relief would come. The people had faith in the efficacy of Mr. Finney's prayers and the chapel was filled to capacity at the hour set for the meeting. After opening the exercise Mr. Finney devoted an hour to what is described as, "An almost fearful explanation of what real prayer is." Toward the close of the hour of service there was a great display of thunder and lightning and pouring rain followed. During the rain Mr. Finney called for a member in the congregation to "come forward" and give thanks. The rain was confined almost altogether to the town of Oberlin.

About two years later a similar condition prevailed and the people once again appealed to Mr. Finney for prayer for rain. A large congregation gathered on the day set apart. The relator says: "We all met in the chapel and then without preliminary exercises to any length, began that almost fearful prayer. All heads and hearts were bowed while Mr. Finney seemed to go up and almost talk with God about the suffering on account of the drought. He pleaded for the fowls of heaven; the birds could no longer sing their sweet songs. The rain came during the prayer and spread over the country. And for a time at least people who had no sympathy with Oberlin did honor to Mr. Finney's prayers."

H. THE FIRST STUDENT HERE

Much of interest and of apparent reliability as to early conditions in and around Oberlin is contained in a letter written to J. B. T. Marsh, then fiscal agent for Oberlin College, by Isaac I. Warren of the class of 1840. Mr. Warren, who then lived at Durham, Iowa, prefaced his discussion of early events with an introduction in which he said: "Even your card has opened in my mind the sealed fountain of other years. With the first decade of Oberlin history I was once very well acquainted and as my wife read your card to me (for I am so blind that I have not read anything for myself for years) the question arose in my mind whether, among all the multitudes of alumni to whom your card would come, there would be one in whose mind would arise so many, so varied, and peculiar reminiscences of their Oberlin life as arise in my own."

After discussing co-education, which had his entire approval, Mr. Warren says: "The admission of colored students to Oberlin was a feature in advance of the age, and awakened great opposition even in its Board of Trustees . . . The founder and agent told me at the time that if the decision had been against the colored people he should have given up all effort or care for the Institution, and that at the time would have meant its ruin. On the other hand because it went in favor of the colored people several members of the board resigned, among whom was Captain Redington, of Amherst. He was the agent of Street and Hughes of whom the land for the college had been obtained, and he told me that had he known colored students would be admitted he would have opposed their parting with any land for the Institution. But it was then too late; the land had been made sure to the Institution by his own action as their agent.

"It was my privilege to be acquainted with Mr. Shipherd long before Oberlin was ever thought of. In his preparation for the ministry he studied under the private instruction of Reverend Josiah Hopkins, pastor of the Congregational Church of New Haven, Vermont, of which he was a member. He was for some time an excellent superintendent of our Sabbath School. Afterward he went to Ohio and became interested in the founding of Oberlin. He made a tour through New England in the spring and summer of 1833 as agent of the board soliciting funds, colonists, and students for the Institution. It is just 45 years today since my connection with the Oberlin enterprise began by my receiving and accepting on the 31st of July, 1833, in New Haven, Vermont, from John J. Shipherd an invitation to join the 'Oberlin enterprise as a student and member of a school that was to be in the woods of Ohio.

"I arrived in Cleveland early in September, 1833, and took the stage to Captain Redington's in South Amherst, five miles from 'Oberlin. I proposed to start immediately for Oberlin, but Mrs. Redington told me that she was fearful I would lose my way through the woods, and advised me to wait until evening and have the company and guidance of Deacon Peter Pindar Pease who had gone from Oberlin to Brownhelm and would return near night. He did return, but later than was expected, and we started into the woods for our five-mile walk through them at dusk. We followed a foot path trail and arrived in Oberlin between 9 and 10 o'clock. We entered at the northeast corner of the public square, and found it all aglow with burning log heaps that cast a low light over the settlement and by its light we passed on to Deacon Pease's cabin at the southeast corner of the square. An elm tree, still standing there, I hope, marked the location of this first cabin ever built in 'Oberlin.[1] The tree stood east of the cabin, directly in front of it, and only a few feet from it. It was preserved as a memorial tree, because up to this tree Deacon Peter Pindar Pease drove his team, fastened them to it, and fed them there when he moved into Oberlin, the first and only family there, and all around was an unbroken wilderness. The second cabin was built directly south of the first and in line with it and close to it. Mrs. Pease told me it was built there so they could have near neighbors in their loneliness. Another elm tree stood directly in front of it and about the same distance from it. If both trees are still standing, the memorial tree is the north one.

"On my long walk through the woods I found Deacon Pease a very sociable gentleman. When he learned where I was from, and why I had come to Oberlin, that I was formerly acquainted with Mr. Shipherd and had, on his invitation joined the Oberlin enterprise as a member of the Institute, he opened his mind to me very freely on Oberlin affairs, spoke of the many difficulties with which they had to contend, and why it was located in the

---

[1] Mr. Warren's statement as to the location of the Peter Pindar Pease cabin, although made many years after his spending his first night as a guest of Mr. Pease, would seem to make it plain that the cabin was made to face the east and stood directly west of the Historic Elm. The second cabin built to the south of the Pease home must have projected beyond the present north line of West College Street.

midst of this wilderness so isolated, it being from three to twelve or fifteen miles out to the nearest houses around in different directions. He informed me that he had moved from Brownhelm to Oberlin on the 19th day of April, a little more than four months previous, and was the first family there; that he was a member of the Board of Trustees and local agent for the Institute, and had the oversight of the work. He said that no students had come in as yet, and that I was the first one on the ground—that I would not find Mr. Shipherd there, as he was with his family still at Elyria, and had not moved in yet for the want of a place, but that it would make no difference with him if I would consider his house my home, although they were very much thronged. He told me there were on the ground forty persons in all, twenty-five of whom were colonists, and the other fifteen were hired helpers to carry forward the work; that some were framing a sawmill and some were clearing off the fifteen-acre college square to put in the fall wheat; that they had raised the first Institute building, which they called Oberlin Hall, and had it partly enclosed, and the work on it had ceased for want of lumber.

"When we arrived at his house he introduced me to his family and household as the first student in Oberlin and they all gave me a very friendly and cordial welcome. We found them becoming very anxious for his safety, as they had expected him home before sunset. The large timber wolves were plenty and their howl had been heard on our trail. It was not thought quite safe to be out in the woods on foot and alone after nightfall. They had kept supper waiting and with him I took my first meal in Oberlin. It was bed time and after family worship something was said about my sleeping in a field bed because they were so thronged. I was puzzled, wondering what a field bed meant, never having heard of that kind of a bed before. Soon a Mr. Harvey Gibbs, a colonist from Hartford, Vermont, (he was afterwards the first justice of the peace and the first postmaster Oberlin ever had), took a light and acted as usher of the bed chamber by ascending the ladder to the loft and standing at the head of it and holding the light so as to shine on those who were coming up and also those who had got up and were going to bed. I found that a field bed meant a bed spread on the floor from one end of the cabin to the other without any division or partition. The first one up took the farthest end and the rest packed along in regular order as they came up, and when all were safely lodged the usher blew out his light and lay down, the last one. On this night some twelve or fourteen of us were thus lodged. Some humorous remarks were indulged in and among the rest there was said that as there was a stranger in the bed they ought all of them to be numbered or labeled, so that there would be no dispute or mistake about the personal identity of each one in the morning. Thus my first night in Oberlin did not furnish me any refreshing sleep. My ride from Cleveland and long walk through the woods, my first experience of a field bed, and my first experience at a concert of owls and wolves made night hideous. The excitement and novelty of the situation, together with the thousand and one thoughts of the past, the present, and the future, kept me in such a state that the first daybreak I ever saw in Oberlin found me wakeful and ready to get up as soon as it should come my turn from the front end of the field bed. It had got noised around that a student had come in with Deacon Pease and after breakfast quite a number made it in their way to call in. They all gave me friendly welcome.

"After the colonists had dispersed to their labors, I went up on the frame of Oberlin Hall, as near the ledge as I could get, to take a look at the town or little hamlet and its improvements. I found that all the improvements consisted of six log cabins finished and occupied, one or two of them only a few days before, two cabin foundations laid but not completed, one Institute building, frame raised and partly covered, a sawmill partly framed, and a log building owned and occupied as a blacksmith shop by Bela Hall from Royalton, Vermont. I found by way of clearing the fifteen-acre college square, the first tier of town lots east and southeast of it, and about an acre south and west of Oberlin Hall, in all twenty acres. This comprised all there was of Oberlin that morning. I found Oberlin a busy hive of earnest workers. Everyone seemed to have a definite object in view, and to go about its accomplishment with a will. I spent my first day there getting acquainted with the place and the people. Mr. Shipherd came in during the day, and the next morning when I reported myself at headquarters as ready to go to work, Mr. Shipherd was there and said there was a very bad place in the wagon trail toward Elyria, and, as all the rest of the men were busy, he and I would go out about a mile and fix it. We went, and after showing me the place he soon left me and returned to the village. I put in my first day's work in Oberlin in repairing the road. I think he did it to test my ability, as he afterwards told me I had done a good job and thought I would do very well as a manual training student. I soon went to work at the bench under the direction of 'Otis Janes, helping to finish off Oberlin Hall.

"The first Sabbath I spent in Oberlin for a meeting house we used the first cabin by placing blocks of wood around the room and placing rails on them for seats, thus accommodating an audience of about forty persons to whom Mr. Shipherd preached. In two or three weeks we finished off two basement rooms under the west part of Oberlin Hall and Mr. Shipherd moved his family from Elyria into the north basement room and I went to live with him."

Mr. Warren relates that while he was the first student on the ground he was not able to attend the first term in the college. He received an invitation to teach at Brownhelm and on the advice of Mr. Shipherd he accepted. Mr. Warren had taught in the East before coming to 'Oberlin. He rode to Brownhelm with Hiram Pease, brother of Peter Pindar Pease, in an ox wagon.

I. AN EARLY INDUSTRY

One of the early industries of Oberlin was an ashery located on East Vine Street. This is an activity which disappeared with the pioneer days. The small factory handled, for the purpose of making potash, the tons of ashes produced when the forests were cleared. This clearing meant not only the cutting down of trees but the burning of stumps and brush to make the soil tillable. There was no market for lumber in those days and logs and branches were thrown into one great heap and fired. The resulting ashes were turned over to the ashery from time to time. Ash-peddlers made regular trips not only around Oberlin but in surrounding territory. Many of the trees reduced to ashes were of great height and diameter. Record is made of an oak tree on a farm west of Oberlin which measured twenty-four feet in circumference. Trees five feet in diameter were not unusual in the early days of the colony.

J. EARLY OBERLIN MAPS

The etching attached to page 21, is made from a photostat copy of the original in the possession of 'Oberlin College and is the oldest map extant showing in detail land ownership and location in the pioneer colony. Accompanying this map is a certificate dated December 23, 1835, and signed by A. Tracy and Nathan P. Fletcher, which reads: "This certifies that the within map plan and design is correct and true, having assembled the same as a committee by order of Oberlin Society (agreeable to the survey and field book on record in the County Clerk Office for the County of Lorain) made and signed by Hiram Davis on a former day employed by the colony—together with Village Lots No. 58 to 62 on the parsonage Lot No. 75—as also Village Lots Nos. 63 to 67 inclusive on the original Lots No. 85 as surveyed by Nathan P. Fletcher."

The Freeman Map

Lorain County Records, Book J, Page 540-541 show a plat and survey of the town or village of Oberlin, signed J. E. Freeman, County Surveyor, and dated July 24, 1837.

This map has peculiar interest in showing that at that early day South Street, Morgan Street, Mill Street, East and West College Street and Lorain Street were the then established streets running east and west. The north and south streets were East Street, Water Street, Pleasant Street, Main Street, and Professor Street. Lots are numbered on the map but names of lot owners are not given. The following certificate bearing the names of early pioneer residents appears on the face of the map: "The undersigned hereby acknowledge that we approve of the plan that is prepared for record in the Clerk's office and signed by J. E. Freeman, dated July 24, 1837; Asahel Munger, Alexander Steele, Joseph H. Marsh, A. H. Boland, Nelson Scoville, Luther Turner, Augustus A. Smith, Bela Hall, Chloe Cummings, Edwin Dowd, Wovener Reed, Anna Butler, James Dascomb, George W. Fletcher, Louis Mills, Phillip James, Robert Cochran, H. C. Taylor, William Hosford, Pringle Hamilton, Steven Hull, Brewster Pelton, Anson Penfield, Isaac Penfield, Sarah Munger, Daniel Morgan, Philo P. Stewart, Otis James, Harvey Gibbs."

For the excellent copy of the 1837 map on file in the office of City Manager Sears the Village is indebted to the thoughtfulness of W. B. Gerrish, former City Engineer.

K. OBERLIN PUBLICATIONS

The first publication regularly issued in the community was the 'Oberlin Evangelist, established in 1838. It was published until 1862, when war conditions forced a suspension. The Peace Maker was launched in 1839, but suspended publication the following year. J. M. Fitch, pioneer book seller, tried on two or three occasions to establish a secular newspaper. The Public Press, which he established in 1844, lasted but one year. Mr. Fitch was not discouraged by this failure and promoted the Village Item in 1852. This paper lasted but a short time and in the fall of that same year he founded the Oberlin Weekly Times, which suspended publication in June, 1853. Lack of advertising patronage was the reason for the suspension of these three papers. The Students Monthly, edited by Oberlin College students, was established in 1858, but suspended publication in 1861, at the outbreak of the Civil War. The Oberlin College Review was established in 1874 and was still published in 1933. Bibliotheca Sacra, edited for many years by Professor G. Frederic Wright, was brought to Oberlin from the East in 1883. The first permanent newspaper in the village was the Lorain County News, later the Oberlin News. It was founded in 1860. The Owl, established by J. L. Kinney, was first published in 1894. It subsequently became the Oberlin Tribune, which was united with the 'Oberlin News in 1930 to make the Oberlin News-Tribune.

L. OBERLIN'S FIRST TABLE

C. S. Hopkins, son of Fay Hopkins, one of the Oberlin builders, tells of "Father" Shipherd's visit to his parents in northern Vermont and of his persuading them to join the Oberlin movement. They finally agreed, and Mr. Hopkins relates that when the family were coming down Lake Champlain his father threw all his pipes and tobacco into the water and "never had any desire to use the stuff afterwards." The trip from Vermont was made in fourteen days, despite the fact that in coming from Elyria to Oberlin Mr. Hopkins found it necessary occasionally to cut out logs so that his family could get through. The Fay Hopkins log cabin was built on the east side of North Main Street north of the Lorain Street intersection. The elder Hopkins improvised a family table by making legs for a single slab or plank. His son thought it was the first table in Oberlin. There was no fire place in the cabin and Mrs. Hopkins used to cook the food for the family out of doors.

M. OBERLIN TELEGRAPH SCHOOL

An industry of an educational character which played an important part in the business life of Oberlin for about four decades, beginning in the early sixties, was the Oberlin Telegraph School, which was organized in 1862 by the Pond Brothers. One member of the firm was Reverend C. N. Pond, for years a resident of Oberlin. In 1868 the school was purchased by C. A. Shearman and A. G. Shearman. A stock company was formed and the new ownership built and operated a commercial telegraph line in connection with their school. The school was located in rooms in the Carpenter block on West College Street opposite the campus. Shearman Brothers conducted the school until 1876, when it was bought by Messrs. Hyatt, Suter, and Peck. C. A. Shearman, accompanied by J. A. Sheridan, removed in 1876 to San Francisco. The following year Mr. Sheridan returned to Oberlin and started an opposition school. Within one year's time he succeeded in getting control of the field and had the only school of the kind in the village. He built the attendance from sixty-five pupils to a peak of two hundred and seventy. The owner finally sold it to a stock company, controlled by Charles T. Beckwith, T. H. Rowland, and Albert Johnson. The school was operated by the company for two years when it was sold to George Durand, who was later succeeded in its operation by George J. Peake.

Mr. Sheridan was recognized a half century ago as one of the best telegraph operators in the country. He built lines to Lorain, North and South Amherst, and Vermilion, having local business, with connections at Vermilion with a postal telegraph company. The school occupied a brick building, on South Main Street, the old Pettis Hall, now Odd Fellows Hall, and the room now used as a club room by Oberlin Lodge of Masons.

N. MAYORS OF OBERLIN

Lewis Holtslander	1847, 1848	Charles A. Metcalf	1884-1888
Isaac Jennings	1849	Arden Dale	1888-1892
O. R. Ryder	1850	Died in office	
J. W. Merrill	1851	O. F. Carter	
Uriah Thompson	1852	Filled vacancy	
James Dascomb	1853	A. G. Comings	1892-1896
O. R. Ryder	1854	Alfred Fauver	1896-1904
J. W. Merrill	1855	Died in office	
David Brokaw	1856, 1857	M. G. Dick	
A. N. Beecher	1858, 1859	Filled vacancy	
Samuel Hendry	1860, 1861	O. F. Carter	1904-1908
J. M. Ellis	1862, 1863	Joseph Wolfe	1908-1910
Samuel Plumb	1864, 1865	Died in office	
E. J. Goodrich	1866, 1867	C. P. Doolittle	
G. W. Shurtleff	1868	Filled vacancy	
W. H. Backus	1869-1873	O. F. Carter	1910-1912
Montraville Stone	1874, 1875	Died in office	
George F. Hutchins	1876, 1877	C. P. Doolittle	
J. B. T. Marsh	1878-1881	Filled vacancy	
J. B. Clarke	1881-1884	J. D. Yocom	1912-1918
		W. H. Phillips	1918-1922
		H. F. Smith	1922-1926

O. OBERLIN POSTMASTERS

This office was established under the name "Russia" on January 10, 1834, with David D. Crocker as postmaster.

POSTMASTER	DATE APPOINTED
Harvey Gibbs	October 20, 1834

The name of the office was changed to "Oberlin" on March 16, 1835.

Harvey Gibbs	March 16, 1835
Grosvenor Reed	December 11, 1839
Timothy Dwight Eells	June 11, 1841
Edward F. Munson	November 25, 1843
Harvey W. Stevens	June 23, 1849
David McBride	February 21, 1850
Edward F. Munson	March 30, 1853
George F. H. Stevens	March 26, 1861
J. Frank Harmon	March 20, 1865
William O. Allen	June 12, 1874
Evan J. Phillips	July 22, 1880
John W. Steele	April 23, 1889
Flavius A. Hart	January 9, 1894
John W. Steele	January 14, 1898
Judson N. Stone	June 2, 1905
Morton A. Houghton	May 4, 1914
Eugene G. Dick	February 9, 1923

Three hundred thirteen

P. OBERLIN BUSINESS MEN
Prior to 1860

Theodore S. Ingersoll
Lewis Holtslander
Dr. Alexander Steele
Brewster Pelton
O. R. Ryder
Jonas Jones
T. Dwight Eells
J. W. Mason
Smith D. Hinman
Thomas Brice
Philo Weed
Woolston Beckwith
George Kinney
Henry G. Carpenter
Hoffman & Straus
S. Kupfer
E. F. Munson
W. H. Plumb
Robert E. Gillette
David McBride
E. J. Goodrich
R. N. Scranton
John Watson
Hiram A. Bunce
Bailey Brothers
George W. Eells
A. N. Beecher

James N. Fitch
L. M. Hall
G. H. Allen
Cyrus Avery
Seth Barthomew
Harvey Gibbs
Addison Tracy
Wilson B. Evans
Henry Evans
John Hennings
Sidney Bedortha
L. W. Butler
Isaac Chamberlain
Henry Wilcox
Seth B. Ellis
David Brokaw
A. C. Platt
W. B. and C. F. Ingersoll
S. M. Mathews
T. Scott
O. S. B. Wall
Samuel Royce
Charles Hill
J. H. Scott
Richard Whitney
John Patterson

In Business in 1860

(This list for 1860 does not repeat names of those noted as in business prior to 1860)

A. Straus
S. S. Calkins
J. Gillanders
Kinney & Reamer
Johnson & Kellogg
H. L. Henry
J. Palmer
J. W. Linder
J. Hayes & Company
J. Jewell

N. H. Townsend
John Watson
H. S. Spencer
W. W. Wright
William Hovey
James Bailey
Frank Hendry
Mrs. M. A. Roberts
J. A. Pindergast

ATTORNEYS

C. B. Baldwin
John M. Langston

Ralph Plumb

DOCTORS—DENTISTS

Homer Johnson
M. P. Hayward

J. F. Siddall
Mrs. E. H. Barry, M. D.

Three hundred fourteen

The Story of a Century

In Business in 1865

A. Straus
G. W. Wright
Attorney O. Bailey, Jr.
First National Bank
William Whitacre
Royce & Hancock
William Bailey
L. A. and J. J. Hill, Builders
J. M. Gardner & Company
Straus & Levy

J. D. Carpenter
P. R. Tobin
C. H. Favel
Waterman & Peek
I. M. Johnson
Dr. William Bunce
T. S. Fuller
Weed & Beckwith
Mrs. E. P. Chapman, M. D.

In Business in 1870

A. Straus
E. P. Brown
D. R. Alden
Platt & Hawley
Attorney I. A. Webster
A. H. Johnson
Fitch & Fairchild
E. J. Goodrich
N. and D. B. Bardwell
V. Hebebrand
H. L. Henry
Moses Levy & Company
Hall, Gillette & Allen
Chapman, Brown & Company
Rogers & Farrar
W. H. Mason
L. E. Bowen
Mayhew & Pope

Eastman & Thompson
Lincoln & Morris
G. S. Pay
Marx Straus
Reamer, Hulberd & Company
Z. A. Clement
Dr. C. D. Noble
Dr. G. T. Smith
Dr. Dudley Allen
J. Brice & Company
Carter, Rogers & Company
Weed & Edwards
Peek & Colburn
Frank Hendry
Locke & Cooley
James Rainey
George H. Fairchild

In Business in 1880

A. Straus, clothing
  Main and West College
Kline and Godley, hardware
  18 South Main
Newton and Searle, groceries
  8 North Main
Pounds & Loweth, city mills
  20 South Main
Cogswell & Newell, shoes
  2 West College
Munson Brothers, fish, oysters
  South Main
Edwin Regal, books
  15 West College
M. Straus, dry goods
  Main and East College
A. K. Bacon, coal
  22 South Main

Harmon & Beecher, drugs
S. Life, shoes
  13 West College
Barnard Brothers, coffee
  5 West College
Moore & Bond, flour and feed
  147 Water
A. B. Johnson, groceries
  14 West College
C. H. Tuttle, jewelry
  3 West College
Johnson, Whitney & Company,
  dry goods, West College
J. H. Lang, attorney
I. A. and F. Webster, attorneys
George P. and Charles A. Met-
  calf, attorneys
Henry Lee, omnibus service

Three hundred fifteen

Oberlin Colony

Oberlin College Writing Department, Uriah McKee proprietor
J. J. Hill and Frank Hill, builders, 41 East Lorain
T. H. Rowland, druggist
6 South Main
J. M. Gardner & Company
South Main
Dr. H. G. Husted, dentist
Carter & Brother, hardware store
Weed & Edwards, hardware store
Pettis & Holter, jewelry
North Main
C. H. Favel, livery service
Dr. Homer Johnson, physician
Dr. Frank P. Johnson, physician
Dr. J. Austin, physician
Dr. Mary L. Briggs, physician
Colburn, Cole & Company, lumber
L. W. Upton, photographs

In Business in 1890

J. A. Barnard, grocer
A. G. Comings, books and wall-paper
Deming & Whitney, millers
L. T. Whitney & Son, clothing
Rowley & Mains, real estate
A. Straus, clothing
The Oberlin Bank Company
A. H. Johnson, president
J. D. Quick, jeweler
Barnum & Godley, hardware
W. C. Bunce, M. D., physician
J. C. Jump, M. D., physician
J. M. Clarke, baker
S. Life, shoes
Oberlin Business College, Uriah McKee and J. T. Henderson
A. B. Johnson, grocery
Lewis Nichols, coal, feed
E. P. Johnson, dry goods
R. B. Ransom, furniture
G. S. Pay & Son, meats
M. G. Dick, grocer
Carter & Huckins, hardware
J. F. Harmon, druggist
A. J. Frederick & Company, dry goods
Cole & Thompson, lumber and coal
Gaston & Stewart, wall paper
H. L. Beecher, boots and shoes
T. H. Rowland, druggist
Oberlin Gas and Electric Company
J. H. Lang, attorney
George P. Metcalf, attorney
C. A. Metcalf, attorney
W. B. Bedortha, attorney
John W. Steele, attorney
J. Burgner, stenographer
G. M. Glenn, barber, draying
J. M. Gardner & Company, druggists
W. H. Haylor, drayman
H. G. Husted, dentist
J. F. Siddall, dentist
Weed & Edwards, hardware
W. J. Fuller, livery
G. W. Gibson, livery
Churches: First Congregational, Rev. James Brand, Pastor; Second Congregational, Rev. Henry M. Tenney, Pastor; First Baptist, Rev. E. J. Rose, Pastor; First Methodist Episcopal, Rev. O. Badgley, Pastor; Chirst Episcopal, Rev. George F. M. Smythe, Rector; Mt. Zion Baptist, Rev. W. H. Lewis, Pastor

In Business in 1900

W. H. Haylor
Alexander Cliff
W. J. Fuller
G. W. Gibson
Booth & Moore, funeral directors
The Oberlin Bank Company
Citizens National Bank

Louis E. Burgner, insurance
9 South Main
E. P. Johnson, dry goods
F. E. Burgess, drugs
H. A. Cook, bicycles
65 South Main

Three hundred sixteen

The Story of a Century

D. A. Gager, watch maker
South Main

Brice & Clark, novelties
9 South Main

Oberlin Coal & Lumber Company
South Main

Huckins & Huckins, hardware
South Main

Hart & Sperry, furniture
South Main

A. G. Comings, books
West College

E. J. Goodrich, books
Main and East College

Thomas Bails, grocery
11 South Main

Wilkinson & Watson, hardware
South Main

M. G. Dick, grocer
North Main

H. F. Smith, druggist
Main and West College

M. Sherburne, coal
South Professor

E. H. Holter, jewler
West College

H. Barnard, grocer
14 South Main

G. S. Pay & Son, meats
20 South Main

A. C. Burgess, sewing machines
9 West College

J. M. Gardner & Company, druggists, South Main

Oberlin Racket Store
South Main

L. T. Whitney & Son, clothing
West College

A. Straus, clothing
West College

Cooley & Fowler, grocers
North Main

S. M. Cole, lumber
South Main

Sage Brothers, grocers
27 West College

Tuttle & Rosecrans

C. W. Persons, drug store
West College

Preston Dry Goods Company
North Main

W. S. Wait, grocer
South Main

Wilcox & Phinney, rugs and novelties, Main and College

The Windecker Company, women's wear, 49 South Main

William Behr's Sons, grocers
North Main

Stewart Sisters, millinery
19 West College

Hiram W. Fobes, insurance
North Main

J. B. Godley, hardware
46 South Main

Fred H. Angle, grocer
12 South Main

W. D. Hobbs, restaurant
15 East College

W. J. Stone, shoes
33 West College

G. E. Newell, shoes
North Main

Anna G. Cooley, milliner
10 East College

J. L. Edwards, grocer
21 West College

L. L. Munson, oysters
South Main

P. D. Probert & Company, grocers
South Main

ATTORNEYS

W. B. Bedortha
A. Z. Tillotson

Frederick Webster
John W. Steele

DENTISTS

H. G. and D. S. Husted

J. F. Siddall

Oberlin Colony

In Business in 1910

Frank J. Dick, grocery
A. C. Burgess, pianos
F. W. Tobin, drug store
Gibson Brothers, bakery
Nellie Cheesman, racket store
The Peoples Banking Company
Fred H. Angle, grocery
Wright & Parsons, grocery
Miles J. Watson, hardware
G. W. Preston, dry goods
Durand's Insurance Agency
J. S. McClelland, cut glass
The Oberlin Racket Store
Yocom Brothers, dry goods
L. T. Whitney & Company, clothing
E. P. Johnson, dry goods
T. J. Rice, real estate
A. G. Comings & Son, books
Oberlin Milling Company, flour, feed
Balson & Campbell, grocery
Louis E. Burgner, insurance
J. L. Edwards, insurance
W. H. Cooley & Son, shoes

A. R. Kimpton, jeweler
The Oberlin Lumber & Coal Co.
Morgan and Cook, coal
The Clean Milk Dairy
A. Straus, clothing
W. P. Carruthers, jeweler
The Oberlin Banking Company
The State Savings Bank Company
W. D. Hobbs, East College
Huckins & Huckins, hardware
E. J. Goodrich, books
Otis E. May, meat market
Squire & Son, clothing and shoes
A. P. Behr, shoes
Dr. W. F. Thatcher, physician
Dr. George C. Jameson, physician
The Sugar Bowl, E. J. Davis, proprietor
Oberlin Business College, J. T. Henderson, president
The McKellogg Clothing Company
Luther Munson, cigars and tobacco
Sperry & Pfaff, grocery
Wade's Hardware
Oberlin Laundry

In Business in 1930

J. V. Hill
V. W. Rosa
The Yocom Brothers Company
Dalton & Crowell
Charles E. Herrick
A. R. Kimpton
The Worcester Dairy
A. G. Comings & Son
Van Kel Pharmacy
B. A. Locke
Tobin's Drug Store
Wood Construction Company
J. L. Edwards
Jarvis Strong
A. C. Burgess
Gulde Chevrolet Company
Henry G. Klermund
Robert F. Gerber
The Apparel & Gift Shop
George T. Sedgeman
Ohly's Corner Drug Store
Maurice S. Schubert

Behr's Boot Shop
The Oberlin Hardware Company
Janby Oil Company
Pfaff & Morris
Oberlin Cash Market
Dairy Service Company
The T. O. Murphy Company
Wilson's Mill
Jones & Jackson
Harry W. Hovey
The Oberlin Laundry
Fink's Dress Shoppe
Henry Revers
Ross Shoe Repair Shop
Louis E. Burgner
The Oberlin Inn
Mahlke & Winder
The Oberlin Dry Cleaning Co.
P. O. Johnson
BeViers, Inc.
Ohio Electric Power Company
Morgan Coal Company

The Story of a Century

Apollo Theatre
Rex Theatre
Sperry & Pfaff
Oberlin Telephone Company
H. A. Cook
Cities Service, C. L. Lyman
Miles J. Watson
The Peoples Banking Company
Southwestern Bus, F. H. Maddock, agent
Hixon-Peterson Lumber Company
Pettiford's Bakery
The Oberlin Savings Bank Co.
Smith Implement Company
The Oberlin Trucking Company
A. E. Cassells
Wade's Hardware Store
The Oberlin Elevator Company
The A & P Tea Company
Fisher Brothers Company
Krogers
Campus Restaurant
Varsity Restaurant
J. R. Haylor

W. E. Powers
Wright & Parsons
H. C. Tuck
Campus Beauty Shop
M. Weiss
A. F. Champney
Oberlin Ice Company
Gibson Brothers
C. D. Smiley
George Chatoian
Clean Milk Dairy
The Oberlin School of Commerce
The Oberlin Printing Company
Rogers & Schafer
A. H. Powers
Bailey & Haas
Sugar Bowl
T. J. Rice
J. E. Collins
N. A. Martin
Wright's Variety
Otis E. May
C. D. Ryals
Dr. J. A. McGrann, optician

PHYSICIANS

Dr. S. E. Miller
Dr. Paul C. Colegrove
Dr. R. D. A. Gunn
Dr. W. R. Gregg
Dr. L. H. Trufant

Dr. H. F. Vaughn
Dr. G. C. Jameson
Dr. Ellen F. Hawkins
Dr. S. W. Stevens

DENTISTS

Dr. C. W. Carrick
Dr. J. E. Barnard

Dr. R. C. Beatty

ATTORNEYS

C. R. Summers

A. Z. Tillotson

Q. OBERLIN SCHOOL OFFICIALS

Presidents

1860-1861	Thomas P. Turner
1861-1867	James H. Fairchild
1867-1868	W. C. French
1868-1872	D. P. Reamer
1872-1884	Judson Smith
1884-1893	C. H. Churchill
1893-1895	W. B. Chamberlain
1895-1904	C. T. Beckwith
1904-1905	E. A. Miller
1905-1924	A. S. Root
1924-1926	J. E. Barnard
1926-1927	J. D. Yocom
1927-1930	D. R. Moore
1930-1932	R. A. Budington
1932-	Lynds Jones

Clerks

1860-1866	John M. Langston
1866-1873	Homer Johnson
1873-1874	C. H. Churchill
1874-1878	Edwin Regal
1878-1878	H. H. Bawden
1878-1895	W. B. Durand
1895-1903	A. B. Spear
1903-1910	C. K. Whitney
1910-1912	J. D. Yocom
1912-1916	E. E. Sperry
1916-1918	H. L. Rawdon
1918-1923	J. E. Barnard
1923-1928	J. W. Schwartz
1928-	C. F. Spitler
Sept. 1, 1928	

Superintendents

1860-1869	Samuel Sedgwick
1869-1876	E. F. Moulton
1876-1878	H. R. Chittenden
1878-1882	H. J. Clark
1882-1900	G. W. Waite
1900-1903	E. A. Miller
1903-1908	W. H. Nye
1908-	H. L. Rawdon

High School Principals

1901-1902	W. H. Nye
1902-1903	B. L. Laird
1903-1905	A. L. Button
1905-1906	H. L. Rawdon
1906-1908	J. B. Crouch
1908-1910	W. H. McCall
1910-1912	Stanley Morris
1912-1922	J. C. Seemann
1922-1924	W. Z. Morrison
1924-1927	C. L. Mackey
1927-	C. E. Wigton

CHURCHES IN 1933

The First Church in Oberlin, Rev. James Austin Richards, pastor.
Christ Church (Episcopal), Rev. L. E. Daniels, rector.
First Methodist Episcopal Church, Rev. Charles F. McBride, pastor.
First Baptist Church, Rev. W. Gaylord James, pastor.
Mt. Zion Baptist Church, Rev. C. H. Brown, pastor.
Sacred Heart Church, Rev. George F. Martin, pastor.
Rust M. E. Church, Rev. R. W. Stennett, pastor.
Christian and Missionary Alliance, Rev. Hiram Maddox, pastor.
East Oberlin Community Church.

INDEX

INDEX

INDEX

INDEX

INDEX

INDEX

Three hundred twenty-seven

INDEX

Wangerien, Henry C., 152, 187, 257, 258, 264, 269, 270, 271
Ward, Artemus, (Charles F. Browne), 107
Warner Hall, 37, 146
Warren, Isaac, I., 305, 306, 307, 308-309
Water Service, Public, 142, 147; $50,000 bond issue for waterplant carries, 149; Judge Steele discovers source of supply, 149; contract for new plant, 150; new plant completed, 151; new reservoir built, 169; total pumpage 1900 and 1932, 189; new conduit line, 254; new reservoir 1915, 268
Watson, John, 87, 98, 127
Watson, M. J., 164, 172, 179, 194, 195, 199, 255
Webber, A. R., Honorable, 189, 198
Webster, I. A., 132
Weed, Philo, 41, 98, 162
Weeks, Charles, 154
West, Amzi, 153
Western Reserve, 13
West, Ira W., 173, 258
West, Lewis F., 169
Westwood Cemetery, 55; formal dedication, 107; presidents and clerks, 108; removal of bodies from old cemetery to, 109; burials 1868, 118; burials 1863-1877, 132
Wheat, William, 103
Whedon, Burt D., Mrs., 225
Whipple, George, 66
Whitney, Charles K., 152, 153, 173, 179, 180, 186, 194, 267
Whitney, L. A., 107
Whitney, Levi T., 152, 153, 164, 267, 282
Whitney, Mark, 260
Wilcox, L. B., 116
Wilkinson, Samuel M., 164
Willard, Frances E., 174

Williams, Amanda Pease, Mrs., 16 (f.n.), 188
Williams, Charles H., Rev., 273, 274
Wilkins, Ernest H., Pres., 283
Wilson, Frank L., 265, 269
Wilson, Woodrow, 174, 279
Wirkler, John E., 257
Wolfe, Joseph, 202, 258
Woman's Christian Temperance Union, 174
Wood, A. N., 107
Wood, George C., 282
Worcester, H. E., 107
Worcester, James, 179
Worcester, James M., 201
Worcester, P. G., 179, 264
Worcester, P. G., Mrs., 264
World War, 250, 251, 265, 269, 270; fuel shortage 1917, 270; heatless Mondays, 271; war committee named, 271; liberty loan record, 272; special war committee, 272; armistice celebration, 272-273
Wright, Albert A., 108, 149, 155, 159, 197, 226
Wright, Clarence J., 288
Wright, Emeline Farnsworth, Mrs., 269
Wright, Fred, 154
Wright, G. Frederick, Prof., 46 (f.n.), 102; story of Monroe, 206, 207; 230
Wright Laboratory, 37
Wright Memorial Park, 288
Wright, S. G., 164
Wright, W. W., Deacon, 115, 142
Wyckoff, M. D., 282

Yocom Brothers Company, 262, 263
Yocom, E. K., 262, 269, 271
Yocom, Ernest, 263
Yocom, Herbert, 263
Yocom, J. D., 166, 194, 260, 262

Zahm, H. V., 279